Agnes Smith Lewis

A Translation of the Four Gospels from the Syriac of the Sinaitic Palimpsest

Agnes Smith Lewis

A Translation of the Four Gospels from the Syriac of the Sinaitic Palimpsest

ISBN/EAN: 9783337241483

Printed in Europe, USA, Canada, Australia, Japan

Cover: Foto ©Lupo / pixelio.de

More available books at **www.hansebooks.com**

A TRANSLATION OF THE FOUR GOSPELS

CAMBRIDGE
PRINTED BY JONATHAN PALMER
ALEXANDRA STREET

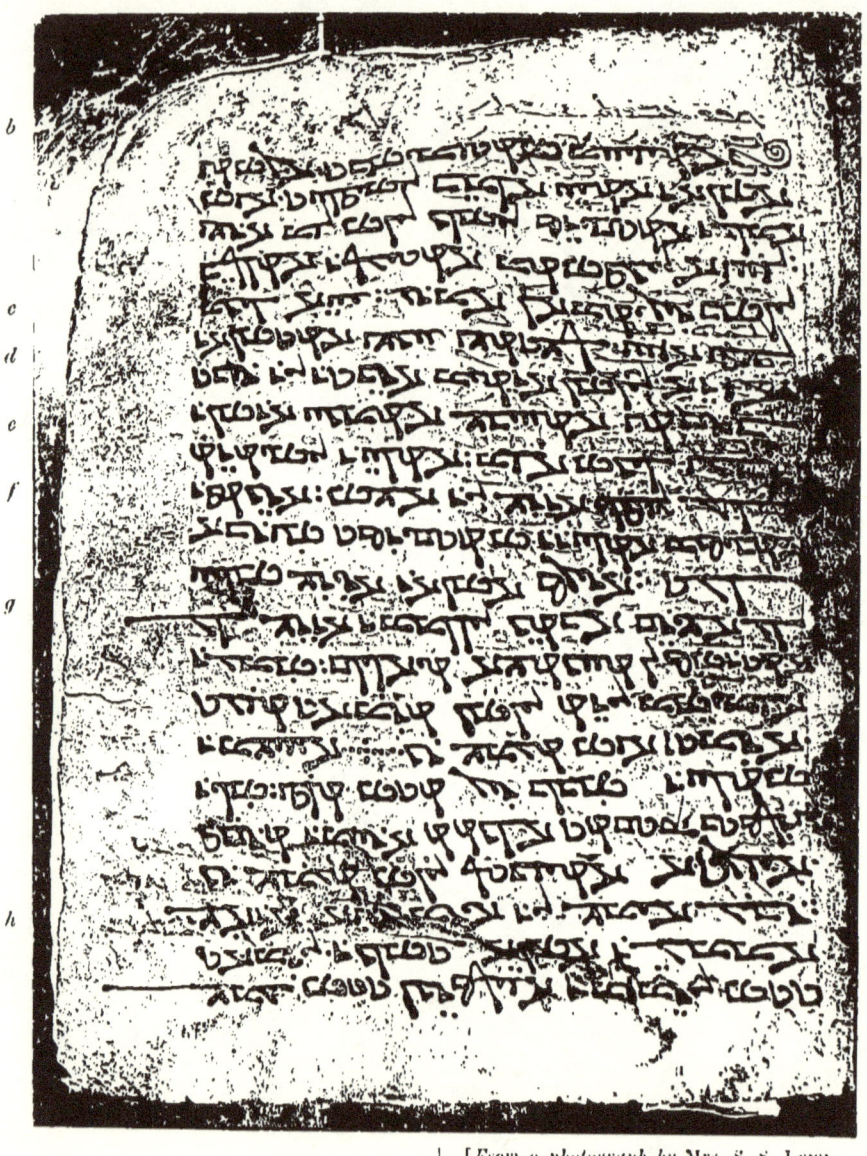

END OF THE GOSPEL OF MARK.

(a) Mark xvi. 1.
(b) Mark xvi. 7.
(c) End of v. 8.
(d) Here endeth the Gospel of Mark (rubric).
(e) Row of dots (red).
(f) Title of Luke (rubric).
(g) Luke i. 1.
(h) "to write" Luke i. 3.
(ii) Blank space between the two columns.

A TRANSLATION

OF THE

FOUR GOSPELS

FROM THE

SYRIAC OF THE SINAITIC PALIMPSEST

BY

AGNES SMITH LEWIS, M.R.A.S.

AUTHOR OF "GLIMPSES OF GREEK LIFE AND SCENERY"
"A CATALOGUE OF THE SYRIAC MSS. IN THE CONVENT OF ST. KATHARINE
ON MOUNT SINAI," ETC.

London
MACMILLAN AND CO.
AND NEW YORK
1894

CONTENTS

	PAGE
INTRODUCTION	ix
GOSPEL OF MATTHEW ...	1
GOSPEL OF MARK	59
GOSPEL OF LUKE	95
GOSPEL OF JOHN	165
APPENDIX I.	209
APPENDIX II.	231

"Jesus said, Let not your heart be troubled; believe in God, and in me ye are believing."—John xiv. 1.

INTRODUCTION.

THE text of the lately-discovered Codex of Old Syriac Gospels is now before the public, and as a translation into English has not been appended to it, the time seems to have come when students of the Bible, who are not Syriac scholars, should be made acquainted with the contents and characteristics of this ancient document. We think that the cause of truth will be best served by placing a translation of the whole text before our readers, and not merely isolated passages, which are apt to be misconstrued when detached from their surroundings. And in order that they may be the better able to form an opinion as to the value of the text, we shall introduce it with—firstly, a short narrative of how the manuscript was discovered and transcribed; secondly, the relation which it is supposed to hold to other Syriac versions; thirdly, a description of the manuscript itself; and fourthly, what appears to us, at first sight, to be a few of its leading features.

I. HOW THE MANUSCRIPT WAS DISCOVERED AND TRANSCRIBED.

The convent of St. Katharine on Mount Sinai stands on the barren granite rocks of a narrow desert valley 4500 feet above the level of the Red Sea, and some 2800 feet below the summit of Jebel Mousa, on whose precipitous side it rests. A community of monks dwelt there from a very early period, keeping alive the traditions which cluster around the spot:

traditions of Moses watering sheep at the well of Jethro; of the rock which gushed with water at the touch of his rod; of the burning bush which flamed on a spot now covered by the apse of the convent church; and of the cave, a thousand feet higher, where Elijah was fed by ravens, and where he heard the still small voice. Several other monasteries flourished in the rocky valleys of that wonderful block of pink granite mountains, of which the lower part is called Horeb, and the upper part Sinai; and numberless are the caves of hermits, chiefly Egyptian, who in those early days burrowed like rabbits amongst the sandstone or limestone cliffs of the desert peninsula. The convent of St. Katharine was in the sixth century turned into a fortress by Justinian, who surrounded it with a massive wall; and we may well imagine that as the smaller convents fell into decay, or were threatened by turbulent or fanatic Bedawin, not only their monks but their manuscripts were transferred to it as to a place of safety.

This may account for the wealth of literary treasures which have been accumulated within these ancient walls, where indeed there is little accommodation for their due keeping. The Greek MSS. catalogued by Gardhausen are about 1223 in number; the Arabic MSS., according to the list published by my sister, Mrs. Gibson, number about 629; the Syriac MSS. 267; and the Iberian MSS. perhaps 100. Some of these are neatly arranged on book-shelves, but the greater part are stored in chests, and are therefore inaccessible to any traveller who cannot make his wants known to the monks, and inspire them with confidence in his own integrity.

Books which have lost their bindings are kept in large baskets, and from one of these probably Tischendorf extracted in 1844 the famous *Codex Sinaiticus*, which, containing as it does a Greek text of nearly the whole Bible, has been of such inestimable value in textual revision. It has been a cause of irritation to the monks that they did not succeed in keeping this treasure in their possession. Partly to this, and partly to the fact that Western scholars are usually ignorant of modern Greek, we may attribute the fact that a chest containing ancient Syriac MSS. has lain there undisturbed for centuries. Professor Palmer saw its contents in 1868, and thus refers to them:

"Amongst a pile of patristic and other works of no great age or interest, are some curious old Syriac books, and *one or two palimpsests*. My hurried visit prevented me from examining these with any great care; but they would no doubt well repay investigation."—*The Desert of the Exodus*, Vol. I. p. 70.

The first real examination of these books was reserved for Mr. Rendel Harris, who in 1889, after a stay of fifteen days at the convent, contrived to disarm all prejudices, and to obtain access to these hidden treasures. How he then found the Syriac text of the *Apology* of Aristides has been told elsewhere, and I refer to it only because it awakened in both Mr. Harris' mind and in my own the conviction that there was something more in the convent, a conviction which induced me and my twin sister, Mrs. James Y. Gibson, to fulfil a long-cherished wish by visiting Sinai in February 1892.

Amongst the ancient volumes which were produced for our inspection by the late Hegoumenos and Librarian, Father Galakteon, was a thick volume, whose leaves had evidently been unturned for centuries, as they could be separated only by manipulation with the fingers; and in the case of ff. 65, 66, by the steam of a kettle. A single glance told me that the book was a palimpsest, and I soon ascertained that the upper writing was a very entertaining account of the lives of women saints, and that its date was, as I then read it, a thousand and nine years after Alexander, that is A.D. 697. After the word "nine" there is a small hole in the vellum, which, as Mr. Rendel Harris believes, occupies the place of the syllable corresponding to the "ty" of "ninety," and the date is thus probably A.D. 778.

I then examined the more ancient writing which lay beneath this. It is in two columns, one of which is always projected on to the margin, and it is written in the same Estrangelo character, but in a much smaller hand than the later writing which covers it. It was also slightly reddish in colour. As I glanced down the margin for over 280 pages, every word that I could decipher was from the Gospels; and so were the lines which at the top or bottom of several pages were free of the later writing. And few indeed were the pages which had not a distinct title, such as "Evangelium," "da Mathai," "da Marcus," or "da Luca." My sister could not at that time read a single letter of Syriac, although she has since acquired enough to give me very material help in the preparation of this volume. I however succeeded in impressing these facts on her mind, and obtained her assistance in photographing the whole of the volume, and I also made an index to it by copying the top lines of each page in the later writing.

Our photographs, though they were the work of novices in the art, were fairly successful; and after we had ourselves developed them, they were shewn to more than one Semitic scholar. Most of our learned friends, however, had not sufficiently keen eyes, nor indeed sufficient time to read what we assured them was a copy of the Gospels written not later than the fifth century. At last they were shewn to Mr. F. C. Burkitt, and he took them to the late Professor Bensly, who was then engaged on a critical edition of the Curetonian Gospels, and to whom the Old Syriac text was therefore most familiar. The decipherment by him and by Mr. Burkitt of a page was sufficient to enable him to pronounce that we had discovered a text of the same type as the Curetonian. But as the whole of it could not be transcribed from my photographs, we at once organized a second expedition, which took place in the early part of 1893.

On this second expedition, Professor Bensly, Lecturer in Aramaic to the University of Cambridge, Mr. J. Rendel Harris, University Lecturer in Palæography, and Mr. F. C. Burkitt went for the purpose of transcribing the text of the Gospels directly from the manuscript, Mr. Burkitt having already copied some thirty pages from my photographs. Two of these gentlemen were accompanied by their wives, whilst my sister and I went in order to ensure their getting access to the volume, as well as to continue our researches.

The monks received us with great cordiality, especially Father Galakteon, who at once entrusted the palimpsest to my keeping. I had already divided my photographs amongst the three transcribers—the first 104 pages to Mr. Rendel Harris, pp. 105 to 200 to Mr. Burkitt, and pp. 201 to 284 to Professor Bensly. This division determined the arrangement of their work, which they accomplished in forty days. None of them could have published his results separately, the four

Gospels having been all interleaved with each other when the vellum was used for the Martyrology. Mr. Burkitt compared what he had already copied with the original, whilst I brought up a great deal of the faded writing by the application of a chemical re-agent—hydro-sulphide of ammonia—recommended to me by Mr. Scott, of the British Museum.

Our return home was saddened by the unexpected death of Professor Bensly. He had seemed to thrive on the hardships of the desert journey, but his health had long been precarious; and the careful nursing of his devoted wife could not ward off the attack of the insidious disease which carried him off only three days after his return to Cambridge.

As some of the pages which had fallen to his lot and to that of Mr. Burkitt were still undeciphered, I placed fresh photographs, representing these, at Mr. Burkitt's disposal after our return home, with the result that a good many *lacunae* in the text were filled up by him.

II. Relation of our Codex to other Syriac Versions.

Syriac, or more properly Christian Aramaic, was the first language into which the New Testament was translated; and as the Greek text itself was written by men who habitually thought in Syriac, the early versions in this tongue have a closer affinity with the original text than those of any other can possibly have, not excepting the old Latin. Aramaic was once popularly supposed to be a corrupt form of Hebrew; but that is a mistake. It is a language quite as regularly formed, and with a grammar quite as distinct, as either Hebrew or Arabic. Almost our first record of its use is from the lips of Laban. In Gen. xxxi. 47 we read that when Laban and Jacob set up a heap of stones as a witness of the covenant between them, Jacob called it, in good Hebrew, Galeed ; and Laban, in equally good Aramaic, Jegar-sahadutha. We therefore conclude that Aramaic was the vernacular of Mesopotamia, the cradle of Abraham's family.

That it was also the vernacular of Palestine in our Lord's time, the language spoken by Him and in which He addressed the multitude, there can be no doubt. Not only the proper names of persons and the names of places which occur in the Four Gospels tell us this, but various Aramaic phrases embodied in the Greek text, such as "Epphatha," "Talitha cumi," and the last despairing cry of our Lord on the cross, "Eloi, Eloi, lama sabachthani," are not translated in this Old Syriac version, for the good reason that they are part of the text itself.

There are also other indications. Semitic peoples delight in puns, and in assonances or jingles of words. We need not go far to prove this. The Qurân derives much of its supposed sanctity from this cause alone. Babylonian royal decrees and Arabic law documents are all enlivened by it. And in the Syriac version of our Lord's discourses it seems as if one word had sometimes suggested another. For instance, John viii. 34 : "He who committeth sin is the slave of sin." Here the word for "commit" and the word for "slave" are both regular forms of the triliteral verb *'bad*. There is a similar play on the same word in Luke vii. 8, "I say to my slave, do this, and he doeth it."

Another, which has been detected by my sister, Matt. x. 30: "But the very hairs of your head are all numbered." The word for "hairs" is *mene*, and the word for "number" is *mna*, both probably from the same root.

Also Matt. xxvii. 6, *dmaya ennōn da dmā*—"the price of blood."

In Matthew x. 13 we have, "And when ye come into an house give peace to it [that is, salute it], and if the house be worthy, your peace shall rest upon it, and if not, your peace shall return unto you." In the Greek text ἀσπάσασθε ("salute") has no verbal relation to εἰρήνη ("peace"). We therefore conclude that our Lord gave this direction in a Semitic tongue, and used either the Hebrew *shalūm* or the Syriac *shalma*.

The alliteration *memath tamōth* of Mark vii. 10 can be reproduced in an English idiom, "die the death," though it is absent from the Greek.

In John xii. 32, "And I, if I be lifted up from the earth will draw all men unto me," the word "lifted up" has the secondary sense of "be crucified."

In John xx. 10 there is in the Greek text an expression, ἀπῆλθον . . . πρὸς ἑαυτούς, which is not classical, and may perhaps be a translation of the Syriac *ezal lahūn*.

And in John xx. 19 the curious grammar of τῇ μιᾷ τῶν σαββάτων is at once explained by the Syriac *had beshaba*. These last two examples may have sprung from the Evangelist's thoughts being habitually in Syriac.

St. Paul must have been thinking in Aramaic when he wrote to the Romans (xiii. 8): *wa lenash medem la tchubun, ella had lehad lemahahbu*—"Owe no man anything, but to love one another." Here the word *hāb* ("owe") is not the same as *habb* ("love"), but the sound is very similar: as in the case of *dmaya* and *dmā*. Our Lord himself may also have made a play on the same words in the story of the two debtors, as recorded in Luke vii. 41, 42. And in the Palestinian Syriac, the words addressed by the risen Saviour to Mary Magdalene are so rhythmical, that we feel as if they must be the very accents which fell from His lips: *Attatha, ma at bakia, leman at baʻia*— " Woman, why weepest thou, whom seekest thou ? "

The Aramaic Christians adopted the name of Syrians, bestowed on them by the Greeks, because they, the Aramaia, did not wish to be confounded with Armaia (the heathen), and the country of Aram was henceforth known as Syria.

The first specimen of literature they possessed was probably a translation of the Old Testament, which was read in their synagogues. The next was a version of the New Testament (if we may not count the original of Matthew's Gospel), and after that, translations of the early Fathers, and of the works of Greek philosophers. Some of these have come down to us in a Syriac dress only. Syriac literature can shew no work of original genius, and it is prized chiefly for the light which it throws upon the history of the New Testament.

One of its most valuable products was the *Diatessarōn*, or Harmony of the Four Gospels, composed by a Syrian named Tatian, in the second century. Whether he made use of a Syriac or of a Greek text is not yet ascertained. But this Harmony was so highly valued, that for three centuries it supplanted every other book in the worship of the Syrian churches. At some period between A.D. 411 and A.D. 435 Bishop Rabbula, of Edessa, promulgated an edict that it must be replaced by the Separate Gospels. From that time copies of Tatian's work began to disappear, and its text is known to us only from quotations in an Armenian version of Mar Ephraim's *Commentary*, and in an Arabic translation, of which two copies exist in the Vatican Library. These have been edited by Ciasca.

The Pĕshĭttā, or "simple" version, which seems to have replaced the *Diatessarōn*, is one which underwent successive revisions in order to bring it into harmony with the Greek codices; and it is, in fact, the Syrian Vulgate.

Quotations in some of the Fathers had suggested to Griesbach, Hug, and others, the existence of a version older than the Pĕshĭttā before the happy discovery by Canon Cureton in 1842 of the British Museum MS., which is now numbered Add. 14,451. This was one of a number of MSS. which had been brought to the Museum from the convent of St. Mary Deipara, in the Nitrian Desert, Egypt, by Archdeacon Tattam. It is written in a clear, distinct hand, only one leaf being palimpsest; and it did not therefore present the same difficulties to a transcriber which our Sinai codex did. But it has been seriously mutilated, and the sum of its contents is as follows:

Matthew i. 1—viii. 22; x. 32—xxiii. 25;

Mark xvi. 17—20;

John i. 1—42; iii. 5—viii. 19; xiv. 10—12; 15—19; 21—23; 26—29;

Luke ii. 48—iii. 16; vii. 33—xvi. 12; xvii. 1—xxiv. 44.
and from some of these verses a few words are missing.

Other Syriac versions are:

The Philoxenian, made by Philoxenus, bishop of Mabbōgh, about A.D. 508. (A revision of this, made by Thomas of Harkel a century later, is called the Harklensian.)

The Palestinian Syriac version, whose origin is attributed by Nöldeke to the fourth or fifth century, and which is now extant only in the form of a Lectionary. Till our visit to Sinai in 1892, only one copy of this was known to exist, that in the Vatican Library, which has been edited by Count Erizzo-Miniscalchi and by Paul de Lagarde. Its date is about A.D. 1029. The copy discovered by me at Sinai in 1892 is dated A.D. 1104, and that which Mr. Rendel Harris found in 1893 A.D. 1118. The translation is from a Greek manuscript quite independent of any that are now extant; yet it agrees in the main with the Codex Sinaiticus and the Codex Vaticanus. A fresh edition is in course of preparation.

III. Description of the Manuscript.

The manuscript is numbered 30 in the convent library, and is a complete book so far as the later writing is concerned. Its material is a strong vellum, the outer pages only being disposed to crumble. Here we find in sober fact what happened only metaphorically in the middle ages the Word of God completely obscured by the legends of the saints. John the Recluse, of Beth-Mari, Kaddish, being in want of vellum, pulled to pieces a copy of the Old Syriac Gospels, and wrote above them his Select Narratives of Holy Women, viz.: Thecla, Eugenia, Pelagia, Mary or Marinus, Euphrosyne, Onesima, Drusis, Barbara, Mary, Irene, Euphemia, Sophia, Theodosia, Theodota, a short Creed, Susanna, Cyprian and Justa, and some verses of a metrical Homily of Mar Ephraim, about Paradise.

The text of the Gospels underlies about 284 pages on 142 leaves of this Martyrology. But it did not suffice for the wants of John the Recluse. To obtain a further supply of vellum for his stories he made use of four leaves from a fourth-century Greek MS. of the Gospels; many leaves from a volume of Syriac Apocrypha containing the Acts of Thomas and the Repose of Mary, and more leaves from another Greek MS. which has not yet been identified.

The stories in the Martyrology are of a very racy character, and throw a curious light on the monastic life at its prime. They have apparently been well read, perhaps by generations of Sinai monks, if we may judge from the thumb-stained margins. Iberian monks have certainly at one period handled the volume, for they have re-numbered its quires in their own tongue. To complete our description of this interesting volume we must state that Mr. Rendel Harris detected the existence of a still more ancient writing beneath that of the Gospels, in this the very oldest specimen of a palimpsest which has as yet come to light.

IV. A FEW OF ITS LEADING CHARACTERISTICS.

Of the titles to the four Gospels two only have been deciphered,—those to Luke and John, with the colophons to Mark, Luke, and John. The spaces between the end of one Gospel and beginning of another were pronounced to be blank, but at Mr. Harris' suggestion I applied my re-agent to them, and they came up in a rich reddish-brown colour. One result of this is that we have their title at the very end. It reads thus:

"Here endeth the Gospel of the *Mĕpharrĕshê* four books: Glory to God and to his Christ, and to his Holy Spirit. Let every one who reads, and hears, and keeps, and does, pray for the sinner who wrote it. May God in his tender mercy forgive him his sins in both worlds. Amen and Amen."

The epithet "*mĕpharrĕshē*" is applied to the Gospels both in Cureton's MS. and in the Sinai one. In our text it bears unmistakeably the two dots which denote the plural. It is therefore a term to be applied to all the four Gospels, just as εὐαγγέλιον in the colophon of our text means "Gospel" generally in the old patristic sense. The question now is, What meaning are we to attach to it?

Cureton applied to Bernstein, who suggested "Evangelium per anni circulum dispositum," a copy of the Gospels divided into lections, or portions appointed to be read throughout the year, and referred to Assemani's *Bibliotheca Orient. Clemen. Vat.*, vol. II. p. 230. Cureton made the obvious objection that there are no indications whatever of such lections in the MS. written at the same period as its title. His judgment is confirmed by the fact that there are also none in our MS.

Another explanation is that *mĕpharrĕshē* means "separate," as distinct from "mixed" *mĕhallĕtē*. In favour of this it has been urged that the canons of Bishop Rabbula of Edessa (A.D. 412—435) ordain that in all churches a gospel of the separated *Evangelion da Mĕpharrĕshē* should be kept and read, obviously that it might supplement the *Diatessarōn* of Tatian, which seems to have been in general use before that period. This is a very strong point.

The difficulty is (1) that the term *mĕpharrĕshē* runs through the whole of Syriac literature, and is applied to the Pĕshittā, probably by inheritance, as well as to the Curetonian; (2) that it is applied to the Psalms as well as to the Gospels.

xxii   INTRODUCTION.

In Dr. Wright's catalogue of the Syriac MSS. in the British Museum, we find that No. CLXVIII. contains the Psalms according to the Pĕshīttā version, with the title, *kutba: da-tashbūchtŭ: da-dawid: da-mĕpharrĕshē.*

In a note to this, Dr. Wright says: "The word *da-mĕpharrĕshē* seems here really to mean 'of the interpreters, or of the translators.' The strange thing is that such titles should be prefixed to the ordinary Pĕshīttā version, and that, too, in a MS. dated A.D. 600."

The meaning "of the interpreters or translators" is corroborated by the title to No. CLXIX. (A.D. 14, 436), to which Dr. Wright draws attention. It runs:

"By the power of the Lord Jesus we begin to write (the Psalms) of David, of the *mĕpharrĕshē*, which we bring out of the Palestinian tongue to the Hebrew, and from the Hebrew to the Greek, and from the Greek to the Syriac."

It is generally allowed that the word פָּרַשׁ sometimes means "to transcribe" in Hebrew. Here are two cases in which it apparently means the same in Syriac; and in a Targum on Isaiah viii. 1, the epithet מפרש is applied to writing in the sense of "clear," "distinct." We must therefore leave the question to further discussion on the part of critics. There is, however, not much hope of their judgment being final until we have the Syriac text of the *Diatessarōn* in our hands. Then the great problem may be solved. Was the *Diatessarōn* compiled in the second century from the version contained in the Curetonian and in the Sinai codices? or did that version come into existence only in the fourth century, when the use of the *Diatessarōn* was discontinued?

Let us now see what our Codex says about the Gospel of Matthew. In chap. i. v. 8 the name of Joram is followed immediately by that of Uzziah; and the three kings, Ahazia, Joash, and Amuzia, who came betwixt them in Cureton's MS., are absent.

In *v.* 16 we come to the most startling variation in our Codex. Although none of the surviving Syriac students, except the transcriber, who were present at Sinai in 1893, knew of this strange reading until months after our return home, and although Professor Bensly has not appended his initials to the foot of the page, we shall not venture to doubt the accuracy of the transcription, which, however, rests upon the evidence of one pair of eyes only. We ask our readers to consider carefully the whole passage, from *v.* 16 to the end of the chapter.

It is hardly possible to find a consistent narrative in this self-contradictory recital. Had *v.* 16 stood alone we might have suspected a clerical error, but the occurrence of the word *lek* ("to thee") in *v.* 21, and *leh* ("to him") in *v.* 25, with the omission of the words, καὶ οὐκ ἐγίνωσκεν αὐτήν, ἕως οὗ, makes it almost certain that the statement in *v.* 16 is an intentional one. Our Codex stands alone in its peculiar readings of these three verses, and doubtless some critics will be inclined to set its authority against that of all the oldest Greek MSS. of all the versions, and of its own sister manuscript, the Curetonian. If so, we hope they will be consistent, and make its text the touch-stone of accuracy everywhere else, not forgetting its reading of *v.* 18, "when they had not come near one to another, she was found with child of the Holy Ghost."

In the meantime, there are some considerations bearing on this subject which we shall do well to keep in mind.

We have in Matthew's narrative, and in Luke's, two genealogies, both of Joseph only. Possibly the one was on the father's side, the other on the mother's side, and both are probably copied from an official register, the last clause of which was perhaps added at the time of the Presentation in the Temple, and was modified by the Evangelist when he became fully acquainted with the story of Mary. It is possible that we have here a partly modified form; but even here Mary is called the Virgin—a title which no one unacquainted with the miraculous birth of her first-born would naturally have given her.

The fact that Joseph was troubled about Mary's condition is simply inexplicable if he were the father of Jesus. And it is difficult to reconcile the idea of his being a just man with that of his wishing to put her away. These circumstances the scribe of our Codex, if he were a heretic, has not been bold enough to suppress.

We have no genealogy of Mary. This is only natural. Our Lord's social position and civil rights were determined by the relation in which He stood to one who was both His reputed father and his foster-father. His disciples were eager that He should claim the throne of David and drive out the Romans, and they therefore laid great stress upon Joseph's ancestry. Even after our Lord's Ascension, as they were disappointed in their expectation that His second coming would take place in their own life-time, they took care that there should be a permanent record of this. We can easily imagine that Mary would make known her wonderful secret to a few only, and that it was not at once published abroad to a nation who would have received it with scornful incredulity. But from the few it was doubtless communicated to many of the disciples, and we can hardly believe that they did not investigate the truth of a statement which most of them sealed with suffering and with death. The seclusion in which Eastern women are kept, not indeed in their houses, but from social intercourse with all members of the other sex who are not of kin to them, and their own gregarious habits, make it highly improbable that Mary could be guilty of a lapse from virtue without the knowledge of some female companion. St. Luke states, chap. i. v. 3, that he had investigated all these things from the beginning, and it is much to be regretted that Luke i. v. 35 occurs on a lost page of our manuscript.

Meanwhile, it is important to remember that we have not ascertained all the facts which may throw light upon the history of this Sinai Codex. In particular, we have not the initial title,—a title whose actual existence has been detected from my photographs by Mr. Rendel Harris. It is on the recto of the page which contains Matthew i. 1—17, and it may yet tell us both the name of the scribe, and the place where the MS. was written.

The various readings in this Codex afford much food for discussion. Those of our readers who are deeply interested in the subject will find many of these for themselves, but we shall point out some which appear to throw fresh light upon the sacred narrative, and some which in our humble opinion indicate an older form of the Old Syriac version than Cureton's manuscript.

In Matthew xix. 29, and in Mark x. 29, our Codex agrees with the judgment of the Revisers by omitting the word "wife" from those whom it is meritorious to leave for our Lord's sake. In Matthew xix. 29 the word "father" is also omitted.

c

In Matthew xx. 12 we have "the burden of the day in the heat," which seems a natural expression.

Matthew xxiii. 13 gives us a graphic picture of priestly pretensions. "Ye hold the key of the kingdom of heaven before men: for ye neither enter in yourselves, nor those that are coming do ye suffer them to enter."

Matthew xviii. 20 gives us a reading similar to that of Codex Bezae, "For there are not two or three gathered together in my name and I not amongst them." We could believe that the Syriac translator had confounded the Greek words οὐ and οὗ, were it not that he has given us a perfectly idiomatic expression.

In Matthew xxvi. 25, and in Mark xiv. 19, the question of the disciples, "Is it I, Lord?" is put in a somewhat stronger and more interesting form. It begins with a word which in Syriac corresponds partly to the Latin *ne . . . forte*, and to the Greek μήπως. This suggests that the question was a deprecatory one, and as it cannot be rendered in English, we have had recourse to the idiom which would probably rise to the lips of one of our own countrymen in a similar case, "Not I, surely, Lord?"

In Matthew xxvii. 56 the companion of Mary Magdalene is called Mary the daughter of James and mother of Joseph. This is repeated in Mark xv. 40. Mary is called the daughter of James also in the two Palestinian Syriac Lectionaries which were found by Mr. Rendel Harris and myself in the Sinai Convent. It is difficult to trace her family connections, but amongst other suggestions one of Mrs. Gibson's may be noted, that perhaps we may link her with the genealogy in Matthew, and that possibly she was the mother-in-law of the Virgin Mary.

If so, she very naturally appears both near the cross and at the sepulchre (see Matthew i. 15, 16).

In Mark x. 50 we are told that blind Timai, son of Timai, put on his garment before he rose and came to Jesus. This, to anyone who has watched Eastern habits, seems a more natural action than if he had cast it away.

The most remarkable feature in our text of Mark is the omission of twelve verses, chap. xvi. 9—20. This occurs in other ancient codices, notably in both the Sinaiticus and the Vaticanus. But in these it is open to question if their absence is not due to cancelling by a later hand. In ours there can be no doubt that they never existed. This is made abundantly clear by the frontispiece to this volume, which represents the page on which St. Mark ends and St. Luke begins. The space betwixt the two is on the left hand column, that is the second column, on the page, for our readers must remember that Syriac is read from right to left; the intervening space is filled up by the words written with red ink, "Here endeth the Gospel of Mark." Then comes a line of ornamental dots, and then, "The Gospel of Luke," also in red.

The subject is too perplexing to enter on here, but it is worthy of remark, that in the Greek codices where these twelve verses do occur, the word τέλος ("end") is always found after verse 8 and also after verse 20. What is very strange is that these verses must exist in Cureton's manuscript, for all that is there preserved to us of Mark's Gospel is xvi. 17, 18, 19, 20. The testimony of the Old Syriac version to their being part of the sacred record is therefore equivocal. We may hope that fresh light will be thrown on this subject through the investigations which have been prompted by

Mr. F. C. Conybeare's remarkable discovery of the signature, *Ariston Erizou* ("Ariston the Presbyter's") to the last twelve verses of Mark xvi. in an Armenian MS. of the tenth century. Our readers will find this interesting subject fully discussed in the *Expositor* for September 1894.

In Luke i. 63, 64 we have the statement, "and they marvelled all" transferred to its natural place, so that it becomes an effect produced by the string of Zacharias' tongue being suddenly loosened, and not simply by his writing the name of John.

In Luke iv. 17 a beautifully characteristic touch is restored to the narrative of our Lord's conduct in the synagogue of Nazareth. Before He stood up to read, He waited modestly until the book of Isaiah the prophet was put into His hand.

In Luke x. 41 our Lord's praise of Mary is accompanied by no reproach to Martha.

In Luke xv. 30 we seem to hear the angry tone of the elder brother as he says, "Thou hast killed for him that fatted calf."

In Luke xvi. 20 we learn that Lazarus was a poor man, but possibly not a beggar.

In Luke xxii. we have a fresh arrangement of the narrative from *v.* 17 to *v.* 21.

In Luke xxiii. 37 we are told that the crown of thorns was placed on our Lord's head whilst He was suspended on the cross.

In Luke xxiv. 47 we have the distinct assertion from His own lips of His divinity, and of His being the Messiah, "and that repentance and remission of sins should be preached in my name."

INTRODUCTION. xxix

In John iv. 36 we are told that the reaper straightway receiveth wages. This, we may safely affirm, agrees with the experience of every earnest worker in the Lord's harvest-field.

In John vi. 59, "These things said he in the synagogue as he taught in Capernaum," becomes "These things said he in Capernaum, in the synagogue, as he taught." This reading would lead us to suspect that our English version of the Gospels shew a misunderstanding of the Greek text—ταῦτα εἶπεν ἐν συναγωγῇ διδάσκων ἐν Καπερναούμ. Here διδάσκων probably refers rather to συναγωγῇ which precedes it, than to ἐν Καπερναούμ which follows.

In John vii. 48 we read, "For who of the chief men or of the Pharisees has believed on him? only this mob, which knoweth not the law."

In John viii. 57 the question, "And hath Abraham seen thee?" follows more naturally on our Lord's previous statement, than the usual reading, "And hast thou seen Abraham?"

In John ix. 35 we observe that our Lord calls Himself Son of man instead of Son of God. All passages in this Codex bearing on the assertion of His divinity must have a special interest, and we therefore note in connection with it the question of the demons in Luke viii. 28, "What have I to do with thee, Jesus, thou Son of God Most High?"

If this assertion is weakened by the statement in our Lord's prayer, as recorded in John xvii. 5, "And now also give me the glory, my Father, from beside thyself, from that which thou gavest me when the world was not yet," instead of "The glory that I had with thee before the world was," we notice that this is only in agreement with the words of v. 24. The assertion of His divinity is as clear and strong as ever in

John xx. 31. And we perceive from John xvii. 5, 6, that some part of this glory at least, is "the men which thou gavest me out of the world."

In John xi. 38 we are told that the grave of Lazarus was an artificial one, hewn out of the rock, like a cave. We can see a vivid picture also of how Martha was startled, when she saw the bystanders obeying our Lord's command, from her exclamation, "Lord, why are they taking away the stone?"

From John xii. 3 we learn that Mary began her loving ministrations to our Lord by pouring the ointment first on His head.

In John xiii. 34 a change in the punctuation shews us that our Lord said, "And now a new commandment I give unto you, that ye love one another."

In John xiii. 37 a similar change shews us that Peter said, "I will lay down my life now for thy sake."

In John xvii. 11 we have an addition to one of our Lord's prayers for His people, "O my holy Father, take, keep them in thy name."

The effect of the transposition of the narrative in John xviii. is to shew that Caiaphas, not Annas, was the high priest who questioned our Lord, and to make the story of Peter's denial an unbroken narrative. It seems as if we had now the episode in something like its original form.

In John xx. 8 Peter shares with John the credit of having been first to see and believe in our Lord's resurrection.

The interpolations in our Codex are not numerous. That which will attract most attention is already known from Codex Bezae in Luke xxiii. 48, "Woe unto us, what hath befallen us? woe unto us, for our sins!"

Another occurs in John xx. 16. Here we are told that Mary Magdalene, when she recognised our Lord by the sound of her own name, "ran towards him, that she might touch him."

In John vi. 63 we are told that it is the Spirit that quickeneth the body; and in John iii. 6 that God is a living Spirit.

Some of these readings, as we have already said, indicate a greater antiquity for the Sinai manuscript than for Cureton's. But on the other hand, there are a few expressions which may point to a later origin.

The chief of these is, as it seems to us, the persistent use of the title, Our Lord, instead of the name Jesus throughout the narrative of all the Evangelists. Also the pleonastic phrase, "He was troubled in his soul, and was disturbed in his spirit," of John xi. 33. This is somewhat puzzling, as one characteristic of our MS., as compared with other early texts, is its conciseness. I believe that the transcribers are willing to assign it to the beginning of the fifth century, that is to an earlier period than Cureton's, or any other Syriac MS. in the British Museum. Their opinion is founded partly upon its orthography. The *facsimiles* of several pages which are now before the world, will enable other scholars to form an independent judgment. We observe from the final colophon, that the MS. must have been written at a period when prayer for departed saints had become a recognised custom.

The Curetonian Gospels have been of inestimable value in the work of New Testament revision. It is a matter of congratulation that the Sinai manuscript, discovered fifty years later, makes the text of the Old Syriac version nearly complete.

Yet the two do not perfectly coincide, as any one who will place this translation beside Cureton's may easily ascertain. Dr. Nestle, of Ulm, and Mr. Rendel Harris have both expressed the opinion that it represents, not a duplicate of the Curetonian, but the very first attempt at rendering the Gospel into Syriac, of which Tatian and the Curetonian are both revisions.

We have endeavoured, by means of the marginal notes, to indicate those variations from our English Authorised Version, which have their equivalents either in the Revised Version, as substantially representing the testimony of the most ancient Greek manuscripts, in Cureton's MS., or in Codex Bezae as the chief representative of the Old Latin.

We have referred to other manuscripts only in the case of remarkable variants, which are justified by none of these three texts. Beyond all these, a number of readings will be observed for which our Codex alone is responsible. And we have added, in an Appendix, a list of Greek words and phrases from the *Textus Receptus* for which the Syriac of our manuscript presents no equivalent.

We would point those of our readers to whom the subject of "various readings" in the text of a divinely inspired book may be new or startling, to the weighty and well-considered statement of the late Dr. Hort, in his Introduction to the *Text of the New Testament in the Original Greek*, the joint work of himself and Dr. Westcott:

"With regard to the great bulk of the words of the New Testament, as of most other ancient writings, there is no variation or other ground of doubt, and therefore no room for textual criticism; and here therefore an editor is merely a transcriber. The same may be said with substantial truth respecting those various readings which have never been received, and in all probability never will be received, into any printed text. The proportion of words virtually accepted on all hands as raised above doubt is very great, not less, on a rough computation, than seven-eighths of the whole. The remaining eighth, therefore, formed in great part by changes of order and other comparative trivialities, constitutes the whole area of criticism. If the principles followed in the present edition are sound, this area may be very greatly reduced. Recognising to the full the duty of abstinence from peremptory decision in cases where the evidence leaves the judgment in suspense between two or more readings, we find that, setting aside differences of orthography, the words in our opinion still subject to doubt only make up one sixtieth of the whole New Testament. In this second estimate the proportion of comparatively trivial variations is beyond measure larger than in the former; so that the amount of what can in any sense be called substantial variation is but a small fraction of the whole residuary variation, and can hardly form more than a thousandth part of the entire text."

Our study of this ancient Syriac version has convinced us that it is not the work of an heretic, and that its peculiar reading of Matthew i. 16 must be explained by some other hypothesis. No man, who entertained the slightest doubt of our Lord's Divinity, would have left John xiv. 1 in its present very interesting form. And Luke surely gives us a strong confirmation of the view that both genealogies are modified copies of an official register, when he prefaces his own account with " Jesus .... as he was called, the son of Joseph." We would entreat our readers not to decide this matter from the consideration of a single passage, but from that of the text as a whole.

In conclusion, I have to thank my sister, Mrs. James Y. Gibson, for her careful revision of my proof-sheets; Mr. J. Rendel Harris for several valuable suggestions; and Dr. Eberhard Nestle, of Ulm, for the solution of some important idiomatic difficulties, also for the marginal references to Luke i. 3, xi. 54, xvi. 25; John viii. 47, xi. 18, and for the changes of punctuation in John xiv. 1, 2, xvii. 24, 25.

AGNES SMITH LEWIS.

Castle-Brae, Cambridge,
December, 1894.

CORRIGENDA.

MATTHEW.

*IX. 9. After "publicans" add ". . . followed him and."
    17. After "spilled" add "and the skins perish."
X. 3. For "Alphæus" read "Halfai."
XXIII. 24. For "gnat" read "gnats."
*XXIV. 39. Add "the flood" before "came."
  *39. Add "shall be . . . of men . . . then two."
XXV. 46. For "punishment" read "torture."
XXVI. 20. For "the twelve" read "his twelve."
    29. For "this fruit" read "the fruit."
XXVII. 28. For "a robe" read "robes."
  *60. For "they departed" read "he departed" (doubtful).

MARK.

I. 38. For "that I may" read "and I will."
III. 7. For "multitude" read "great multitudes."
    19. For "Iscariot" read "Scariota," *passim*.
V. 23. For "hands" read "hand."
*VII. 35. After "Be opened" add "and in that . . . were opened."
  *36. Before "a great deal more" add ". . . them . . ."
*VIII. 23. After "in his eyes" read "hand."
*IX. 15. After "and straightway" read "when they saw him, they."
  *22. Omit "to destroy" (doubtful).
    23. For "the house" read "his house."
X. 7. For "for this cause" read "therefore."
    30. For "mothers" read "mother."
  *40. For "others" read "another." (The word is masculine singular. Professor Bensly gave it the seyâmé points which denote the plural; and but for my photograph, it might have been edited in the plural. The parallel passage, Matt. xx. 21, has a plural pronoun.)

* See Note on next page.

CORRIGENDA.

MARK—*continued*.

X. 52. For "Jesus" read "He."
XI. 11. For "and when" read "but when."
XIV. 44. After "saying" add "unto them."
XV. 3. After "give" add "them."
*7. For "because of murder" read "there was a man who had done evil and committed murder."
*12. Add "again" after "answered."
*15. Add "to be crucified" before "And the soldiers."

LUKE.

I. 7. For "And" read "But."
50. For "on the generation" read "unto the generation."
II. 36. For "her husband" read "a husband."
*XXIV. 34. Omit "came."

* Those marked with an asterisk are owing to additions and alterations having been made from my photographs by the transcribers on the last revise of their proof-sheets, and which did not come under my observation in time to be included in this volume.—A. S. L.

EMENDATIONS SUGGESTED IN THE SYRIAC TEXT.

MARK	X. 12,	for	ܐܢܬܬܐ	read	ܐܢܬܬܗ
,,	XIV. 5,	,,	ܘܡܬܚܫܒܝܢ	,,	ܘܡܬܚܫܒܝܢ
,,	XV. 20,	,,	ܒܥܘܗܝ	,,	ܕܒܥܘܗܝ
LUKE	I. 53,	,,	ܣܒܥܘ̈ܗܝ	,,	ܣܒܥܘ̈ܗܝ
,,	I. 70,	,,	ܕܐܦ	,,	ܕܐܡܪ
,,	V. 1,	,,	ܣܦܬܐ	,,	ܣܦܬܐ
,,	XIV. 21,	,,	ܘܟܘܣܡܝܐ	,,	ܘܟܘܣܡܝܐ
,,	XX. 34,	,,	ܢܣܒܝܢ	,,	ܢܣܒܝܢ
,,	XXIV. 23,	,,	ܘܐܡܪܝܢ ܕܚܙܘܗܝ	,,	ܘܐܡܪܝܢ ܕܚܙܘܗܝ
JOHN	VI. 49,	,,	ܗܘܐ	,,	ܚܢܢܐ
,,	VI. 64,	,,	ܕܡܢ ܡܗܝܡܢܝ̈ܢ	,,	ܡܢ ܕܡܗܝܡܢܝ̈ܢ
,,	X. 9,	,,	ܢܚܐ	,,	ܢܚܐ
,,	XI. 17,	,,	ܕܟܒܪ	,,	ܠܟܒܪ
	XVII. 7,	,,	ܡܕܡ	read perhaps	ܡܪܟ
,,	XXI. 16,	,,	ܚܒܣܝܢ	,,	ܚܒܣܝܢ

THE FOUR GOSPELS

THE GOSPEL OF MATTHEW

1 The book of the generations of Jesus the Christ,
2 the son of David, the son of Abraham. Abraham begat Isaac; Isaac begat Jacob; Jacob begat Juda
3 and his brethren; Juda begat Phares and Zara of Thamar; Phares begat Hesron; Hesron begat Aram;
4 Aram begat Aminadab; Aminadab begat Nahson;
5 Nahson begat Shela[1]; Shela[1] begat Boaz of Rahab; [1 Cureton.]
6 Boaz begat Obed of Ruth; Obed begat Jesse; Jesse begat David the king; David[2] begat Solomon of the [2 R. V. Cureton.]
7 wife of Uria; Solomon begat Rehoboam; Rehoboam
8 begat Abia; Abia begat Asa; Asa begat Josaphat;
9 Josaphat begat Joram; Joram begat Ozia; Ozia begat Jotham; Jotham begat Achaz; Achaz begat
10 Hezekia; Hezekia begat Manassa; Manassa begat
11 Amon; Amon begat Josia; Josia begat Juchonia
12 and his brethren in the captivity[3] of Babylon; And [3 Cureton.] after the captivity[3] of Babylon, Juchonia begat Sheal-
13 tiel; Shealtiel begat Zorobabel; Zorobabel begat Abiur[4]; Abiur[4] begat Eliakim; Eliakim begat Azor; [4 Cureton.]
14 Azor begat Sadoc; Sadoc begat Achin[5]; Achin[5] begat [5 Cureton.]
15 Eliud; Eliud begat Eleazar; Eleazar begat Matthan;
16 Matthan begat Jacob; Jacob begat Joseph; Joseph, to whom was betrothed Mary the Virgin, begat Jesus, who is called the Christ.
17 All these generations from Abraham until David are fourteen generations; and from David until the captivity of Babylon are fourteen generations; and from the captivity[6] of Babylon until the Christ are [6 Cureton] fourteen generations.

And the birth of the Christ was on this wise: 18 When Mary his mother was espoused to Joseph, when they had not come near one to the other,¹ she was found with child of the Holy Ghost. Then 19 Joseph her husband, because he was just, did not wish to expose Mary, and was minded quietly to repudiate her.² But while he thought on these 20 things,³ the angel of the Lord appeared to him in a vision, and said unto him, Joseph, son of David, fear not to take Mary thy wife: for that which is begotten⁴ from her is of the Holy Ghost. And she 21 shall bear to thee a son, and thou⁵ shalt call his name Jesus: for he shall save his people from their sins. Now this which happened was that it might be 22 fulfilled which was spoken of the Lord by Isaia⁶ the prophet, who said, Behold a virgin shall be with 23 child, and shall bring forth a son, and they shall call his name Emmanuel, which being interpreted is, God with us. When Joseph arose from his sleep, 24 he did as the angel of the Lord had commanded him, and took his wife: and she bore to him a son, and 25 he called his name Jesus.

And when Jesus was born in Beth Lehem of 2 Judæa in the days of Herod the king, behold, there came wise men from the east to Jerusalem, and 2 said, Where is the King of the Jews that is born⁷? for we have seen his star from the east, and are come to worship him. And when Herod the king 3 heard, he was troubled, and all Jerusalem with him. And he assembled all the chief priests and 4 scribes of the people, and said to them, Where is the Christ born? They say unto him, In Beth 5 Lehem of Judæa, for thus it is written by the

¹ Cureton.

² Cureton. Bezae.
³ Cureton.

⁴ R.V. marg.
⁵ Or 'she shall call.'

⁶ Bezae

⁷ Cureton.

6 prophet, And thou too, Beth Lehem of Juda art
not the least of the kings of Juda: for out of thee
shall come a king, who shall shepherd[1] my people [1 R. V. Cureton. Bezae.]
7 Israel. Then Herod called those wise men privily,
and enquired of them that he might know at what
8 time the star appeared to them. And he sent them
to Beth Lehem, and said unto them, Go search concerning him, the child; and when ye have found
him, come and shew me, that I also may go and
9 worship him. They then, when they had received
the commandment[2] of the king, departed: and there [2 Cureton.]
appeared[3] to them the star which they had seen in [3 Cureton.]
the east; it went before them till it came and stood
10 there where the child was. And they, when they saw
11 the star, rejoiced with great joy. And they came into
the house, and saw the child with Mary his mother,
and fell down and worshipped him: and they opened
their treasures, and presented unto him gifts; gold,
12 and myrrh[4] and frankincense. And it appeared to [4 Cureton.]
them in a vision that they should not return unto
Herod,[5] and they departed by another way into their [5 Cureton.]
13 country. And after them[6] there appeared to Joseph [6 Cureton.]
the angel of the Lord in a dream, and said unto
him,[7] Arise, take the child and his mother, and flee [7 Cureton.]
into Egypt, and be thou there until I tell thee: for
Herod is about to seek the young child to destroy
14 him. And Joseph[8] arose, and took the child and his [8 Cureton.]
mother by night: and departed into Egypt: and was
15 there until Herod the king[9] was dead: that it might [9 Cureton.]
be fulfilled which was spoken of the Lord by the
mouth of Isaia the prophet, who had said, Out of Egypt
16 did I call my son. Then Herod, when he saw that
the wise men had mocked him, was exceeding wroth,

and sent and slew the children, all that were in Beth Lehem and in its borders, from two years old and under, according to the time which the wise men had said to him. Then was fulfilled the word which 17 Jeremia the prophet[1] had spoken. A voice was heard in Ramtha, wailing and weeping, and much 18 sighing, the voice[2] of Rachel who was weeping for her children, and she would not be comforted because they are not.

But when Herod the king[3] was dead,[4] there 19 appeared unto Joseph in Egypt an angel of the Lord, saying to him[5] in a dream, Arise, take the 20 child and his mother, and go into the land of Israel: for they are dead that sought the child's life. And 21 he arose, took the child and his mother, and came into the land of Israel. But when Joseph[6] 22 heard that Archelaus was king in the room of his father Herod, he was afraid to go thither: and it appeared[7] in a dream that he should go into the region of Galilee: and he came thither,[8] and dwelt in 23 a city which is called Nazareth: and the word was fulfilled which was spoken by the prophet, that he should be called a Nazarene.

In those days came John the Baptist, preaching 3 in the wilderness of Judæa, saying, Repent ye: for 2 the kingdom of heaven is at hand. This is he 3 that was written[9] about by Isaia the prophet, who said, Prepare ye a way for the Lord. And the same 4 John was clothed[10] in raiment of camel's hair, and was girded about his loins with a girdle; and his meat was locusts and honey of the mountain.[11] Then 5 went to him they of Jerusalem, and all Judæa, and all from beyond the river[12] Jordan, and he bap- 6

[1] Cureton.
[2] Cureton.
[3] Cureton.
[4] Cureton.
[5] Cureton.
[6] Cureton.
[7] Cureton.
[8] Cureton.
[9] Cureton.
[10] Cureton.
[11] Palestinian Syriac.
[12] Cureton.

tized them in the river¹ Jordan, each² man con- ¹ Cureton.
7 fessing his sins. But when he saw many of the ² Cureton.
Pharisees and Sadducees who were coming to his
baptism, he said to them, O generation of vipers, who
hath shewn you to flee from the wrath that is about
8 to come³? Bring forth therefore fruits which are ³ Cureton.
9 meet for repentance: and say not,⁴ We have ⁴ Cureton.
Abraham for our father: for I say unto you, that
God is able of these stones to raise up children unto
10 Abraham. And behold,⁵ the axe has reached the roots ⁵ Cureton
of the trees: and every tree that bringeth not forth
11 fruit is cut down, and is cast into the fire. For I
baptize you with water unto repentance: but he that
cometh after me is mightier than I, whose shoes
I am not worthy to bear: he shall baptize you with
12 fire, and with the Holy Ghost: he who holds⁶ the ⁶ Cureton.
fan in his hand, and will cleanse his threshing-
floor, and will gather the wheat into his garner;
but the chaff he will burn up with unquenchable
fire.

13 Then cometh Jesus from Galilee unto John that he
14 might baptize him in the Jordan, and John forbad him,
saying unto him,⁷ I have need that thou shouldest⁸ ⁷ Cureton.
⁸ Cureton.
15 baptize me, and thou art come to me. Jesus answered
and said unto him, Suffer it now: for thus it
becometh us to fulfil all righteousness. Then he
16 suffered him to be baptized.⁹ And when he¹⁰ was ⁹ Cureton.
¹⁰ Cureton.
baptized and went up out¹¹ of the water, lo, the ¹¹ Cureton.
heavens were opened, and he saw the Spirit of God
descending in the likeness of a dove, and it abode
17 upon him: and a voice was heard¹² from heaven, ¹² Cureton.
saying to him, Thou art my Son and my beloved,¹³ in ¹³ Cureton.
thee I am well pleased.

Then Jesus was led up of the Spirit into the 4 wilderness, to be tempted of the devil. And after 2 forty days and forty nights that he had fasted, he hungered. And the tempter came near and said 3 unto him,[1] If thou be the Son of God, say to these stones that they become[2] bread. Jesus[3] answered and 4 said[4] unto him, It is written, Not by bread alone shall man live, but by every word that proceedeth out of the mouth of the Lord.[5] Then the devil led 5 him and brought him into the holy city, and set him on the pinnacle of the temple, and said unto him, If 6 thou be the Son of God, cast thyself from hence: for it is written, that to his angels he shall command concerning thee to keep thee, and on their arms they shall bear thee up, lest thou shouldest strike with thy foot on a stone. Jesus said unto him, It is 7 written, Thou shalt not tempt the Lord thy God. Again Satan led him and took him up, and set him 8 on a mountain which was very high, and shewed him all the kingdoms of this world; and said unto him, 9 These kingdoms and their glory thou hast seen; to thee will I give them, if thou wilt fall down and worship before me. Then said Jesus unto him, 10 Get behind with thee, Satan: for it is written, The Lord thy God shalt thou worship, and him only shalt thou serve. Then the tempter withdrew from 11 him until the time, and angels came near and were ministering unto Jesus.

And when he[6] heard that John was apprehended, 12 he withdrew into Galilee; and left Nazareth, and 13 came to Capernaum, which is beside the sea, in Zebulon and in Naphtali: that the word might be 14 fulfilled which was spoken by Isaia the prophet,

---

[1] Cureton. Bezae.
[2] Cureton. Bezae.
[3] Cureton.
[4] Cureton.
[5] Cureton.
[6] R. V. Bezae.

15 saying, The land of Zebulon, and the land of Naphtali, the way of the sea, and beyond the river Jordan,
16 Galilee of the nations; the people that sat in darkness saw a light; and those who sat in sadness and
17 the shadows of death light is sprung up on them. From that time began Jesus to preach, saying,[1] The king-
18 dom of heaven hath come near. And as .... was by .... the shore of the sea, he saw two brethren, Simon and Andrew his brother, preparing their nets and casting [them] into the sea: for they were fisher-
19 men.[2] He saith unto them, Follow me, and I will
20 make you fishers of men. And they in that hour
21 left their nets and followed him. And again he came near, and saw two other brethren, James and John, sitting[3] in the ship with Zebedee their father,
22 and preparing their nets, and he called them. And they left their father in the ship, and followed him.
23 And Jesus went round about in all Galilee, teaching in their synagogues, and preaching the gospel of the kingdom, and healing all disease and all sickness
24 which were among the people. And they brought unto him many that were tormented with hateful torments, and with sore sicknesses, and on each of them he laid his hand; and he healed everyone.
25 And when there was a great multitude who were from Galilee, and from Decapolis, and from Jerusalem, and from Judæa, and from beyond
5 Jordan, when he saw the great multitudes, he went up the mountain: and when he had sat down, his
2 disciples came unto him: and he began to say unto them,
3 Blessed are the poor in spirit: for theirs is the kingdom of heaven.

[1] Cureton.
[2] Syriac—'hunters of fish.'
[3] Cureton.

Blessed are they that mourn: for they shall be comforted. 4

Blessed are the meek: for they shall inherit the earth. 5

Blessed are they which do hunger and thirst for justice: for they shall be satisfied. 6

¹ Cureton.

Blessed are the merciful: for upon¹ them shall be mercies. 7

² Cureton.

Blessed are those² who are pure in heart: for they shall see God. 8

Blessed are the peacemakers: for they shall be called the children of God. 9

Blessed are they which are persecuted for righteousness' sake: for theirs is the kingdom of heaven. 10

Blessed are ye, when men shall hate you, and persecute you, and when they shall say against you what is evil, for my own name's sake. 11 But rejoice ye, 12

³ Cureton.

and be glad in³ that day: for great is your reward in heaven: for so persecuted their fathers the prophets.

Ye are the salt of the earth: if the salt have become insipid, wherewith shall it be salted? it is good 13

⁴ Cureton.

for nothing, but to be cast out, and men⁴ shall trample upon it. Ye are the light of the world. And a city 14

⁵ Cureton.
⁶ Cureton.

that is built⁵ on a hill cannot be hid. And a man⁶ doth 15 not light a lamp, and set it under a bushel, but he setteth it on the top of a candlestick; and it giveth light unto all that are in the house. So let your 16 light shine before men, that they may see your good works, and glorify your Father which is in heaven.

Think not that I am come to destroy the law and the prophets: I am not come to destroy, but to fulfil 17

⁷ Cureton.

them.⁷ For verily I say unto you, till heaven and 18 earth pass away, one letter iota shall not pass from

⁸ Syriac—
'relax.'

the law, till all shall be. And whosoever shall destroy⁸ 19

19 one of these small commandments, and shall teach men so, he shall be called little in the kingdom of heaven:
20 but whosoever shall do and teach thus... cal... except
21 your uprightness shall exceed.... Ye have heard.... to them of old time, Thou shalt not kill; and whosoever
22 shall kill shall be condemned in the judgment: but I say unto you, that whosoever is angry with his brother without a cause shall be condemned in the judgment: and whosoever shall say to his brother, Raca, shall be condemned by the council: and whosoever shall say to his brother,[1]... shall be condemned to the Gehenna of fire.
23 If therefore.... thine offering on the altar, and
24 there r... hath enmity against thee, leave [it] there on the altar, and go... be reconciled to thy brother, and
25 then come, offer thine offering... Be agreed with thine adversary quickly, whilst... in the way... into
26 prison.... unto thee... no... thence, till...
27 shalt pay the last farthing. Ye have heard that it
28 was said,[2] Thou shalt not commit adultery: but I say unto you, That whosoever looketh on a woman and lusteth after her, hath committed adultery with her[3]
29 in his heart. And if thy right eye offend thee, pluck it out, and cast it from thee: for it is profitable for thee that one of thy members should perish, and not that thy whole body should go to hell.
31 [4]It hath been said, whosoever shall leave his wife, let him give her a writing of divorcement: but I say
32 unto you, That whosoever putteth away his wife, against whom adultery hath not been alleged,[5] he causeth her to commit adultery. And whosoever taketh a forsaken one committeth adultery.
33 Ye have heard that it hath been said, Thou shalt not forswear thyself, but shalt give[6] unto the Lord an

[1] Cureton.
[2] R.V.
[3] Cureton.
[4] Omit v. 30. Bezae.
[5] Cureton.
[6] Cureton.

oath: but I say unto you, Swear not at all; not by 34 the heavens¹; for they are the throne of God: and 35 not by the earth; for it is the footstool beneath his feet²: and not by Jerusalem; for it is the city of the great King. And swear not by thy head, because 36 thou canst not make one hair of the hair on it black or white. But let thy word be, Yea, yea; and Nay, nay: 37 whatsoever is more than these is of the evil³ one.

Ye have heard that it hath been said, An eye for 38 an eye, and a tooth for a tooth: but I say unto you, 39 That ye resist not evil: but whosoever shall smite thee on thy cheek, offer to him the other. And who- 40 soever will go to law with thee, and take thy coat, leave⁴ to him also thy cloke. Whosoever shall compel 41 thee to go with him a mile, go again with him other⁵ twain. And whosoever asketh of thee, give to him, and 42 whosoever desireth to borrow of thee, refuse him not.

Ye have heard that it hath been said, Thou shalt 43 love thy neighbour, and hate thine enemy. But I say 44 unto you, Love your enemies, and pray for them who persecute you,⁶ that ye may be the children of your 45 Father which is in heaven: he who maketh his sun to rise on the good and on the evil, and letteth down⁷ his rain on the just and on the unjust. For if ye love 46 them which love you, what reward have ye? the publicans do thus. Be ye therefore perfect, even as 48 your Father which is in heaven is perfect.

And do not your alms in the presence⁸ of men, **6** that ye may be seen by them, and no reward be yours with your Father which is in heaven.

When thou doest alms, do not sound a trumpet 2 before thee, as the hypocrites do in the synagogues and in the streets, that they may be glorified

---

¹ Cureton.
² Cureton.
³ R. V. Cureton. Bezae.
⁴ Bezae.
⁵ Cureton. Bezae.
⁶ Cureton.
⁷ Cureton.
⁸ Syriac — 'eye.'

of men. Verily I say unto you, they have received
3 their reward. But when thou doest alms, let not thy
4 left hand know what thy right hand doeth: that
thine alms may be in secret: and the Father, which
6 seeth in secret, shall reward thee openly. [1]But thou, [1] Omit v. 5.
when thou prayest, enter into the closet, and shut the
door, and pray to thy Father in secret; and thy Father,
7 who seeth in secret, he shall reward thee. And when
ye pray, do not say vain things, like the heathen: who
think that with much speaking they shall be heard.
8 Be not ye therefore like unto them: for he, your
Father, knoweth, when ye have not yet asked him,
9 what is wanted by you. After this manner therefore pray ye. Our Father which art in heaven,
Hallowed be thy name. And let come . . . .

[vi. 10 *to* viii. 3 *is on pages which have been lost from the original MS. before John the Recluse used it in* A.D. 778.]

8 Our Lord . . . . his hand, and touched him, say-
3 ing to him, I will: be thou clean. And immediately
4 the leprosy was cleansed from him. Our Lord said
unto him, See thou tell no man; but go thy way,
shew thyself to the priest, and offer the sacrifice as
Moses commanded, that it may be a testimony unto
them.
5 After these things[2] a chiliarch[3] came to him . . . . [2] Cureton.
6 saying, My servant is paralyzed, and lieth at home[4] in [3] Or 'military tribune.'
7 great torment. He[5] saith unto him, I will come . . . . [4] Cureton.
[5] R. V.
8 The chiliarch answered and said unto him, Lord, I am
not worthy that thou shouldest enter under my roof:
but speak[6] with a word, and my boy shall be healed. [6] R. V. marg.
9 For I also am a man who has authority, and soldiers
are under me[7]: and I say to this man, ... [7] Syriac— 'my hand.'

Come, and he cometh; and I say to my servant, do such
a thing, and he doeth it. When our Lord heard this, 10
he marvelled, and said to them that followed, Verily
I say unto you, I have not found faith like this even
among Israel. I say unto you, That . . . . shall come 11
from the east and from the west, and shall sit down
with Abraham and Isaac and Jacob, in the kingdom
of heaven . . . . the kingdom shall go[1] out into outer 12
darkness: there shall be weeping and gnashing of
teeth. Then our Lord said unto the chiliarch, Go: 13
as thou hast believed so be it to thee. And in
that hour his boy was healed.

And Jesus came into the house of Simon C[epha] 14
and saw his wife's mother laid, and sick of a fever.
And he touched her hand, and immediately the fever 15
left her: and she arose, and ministered to them.
And . . . . sunset . . . . they brought to him all those 16
who had demons: and he cast them out with a word,
and those that . . . . he healed: that it might be ful- 17
filled which was spoken by Isaia, saying, He will take
our infirmities, and bear our sicknesses. Now when 18
our Lord saw a great multitude about him, he commanded that they should depart thence to the other
side. And a certain scribe came near, and said unto 19
him, Master, I will follow thee whithersoever thou
goest. Our Lord said, The foxes have holes, and the 20
birds of the heaven[2] have nests; but the Son of man
hath not where to lay his head. And another of his 21
disciples said unto him, Suffer me first to go and bury
my father, and I will come. He said unto him, Let 22
the dead bury their dead; . . . . come after . . . .
And he went up . . . . and his disciples followed 23
him. And there was a tempest in . . . . was almost 24

[1] Cureton.
[2] R. V. Cureton.

THE GOSPEL OF MATTHEW

25 covered with the waves: but he was asleep. And they came near .... and awoke him, ... to him,
26 Our Lord, save us: for behold, we perish. He said .... Why are ye fearful? Then he arose, and rebuked the wind and the sea; and there was a great
27 calm. But the men marvelled, saying, ... this, that the sea and the wind obey him!
28 And when he was come to the country of the Gadarenes,[1] there met him two men .... demons,[1 R.V.] and were very wicked, ... so that no man could pass
29 by that way.... What have we to do with thee, ...
30 of God? art thou come .... was feeding a good

[In many parts of this page the writing has been completely scraped out with a knife.—J.R.H.]

31 way off from them. And these demons besought him, saying, If thou cast us out, send[2] us into that [2 R.V. Bezae.]
32 herd of swine. He said unto them, Go. And they came out, and entered into the swine: and the whole herd ran to a steep rock and fell into the sea, and the
33 h[erdsmen] fled, and entered into the city, and told
34 all .... of the demons .... the whole city ....

9
2
to
5 .... whether is easier to say, Thy sins be for-
6 given thee; or to say, Arise, walk? But that ye may know that the Son of man hath power on earth to forgive sins, (then saith he to the sick of the palsy), Arise, take up thy bed, and go unto thine house.
7 And he arose, and took up his bed, and went to his
8 house. But when the multitudes saw it, they were

afraid, and glorified God, who had given this power unto men.

And he departed thence, and when our Lord was passing, he saw a certain man sitting amongst the publicans: 10
. . . . 11
. . . . But when he¹ heard it, he said,² They that are whole need not a physician, but they that are sick. But go ye and learn what that is, I seek mercy, and not sacrifice: for I am not come to call the righteous, but sinners to repentance. Then came the disciples of John, saying, Why do we and the Pharisees fast assiduously, but thy disciples fast not? Our Lord said unto them, The children of the bride-chamber cannot keep a mourning as long as the bridegroom is with them: but the days will come, when the bridegroom shall be taken from them, and then shall they fast.

No man putteth a piece of new cloth on a worn-out garment, lest the filling-up of the new piece should draw away the weak parts of the worn-out one, and the rent should be worse than before. And also they do not put new wine into worn-out wine-skins, lest the wine split these wine-skins, and the wine be spilled: but they put new wine into new wine-skins, and both are preserved. While he spake with them, behold, a certain ruler of their synagogue came, and falling down, worshipped him, saying, My daughter is now dead: but lay thy hand, and she shall live. And our Lord arose, and went with him, he and his disciples. And behold, a woman, who had an issue of blood twelve years, came and touched the hem of his garment: for she said within herself, If I may

¹ R. V.
² R. V.

but touch the hem of his garment, I shall be healed.
22 And he turned, and said unto her, Daughter, thy faith hath saved thee. And from that hour that woman
23 was made whole. And when our Lord came into the house of that ruler of the synagogue, and saw the minstrels and the crowd who were making a tumult,
24 he said unto them, Give place: for the maid is not
25 dead, but sleepeth. And they laughed at him. And when he had put out the crowd, he came and touched
26 her hand, and immediately she arose. And the fame
27 hereof went abroad into all that land. And as our Lord passed by, two blind men followed him, crying with a loud voice, Have mercy on us, thou son of
28 David. And when he was come into the house, the blind men came to him: he saith unto them, Believe ye that I am able to do this? They say unto him,
29 Yea, our Lord, we believe. Then touched he their eyes, saying, According as ye believed be it unto you.
30 And immediately their eyes were opened; and our Lord charged them, saying unto them, Behold, see
31 that ye tell it to no man. And when they had gone out, they made it known to every man in that
32 country. And after they had gone out, they brought
33 to him a dumb man[1] possessed with a demon. And when the demon had gone out of him, the dumb spake: and the multitudes marvelled, saying, It was never so seen in Israel.

35 [2]And our Lord went among the cities and villages, teaching in their synagogues, and preaching the gospel of the kingdom, and healing every sickness
36 and every disease. But when he saw the multitudes, he had compassion on them, because they were weary, and were scattered as sheep having no shepherd.

[1] Syriac—'whom a demon rode upon.'
[2] Omit v. 34.

Then saith he unto his disciples, The harvest is 37 plenteous, and the labourers few; pray ye therefore 38 the Lord of the harvest, that he will send forth labourers into his harvest.

And he called his twelve, and gave them power 10 to cast[1] out unclean spirits, and to heal every sickness and every disease. Now these are the names of his 2 twelve disciples; The first, Simon Peter, and Andrew his brother; and James and John the sons of Zebedee; and Philip and Bar-Tholomi; and Thomas, and 3 Matthew the publican; and James the son of Alphæus; and Simon the Zealot, and Juda the 4 son of James, and Juda Iscariot, he who was the betrayer. And our Lord sent forth these his twelve 5 disciples, and commanded them, saying unto them, Go not into the way of the Gentiles, and into any city of the Samaritans enter ye not: but go to the 6 lost[2] sheep of the house of Israel. And as ye go, 7 preach, saying, The kingdom of heaven cometh near. Heal the sick, raise the dead, cleanse the lepers, cast 8 out demons: freely ye have received, freely give. Provide neither gold, nor silver, nor brass in your 9 purses, nor scrip for the way, neither two coats, 10 neither shoes, nor yet staves: for the workman is worthy of his meat. Into whatsoever city ye enter, 11 inquire who is worthy; and be there till ye go thence. And when ye come into an house, salute[3] 12 that house. And if that house be worthy, your 13 peace shall be on it[4]: but if not, your peace shall return upon you. Whosoever shall not receive you, nor hear 14 your words, when ye depart out of that house or out of that city, shake off the dust of your feet. And verily I say unto you, that for the land of Sodom 15

[1] Bezae.

[2] Syriac—'wandering.'

[3] Syriac—'give peace to.'

[4] Bezae.

and of Gomorra it shall be more tolerable in the day
16 of judgment, than for that city. Behold, I send you
forth as lambs in the midst of wolves: be ye therefore
wise as serpents, and simple¹ as doves.   ¹ Bezae.

17 Beware of men: who will deliver you up to law
courts, and will scourge you in their synagogues;
18 and before kings and governors shall ye stand for my
name's sake, for a testimony to them and to the
19 nations. When they bring you near, take no thought
what ye shall speak: for it shall be given you in that
20 hour what ye shall speak. For it is not ye that
speak, but the Spirit of your Father speaketh in
21 you. For the brother shall deliver up his brother to
death, and the father his son to death: and children
shall rise up against their parents, and cause them
22 to be put to death. And men shall hate you for my
name's sake: but he that endureth to the end, he
shall be saved.

23 When they persecute you in this city, flee ye
from it to another: and if they persecute² you in the   ² Bezae.
other city, flee ye to another: for verily I say unto
you, Ye shall not have finished all the cities of the
24 house of Israel, till the Son of man be come. A
25 disciple is not greater than his master. It is enough
for the disciple that he be as his master, and for the
servant as his lord. And if they have called the
master of the house Beelzebub, what shall they call
26 them³ of his household? Therefore fear them not: ³ Syriac—'the sons of his house.'
for there is nothing covered that shall not be revealed; nor hid, that shall not be made known.
27 What I tell you in darkness, speak ye in the light:
and what ye hear in your ears, proclaim upon the
28 house-tops. And be not afraid of them which kill

the body, but the soul they have no power to kill: 28 but rather fear him who is able to cast both body and soul into hell. Two sparrows are sold for a 29 farthing; and one of them doth not fall on the ground without your Father. But even the hairs of your 30 hair are all numbered. Fear not therefore, for ye 31 are of more value than many sparrows. Every man 32 who shall confess me, I also will confess him before my Father which is in heaven. And whosoever shall 33 deny me before men, I also will deny him before my Father which is in heaven. Think not that I came 34 to sow[1] peace on this earth: I came not to sow peace, but a sword. For I came to separate[2] a son from his 35 father, and the daughter from her mother, and the daughter-in-law from her mother-in-law. And a 36 man's foes shall be they[3] of his household. But he 37 who loveth his[4] father and his[4] mother more than me, is not worthy of me: and he who loveth his son or his daughter more than me, is not worthy of me. And whosoever doth not take up his cross and follow 38 me, is not worthy of me. For whosoever will find his 39 life shall lose it: and whosoever will lose his life for my sake shall find it. He that receiveth you receiveth 40 me, and he that receiveth me receiveth him that sent me. For whosoever receiveth a prophet in the 41 name of a prophet, receiveth a prophet's reward; and whosoever receiveth a righteous man in the name of a righteous man, shall take a righteous man's reward. And whosoever shall give to drink a 42 cup of cold water unto one of these little ones in the name of discipleship,[5] verily I say unto you, his reward shall not be lost.

And it came to pass, when our Lord had made an 11

[1] Syriac—'cast.'
[2] Cureton.

[3] Syriac—'the sons of his house.'
[4] Cureton.

[5] Cureton.

end of commanding his twelve disciples, he departed
2 thence to t . . . . and to preach . . . . John . . . .
3 of our Lord he sent . . . . . unto him . . . . . who
4 should come . . . .
5
6 . . . .
7
8 . . . . what . . . . to say unto the multitude
9 . . . . they . . . . king's . . . . But what went ye
out for to see? A prophet? yea, I say unto you, and
10 he is more than a prophet. This is he of whom it
is written, Behold, I send my messenger before thy
11 face, which shall prepare the way before thee. Verily
I say unto you, there hath not arisen among them
that are born of women a greater than John the
Baptist: but he that is little[1] in the kingdom of [1] R.V. Cureton.
12 heaven is greater than he. From the days of John
the Baptist until now the kingdom of heaven suf-
13 fereth violence, and the violent . . . . it . . . . For all
14 the prophets . . . . until John . . . . receive it . . . .
15 which was . . . . Who hath ears, let him hear.
16   . . . . this generation? It is like unto children
sitting in the market, and sending[2] to their fellows, [2] Cureton.
17 We have piped unto you, and ye have not danced;
we have mourned unto you, and ye have not lamented.
18 For John came neither eating nor drinking, and they
19 say, He hath a demon. And the Son of man came eating and drinking, and they say, Behold a man gluttonous and a wine-bibber, and a friend of publicans and
sinners. But wisdom is justified of her children.
20   Then began . . . . to upbraid . . . . . those
21 . . . . repented . . . . of Sidon . . . . would have
22 . . . . in sackcloth . . . . repented . . . . I say unto
you, It shall be more tolerable for Tyre and Sidon at
23 the day of judgment than for you. . . . . which art

exalted . . . . . . shalt be brought down to Sheol; 23
. . . . in Sodom . . . . . mighty works that have
been seen in thee 24
. . . . from the wise, and hast revealed them unto $^{to}_{26}$
babes . . . . before thee. All things are delivered 27
unto me of my Father: and no man knoweth the
Son but the Father; neither . . . . any man the
Father, but . . . . Come unto me all ye . . . . laden, 28
and I . . . . my yoke . . . . and learn . . . . I am lowly 29
in heart . . . . rest unto your souls, for my yoke is 30
gentle, and my burden is small.[1]

At that time he walked 12
. . . . $^{2}_{to}$
. . . . had known 7
mercy . . . . sacrifice 8
and will he not draw, lifting . . . . $^{to}_{11}$
How much then . . . men than . . . lawful . . . well . . . 12
Then . . . to the man . . . thy hand. And he stretched 13
forth . . . . and it was restored like as . . . . And 14
as they went out . . . . how . . . . that it might $^{to}_{17}$
be fulfilled . . . . . heard . . . . . not demons, but $^{to}_{24}$
by . . . . of the [demons]. And when he saw 25
sins and blasphemies shall be forgiven unto men: $^{to}_{31}$
but whosoever shall blaspheme against the Spirit it
shall not be forgiven him. And whosoever speaketh 32
a word against the Son of man, it shall be forgiven
him: but whosoever blasphemeth[2] against the Holy
Spirit, it shall not be forgiven him, neither in this
world, nor in the world to come. Either make the 33
tree good, and his fruit good; or make the tree
corrupt, and his fruit corrupt: for the tree is known
by his fruit. O generation of serpents, how can ye, 34
when ye are evil, speak good things? for out of the

[1] Cureton.

[2] Cureton.

35 abundance of the heart the mouth utters. And a
good man, out of the good treasures which are in[1] his   [1] Cureton.
heart, bringeth forth good things; and an evil man
out of the evil treasures that are in his heart,
36 speaketh evil things. But I say unto you, That
every idle word that men shall speak, they shall give
37 account of it in the day of judgment. For by thy
words thou shalt be justified, and by thy words thou
shalt be condemned.

38   Then certain of the scribes and of the Pharisees
said unto him, Teacher, we would see some sign from
39 thee. But he answered and said unto them, An evil
and adulterous generation seeketh a sign; no sign
shall be given to it, but the sign of Jona the
40 prophet. And as Jona the prophet was in the
belly of the fish three days and three nights, so shall
the Son of man be three days and three nights in
41 the heart of the earth. The men[2] of Nineveh shall   [2] Syriac—'men, the sons of Nineveh.'
rise in the judgment with this generation, they shall
condemn it: for they repented at the preaching of
Jona; and behold, a greater than Jona is here.
42 The queen of the South shall rise up in the judgment
with this generation, and shall condemn it: for she
came from the uttermost parts of the earth to hear
the wisdom of Solomon; and behold, a greater than
Solomon is here.

43   When the spirit of uncleanness is gone out of
a man, it goeth wandering about through places,
where no water is, to find rest; and when it hath
44 not found it, it saith, I will return and go to
my house, from whence I came out; and if it
cometh, it findeth it empty, and swept, and gar-
45 nished. Then it goeth, and taketh seven spirits

worse than itself, and they enter in and dwell in it: and the last state of the man is worse than his first. Even so shall it be unto this wicked generation. While he yet talked to the multitude, behold, his mother and his brethren stood without, desiring to speak with him. ¹But he answered and said unto him that told him, Who is my mother? or who are my brethren? And he stretched forth his hand towards his disciples, and said, These are my mother and my brethren; for whosoever doeth the will of my Father which is in heaven, he is my brother and my sisters and my mother.

The same day Jesus went out, and sat by the sea-side. And great multitudes were gathered together unto him, and he went up and sat in a ship; and the whole multitude stood on the shore of the sea. And he spake with them many things in parables, saying, Behold, a sower went forth to sow seed; and when he sowed, some fell by the way-side, and the fowls came and picked it up: and some fell on the rock: and because the sun rose, and there was not much earth, forthwith it sprung up: and with the shining of the sun which was upon it, it sank down: and because it had not struck root, it withered. And some fell among thorns; and the thorns sprang up with it, and choked it; but other fell into good ground, and gave fruit, some an hundred-fold, some sixty-fold, some thirty-fold. Everyone that hath ears² let him hear.

And his disciples came near, and said unto him, Why speakest thou unto them in parables? But he answered and said unto them, Because it is given unto you to know the mysteries of the kingdom, but to

12 them it is not given. For whosoever hath, to him shall be given: and whosoever hath not, from him 13 shall be taken away even that he hath. Because of this speak I with them in parables: that what they see they may not see; and what they hear they may not hear, and may not understand, and they[1] may never 14 be converted; and in them may be fulfilled the prophecy of Isaia the prophet,[2] who said, By hearing ye shall hear and shall not understand; and 15 seeing ye shall see, and shall not see: for this people's heart is waxed gross, and their ears have they made heavy, that they may not hear,[3] and their eyes have they closed; lest they should see with their eyes, and hear with their ears, and should understand with their heart.

16 But as for your eyes, blessed are they, for they see: 17 blessed[4] are your ears, for they hear. For verily I say unto you, That many prophets and righteous men have desired to see those things which ye see, and have not seen them; and to hear those things which 18 ye hear, and have not heard them. Hear ye therefore 19 the parable of the sower. When a man[5] heareth the word of the kingdom, and understandeth not, the wicked one cometh, and snatcheth the seed from his heart.[6] This is he which receiveth seed by the way- 20 side. And that which was sown on the rock, this is he that heareth the word and with joy receiveth it; 21 because[7] he hath not root in himself, a short time it stays in him: but when there is distress or persecution 22 because of the word, quickly[8] he is offended. And that which fell among the thorns is he that heareth the word, and is in the care of this world, and in the deceitfulness of riches; and these choke it, and it

[1] Cureton. Bezae.
[2] Cureton.
[3] Cureton.
[4] Cureton.
[5] Syriac— 'every man who.'
[6] Cureton.
[7] Cureton.
[8] Cureton. Bezae.

becomes without fruit.[1] And that which fell upon 23
good ground is he that heareth the word, and understandeth
it; and then giveth fruit, and produceth,
some an hundred, and some sixty, and some thirty.

Again he continued, and spake another parable 24
unto them, The kingdom of heaven is like unto
a man which sowed good seed in his field: but while 25
men slept, the enemy came and sowed tares among
the wheat, and went his way. But when the blade 26
was sprung up, and brought forth fruit, the tares
appeared.[2] The servants drew near to their lord, saying 27
unto him, Our Lord, didst thou not sow good seed
in thy field? whence the tares in it[3]? He said unto 28
them, A man, an enemy, hath done this. His servants
say unto him, If thou wilt, we will go and gather
them up.[4] He said unto them,[5] Nay; lest while ye 29
gather up the tares, ye root up also the wheat with
them. But[6] let them grow together until the harvest: 30
and in the time of harvest I will say to the
reapers, Gather ye together first the tares, and bind
them in bundles as for the fire[7]: but gather the
wheat into the barns.

And he spake another parable unto them: The 31
kingdom of heaven is like to a grain of mustard-seed,
which a man taking, sowed it in his field. And 32
it is the least of all seeds: but when it is grown, it is
the greatest of all[8] herbs, and becometh a tree, and
the birds come and lodge in its branches. Another 33
parable: The kingdom of heaven is like unto leaven,
which a woman took, and hid in three measures of
meal, till the whole was leavened. All these things 34
spake Jesus unto the multitude in parables; and
without a parable spake he not unto them: that it 35

---

[1] Cureton.
[2] Cureton.
[3] Cureton.
[4] Cureton.
[5] Cureton. Bezae.
[6] Cureton.
[7] Cureton.
[8] Cureton.

might be fulfilled which was spoken by the prophet, who said, I will open my mouth in parables; I will
36 speak hidden things which are from of old.¹ Then
he² sent the multitude away, and went into the house: and his disciples came, saying unto him, Declare unto us the parable of the tares of the field.
37 He answered and said unto them, The sower of the
38 good seed is the Son of man; and the field is the world; and the good seed are the children of the kingdom; and the tares are the children of the
39 wicked one. And the sower of them is the wicked one³; and the harvest is the end of the world; and
40 the reapers are the angels. As therefore the tares are gathered and burned in the fire; so shall it be in
41 the end of the⁴ world. The Son of man shall send forth his angels, and they shall choose⁵ out of⁶ his
42 kingdom all things that offend, and all the doers of iniquity; and shall cast them into a furnace of fire:
43 there shall be weeping⁷ and gnashing of teeth. And then shall the righteous shine in the kingdom of their Father. Who hath ears to hear, let him hear.
44 ⁸The kingdom of heaven is like unto treasure hid in a field; which whoso hath found, he hideth it, and with joy he goeth and selleth all that he hath, and buyeth that field.
45 Again, the kingdom of heaven is like unto a
46 merchant man seeking pearls: and when he had found one good⁹ pearl of great price,⁹ he went and sold all that he had, and bought it.
47 Again, the kingdom of heaven is like unto a great¹⁰ net, which was cast¹⁰ into the sea, and gathered
48 of every kind: and when they had filled it, they drew it to the shore of the sea, and sat down, and chose the

¹ Cureton.
² Cureton. Bezae.
³ Cureton.
⁴ R.V. Cureton. Bezae.
⁵ Cureton.
⁶ Syriac— 'the house of.'
⁷ R.V. Cureton.
⁸ Cureton. Bezae.
⁹ Cureton.
¹⁰ Cureton.

very¹ good fishes, and cast the bad away. So shall 49 it be at the end of the world: the angels shall come forth, and sever the wicked from among the just, and shall cast them into the furnace of fire: there 50 shall be weeping² and gnashing of teeth. Have³ ye 51 understood all these things? They say unto him, Yea.⁴ He⁵ said unto them, Therefore every scribe 52 which is instructed unto the kingdom of heaven is like unto a man that is an householder, which bringeth forth from his treasure things new and old. And⁶ when Jesus had finished these parables, he 53 departed thence, and came to his city.⁷ And he 54 taught them in their synagogues, insomuch that they were astonished, and said, Whence hath this man all this wisdom and mighty works? Is not this the son 55 of Joseph? and is not his mother's name Mary? and his brothers, James, and Joseph, and Simon, and Juda? and his sisters, are they not all with us? Whence 56 then hath this [man] all these things? And they 57 were offended in him. Jesus said unto them, ... who is despised, except . . . and in his house . . . . because . . . . belief. 58

At . . . . time Herod the tetrarch heard of the 14 fame of Jesus, and said unto his servants, ... 2 John the Baptist; he is risen from the⁸ dead; therefore great is his power.⁹ For Herod had laid hold 3 on John, and cast him into prison for Herodia's sake, his brother Philip's wife. For John had said unto him, 4 It is not lawful for thee to take her. And he would 5 have put him to death, and he feared the people, because they held him as a prophet. But when it 6 was Herod's birthday, the daughter of Herodia came in,¹⁰ and danced, and pleased Herod. And he promised 7

---

¹ Cureton.

² Cureton.
³ R.V. Bezae.
⁴ R.V. Cureton. Bezae.
⁵ Cureton. Bezae.

⁶ Cureton.
⁷ Cureton.

⁸ Syriac—'midst of the.'
⁹ Cureton.

¹⁰ Cureton.

her with an oath that whatsoever she would ask him
8 he would give her. And she, because¹ .... was ....   ¹ Cureton.
of her mother, said, Give me [here] on a charger the
9 head of John the Baptist .... and because of ....
and because of them which sat at meat, he commanded
10 it to be given .... And he sent, and took off the
11 head of John from the prison. And they brought the
head of John in a charger,² and it was given to the   ² Cureton.
12 damsel: and she carried it to her mother. And his
disciples took up his body, and buried him, ...
13 told Jesus. When Jesus heard of it, he departed
14 thence to a place ..... apart: .... the people
15 who were from .... they came to him .... that
16 they should buy themselves ..... He said unto
them, ... to them to go .... you to eat. ....
17 to him, there is not .... five .... them ....
18
19 to .... and he commanded the multitude to sit
down on the green, and took these five loaves, and
two fishes, and looked to heaven, and blessed, and
brake the bread, and gave it to his disciples, and his
20 disciples gave³ to the multitude. And they did all   ³ Cureton.
to eat, and were filled: and they took up .... which
24 were broken from ... and they were troubled ...
25 the lake ... contrary to them ... but [in] the fourth
26 ... came unto ... walking .... when they saw
that he was w .... waves of the sea .... saying
27 .... and for fear .... a cry; and Jesus .....

[This page is on a leaf in the binding of the book; some of it could have been read by detaching the flap. This Mr. Rendel Harris could not venture to do as the MS. was not our property.]

32 didst thou doubt? And when they were come
33 into the ship, the wind ceased. And they that

were in the ship came near and worshipped him, 33
saying, Of a truth thou art the Son of God. And 34
when they went up to the dry land, they came
to Gennesar.¹ And the men of that place had 35
knowledge of him, and sent to their country, and
brought unto him all that were very sick; and 36
besought him that they might only touch the hem
of his garment: and as many as touched were made
whole.

Then came to him² from Jerusalem scribes and 15
Pharisees, saying unto him, Why do thy disciples 2
transgress the commandment³ of the e[lder]s? they
wash not their hands and eat br[ead]. He answered 3
and said unto them, Why do ye also transgress the
commandment of God, because of your commandments? For God said,⁴ Honour thy father and thy 4
mother: and whosoever curseth his father or his
mother, let him die the death. But ye say, Whoso- 5
ever shall say to his father or to his mother, It is an
offering, if thou mightest be profited by me; and he 6
honoureth not his father⁵ or his mother. Thus
have ye made the word of God of none effect because
of your commandments. Ye hypocrites, well did 7
Isaia the prophet⁶ prophecy concerning you, saying,
This people honoureth⁷ me with its lips, and in 8
its heart it is far from me. But in vain do 9
they fear me, teaching doctrines of the commandments of men. And he called the multitude, and 10
said unto them, Hear and understand: not that 11
which goeth into the mouth defileth a man; but that
which cometh out of the mouth, this . . . . a man.
Then came near his disciples, and said unto him, 12
Knowest thou that the Pharisees when they heard

¹ Cureton. Bezae.
² Bezae.
³ Cureton.
⁴ R.V. Cureton. Bezae.
⁵ R.V. Cureton. Bezae.
⁶ Cureton.
⁷ R.V. Cureton. Bezae.

13 this saying were offended? But he answered and said, Every plant, that the Father which is in heaven
14 hath not planted, shall be rooted up. Let them alone: they be leaders of the blind. And the blind man who leads the blind man shall fall with him
15 into the ditch. Simon[1] Cepha answered and said unto
16 him, Expound unto us this parable. He[2] said unto
17 him, Do ye not yet understand? Do ye not know that whatsoever entereth in at the mouth goeth into the belly, and is cast out thence into the cleansings?
18 And whatsoever proceeds out of the mouth, comes
19 forth .... and that defiles the man. For out of the heart proceed evil thoughts of murders, and adulteries,
20 and fornications, and thefts, and false witness, and blasphemies: these are the things which defile a man: but when a man eats bread[3] with unwashen hands, the
21 man is not defiled. And Jesus went forth from thence,
22 and went into the coasts of Tyre and Sidon. And behold, a Canaanite woman came out of these coasts, and cried,[4] saying, Have mercy upon me, O Lord, thou Son of David; my daughter is grievously vexed with
23 .... But he gave her no answer. And his disciples came near and besought him .... for behold, she
24 cried, and followeth[5] us. But he answered and said to them,[6] I am not sent but to the lost[7] .... of the
25 house of Israel. Then she came near and worshipped
26 him, ... to him, Lord help me. But he answered and said unto her,[8] It is not meet to take the
27 children's bread and cast it to dogs. She said to him, Yea,[9] Lord, even the dogs eat from the tables of their
28 masters, and live.[10] Then he[11] answered and said, O woman, great is thy faith: be it unto thee even as thou wilt. And from that very hour her[12] daughter

[1] Cureton.
[2] R.V. Cureton. Bezae.
[3] Cureton.
[4] R.V. Cureton.
[5] Cureton.
[6] Cureton.
[7] 'wandering.'
[8] Cureton.
[9] R.V.
[10] Cureton.
[11] Cureton. Bezae.
[12] Cod. 'thy.'

was made whole. And Jesus departed from thence, 29 and came to the shore of the lake of Galilee; and went up, and sat down on a mountain. And great 30 multitudes came near unto him, having with them the lame, the blind, the maimed, the dumb, and many others, and cast them down at his[1] feet; and he healed them: and the multitude wondered, for 31 they saw the dumb who spake,[2] the lame who walked, and the blind who saw: and they glorified the God of Israel. And Jesus called his disciples, and said, I 32 have compassion on this multitude, for behold, three days they continue with me, and have nothing to eat: and I do not wish to send them away fasting, lest they faint in the way. His disciples say unto him, Whence 33 should we have bread in the wilderness, to feed all this multitude? Jesus said unto them, How many 34 loaves have ye? They said, Seven loaves, and a few fishes. And he commanded the multitude to sit 35 down on the ground. And he took these seven loaves 36 and the fishes, and gave thanks and brake, and gave to his disciples, and his disciples placed them before the multitude. And they did all eat, and were satisfied: 37 and they took up from before them what was left of the loaves seven baskets full. And the men that did 38 eat were four thousand, besides women and children. And he sent away the multitude, went up, and sat in 39 a ship, and came into the coasts of Magdan.[3]

And the Pharisees and Sadducees came near, 16 tempting him, and asking him to shew them a sign from heaven. But he answered and said,[4] A wicked 2 and adulterous generation seeketh a sign; and no 4 sign shall be given unto it, but the sign of Jona the prophet. And he left them and departed. And 5 6

[1] R.V. Cureton. Bezae.
[2] Cureton.
[3] Cureton. Magdon.
[4] Omit part of v. 2; omit v. 3. R.V. marg. Cureton.

when they were come to the other side, his disciples had forgotten to take bread with them. Jesus said unto them, Beware[1] of the leaven of the Pharisees, 7 and the Sadducees. Then they reasoned among themselves,[2] that[2] they had not taken bread with 8 them. And Jesus knew it, and said,[3] Why reason ye among yourselves, O ye of little faith, because ye 9 have brought no bread? do ye not yet understand, do ye not remember the five loaves, and the five thousand who ate them, and how many baskets[4] ye 10 took up from before them[5]? nor yet those seven loaves, ... of the four thousand who ate of them, and how 11 many baskets[4] ye took up from before them? How is it that ye do not understand that it was not concerning bread I said to you, Beware of the leaven of the 12 Pharisees and the Sadducees? Then they understood that it was not of the leaven he bade them beware, but of the doctrine of the Pharisees and of 13 the Sadducees. And when Jesus came into the borders of Cesarea Philippi, he asked his disciples saying, What do men say concerning me? who then 14 is this Son of man? They say to him, Some say he is[6] John the Baptist; others say he is[6] Elia; others say he is Jeremia; others say he is[6] one of the 15 prophets. He saith unto them, Ye . . . . . .

[1] Cureton.
[2] Cureton.
[3] R.V. Bezae.
[4] 'baskets' in vv. 9 and 10 represent different Syriac words borrowed from the Greek.
[5] Cureton.
[6] Cureton.

[xvi. 15 to xvii. 11 is lost.]

17 . . . . things. But I say unto you, that Elia also is come, and they knew him not, but have done unto him whatsoever they listed. And the Son of man 13 shall suffer of them. Then his[7] disciples understood that he spake unto them of John.

14   And when Jesus[8] came to the multitude, there

[7] Cureton.
[8] Cureton.

came a certain man, and fell on his knees, and said, Have mercy on me; my son, a spirit of epilepsy seizes on him, and he is sore vexed: and oft-times he falleth into the fire, and oft-times into the water. And I brought him to thy disciples, and they could not cure him. Jesus answered and said, O perverse¹ and faithless generation, how long shall I be with you, and suffer you? Bring thy son hither to me. And Jesus rebuked him²; and the demon³ departed from him: and from that hour the child was cured. Then his disciples came near to him apart, and said, Why could not we cure him? He⁴ said unto them, Because ye have no faith: for verily I say unto you, If ye had faith as a grain of mustard seed, ye should then have said unto this mountain, Remove, and it shall remove; and nothing shall prevail against you. ⁵And while they went about⁶ in Galilee, Jesus said unto them, The Son of man shall be betrayed into the hands of men: and they shall kill him, and after three days he shall rise again. And they were exceeding sorry. And when they were come to Capernaum, they that collected drachmas came and said unto Simon, Thy master, doth he not give his drachmas? He saith, Yes. And when he was come into his house, Jesus spake first to him, saying, What thinkest thou, Simon? of whom do the kings of the earth take custom and tribute? of their children, or of strangers? He⁷ said unto him, Of strangers. Jesus saith unto him, Then are the children free. But that we may not offend them, go, cast a hook into the sea, and the first fish that cometh up, take; and open his mouth, and thou shalt find there⁸ a stater: give to them for me and for thee.

---

¹ Cureton.
² R.V. Cureton. Bezae.
³ Cureton.
⁴ R.V. Cureton. Bezae.
⁵ Omit v. 21. R.V. Cureton.
⁶ Cureton. Bezae.
⁷ Bezae.
⁸ Cureton. Bezae.

18 On that day his disciples came near, saying unto him, Who then shall be great in the kingdom of 2 heaven? Jesus called a certain child, and set him 3 amongst them, and said, Verily I say unto you, Except ye be converted, [and] become as children, ye 4 shall not enter into the kingdom of heaven. For whoso shall humble himself as this child, he shall be 5 great in the kingdom of heaven. And whoso shall receive such as one of these[1] children in my name, receiveth me. And whosoever shall offend one of 6 these little ones which believe in me, it were better for him that the mill-stone of an[2] ass were cast about his neck, and that he were drowned in the depth of the sea.

7   Woe unto the world because of the offences that are coming[3]! for the offences are ready to come; but woe to the man by whose hand[4] they shall come! 8 If then thy hand or thy foot offend thee, cut it off, and cast it from thee: for[5] it is profitable[5] for thee that thou shouldest come into life whilst thou art halt or whilst thou art maimed, and not whilst thou hast two hands or two feet, thou shouldest go into 9 eternal fire. If thine eye offend thee, pluck it out, cast it from thee: for it is profitable for thee to enter into life, having . . . . eye, and not whilst thou hast two, that thou shouldest go into the hell[6] of fire.
10 See that ye despise not one of these little ones; for verily I say unto you, That their angels do always behold the face of my Father which is in heaven.
12 [7]How think ye? if a man have an hundred sheep, and one of them go astray, doth he not leave the ninety-and-nine on the mountain, and go seeking 13 that which is gone astray? And when he hath

[1] Cureton.
[2] R.V. marg. Cureton. Bezae.
[3] Cureton.
[4] Cureton.
[5] Cureton.
[6] Gehenna.
[7] Omit v. 11. R.V. Palestinian Syriac.

found it, ... I say unto you, he rejoiceth more over it than over the ninety-and-nine which went not astray. Even so my Father which is in heaven willeth not that one of these little ones should perish.

But if thy brother sin against thee, reprove him between thee and him: if he hear thee, thou hast gained thy brother. But if he will not hear thee, take with thee again one or two, that in the mouth of two or three witnesses every word may be established. But if he will not hear them, tell it unto the synagogue: and if he will not hear the synagogue, let him be accounted by thee as a heathen . . . . publican. . . . . I say unto you, Whatsoever ye shall bind on earth, shall be bound in heaven: and whatsoever ye shall loose on earth, shall be loosed in heaven. Again, verily I say unto you . . . . about any . . . . they shall ask, it shall be to them from my Father which is in heaven. For there are not two or three gathered together in my Name, and I not amongst them.[1]

Then came Simon Cepha, and said, Lord, how oft-times if my brother sin against me shall I forgive him? till seven times? He saith unto him, Not until seven, but until seventy times seven seven.[2]

Therefore the kingdom of heaven is likened unto a man, a king, which would take account from his servants. And when he began to reckon, there came to him one which owed him ten thousand talents. And when he had nothing to pay, he commanded to sell him, ... and his children, and everything that he had to be taken.[3] And he

[1] Bezae.
[2] 'seven' is repeated also in the Syriac text of Cureton and of the Peshitta.
[3] Cureton.

fell down, ... to his lord. . . . . patience, and I
27 will pay¹ all. He had compassion on him, and ¹ Bezae.
28 loosed him, and forgave him also the debt. That
servant went out, and found one of his fellow-
servants, which owed him one hundred pence: and
he seized on him, and throttled him, and said, Give
29 me that thou owest me. And his fellow-servant fell
down,² beseeching him and saying, Have patience ² R.V.
Cureton.
30 with me, and I also will pay thee.³ And he did not Bezae.
³ R.V.
receive his entreaty⁴: but cast him into prison, till he Cureton.
Bezae.
31 should pay what he owed. But when his fellow- ⁴ Cureton.
servants saw what had happened, they were sorry, and
came . . . unto their lord all . . . that had happened.
32 Then his lord called him, and said unto him, O
wicked servant, lo, I forgave thee all the debt,
33 because thou desiredst me: shouldest thou not have
had pity on thy fellow-servant, even as I had pity
34 on thee? And his lord was wroth against him,⁵ and ⁵ Cureton.
delivered him to be scourged,⁶ till he should pay ⁶ Cureton.
35 that⁷ which he owed. So shall my Father which is ⁷ Bezae.
in heaven do unto you, unless ye from⁸ your heart ⁸ Cureton.
forgive every one his brother.⁹ ⁹ Cureton.

19 And it came to pass, when Jesus had finished
these sayings, he departed from Galilee, and came to
2 the borders of Judæa beyond Jordan; and great
multitudes followed him, and he healed them.
3 And the Pharisees came unto him there, tempting
him and saying,¹⁰ Is it lawful for a man to put away ¹⁰ R.V.
Cureton.
4 his wife for every cause? And he answered and
said unto them, Have ye not read, that he who
5 made the male made also the female¹¹? For ¹¹ Cureton.
this cause shall a man leave his¹² father and his¹² ¹² Cureton.
mother, and shall cleave to his wife: . . . . twain

one. . . . . Wherefore they are not twain, but one 6 . . . . joined, let not man put asunder. They say 7 unto him, Why then did Moses command,¹ Whoso will put away his wife let him give her a writing of divorcement²? He saith unto them, Moses, because 8 of the hardness of your heart, suffered you to put away your wives: but from the beginning it was not so. I say then unto you, Whoso shall put away his 9 wife, when there is no adultery, and shall take another, committeth adultery.³ His disciples say 10 unto him, If the case be so between a man and wife, it is not profitable to take a wife. He said unto 11 them, Not . . . . every man . . . . this saying, but [those] to whom it is given. For there are eunuchs, 12 which were . . . . from their mother's womb: . . . . there are eunuchs, whom men have made: and there are some who have made themselves eunuchs for the kingdom of heaven's sake. . . . . able to bear it, let him bear it.

Then . . . . children, that he should put his 13 hand on them, and pray; and the disciples rebuked 14 them. Jesus said unto them, Suffer the children to come unto me, and forbid them not, for of such as are like them,⁴ theirs is the kingdom of heaven. And he laid his hand on them, and departed. 15

And⁵ a certain man came and said unto him, 16 Good Teacher, what good thing shall I do, that I may inherit⁶ eternal life? He said unto him, Why askest 17 thou me concerning the good⁷? for one is the good one.⁸ If thou then wilt enter into life, ... He saith unto 18 him, Which ones? Jesus said unto him, Thou shalt not kill, thou shalt not commit adultery, ... to saith unto him . . . . I have kept . . . . youth 20

¹ Literally, 'what is that which Moses commanded?'
² Cureton.
³ Omit— 'and whosoever marrieth her which is put [away doth commit adultery.' R.V. marg Cureton. Bezae.
⁴ Cureton.
⁵ Cureton.
⁶ Cureton.
⁷ R.V. Bezae.
⁸ Omit 'God.' R.V. Bezae.

21 .... Jesus .... unto him, If thou desirest to be perfect, go, sell all that thou hast, and give to the poor, and thou shalt have treasure in heaven: and
22 come f.... When the young man heard that saying, he went away: .... for he was rich with
23 good possessions. Jesus .... Verily I say unto you, That it is hard for a rich man to enter into the
24 kingdom of heaven. And again I say unto you,
25 That it is easier for a camel .... disciples, ...
26 saying, Who then can be saved? .... and said
27 unto them, ... God all things .... Then .... Cepha and said unto him, We have forsaken all,
28 .... what shall we have .... the Son of man on .... of his glory, ... the twelve tribes of the
29 house of Israel. And every one that hath forsaken houses, or brethren, or sisters, or mother, or children, or lands, for my name's sake, shall receive
30 an hundredfold, and shall inherit eternal life. For there are many first who shall be last, and last who shall be first.

20   The kingdom of heaven is like to a man, a householder, which went out early in the morning to hire
2 labourers into his vineyard. And he agreed with them for one penny for one workman[1] for one day, [1] Cureton.
3 and sent them into his vineyard. And he went out at the third hour, and saw others standing idle in the
4 marketplace. He said unto them, Go ye also into the vineyard, and whatsoever is right I will give you.
5 Again he went out at the sixth and ninth hour, and
6 did likewise. And he went out at the eleventh hour, and saw others who were standing.[2] He saith unto [2] R.V. Cureton. Bezae.
7 them, Why stand ye here all the day idle? Thay say unto him,[3] No man hath hired us. He saith unto [3] Cureton.

Bezae. R.V. Bezae.	them, Go ye also into my¹ vineyard.² And so when it 8 was evening, the lord said unto his steward, Call the labourers, and give them their wages: and he began from the last unto the first. And when they came, 9 who were in the eleventh hour, they took up every man a penny. And when the first came, they 10
Cureton.	supposed that he would give them more³; and they also received every man a penny. And when they 11
Cureton.	saw⁴ it, they murmured against the master of the house, saying, These last, which have wrought one 12 hour, thou hast made equal with us, who have borne the burden of the day in the heat. But he 13 answered and said to one of them, Friend, I wrong thee not: was it not for a penny that I agreed with thee? Take thy penny, and go: if I wish to give to 14 this last one, even as unto thee, have I not power 15
Or 'within mine own.'	to do what I will with⁵ mine own? or is thine eye evil, because I am good? So the last shall be first, and 16 the first last: many be called, but few chosen.
Cureton. Bezae.	And when Jesus was going up to Jerusalem, he 17 took with him his⁶ twelve in the way, and said unto them apart, Behold, we go up to Jerusalem; and 18 the Son of man shall be betrayed unto the chief priests and unto the scribes, and they shall condemn him to death, and shall deliver him to the people, 19 and they shall mock him, and scourge him, and crucify him: and on the third day he shall rise.
Cureton.	Then came to him the mother of Zebedee's 20 children, she and her sons, and she fell down,⁷ and worshipped him, and desired something of him. And 21 he said unto her, What wilt thou? She saith unto him, Lord, that these my two sons may sit, one on thy right hand, and the other on thy left, in thy

22 kingdom. Jesus answered and said unto them, Ye know not what ye ask. Are ye able to drink of the cup that I shall drink of[1]? They say, We are able.
23 Jesus[2] saith unto them, Ye shall drink of my cup,[2] but to sit on my right hand, and on my left, is not mine to give to you, except to those for whom my
24 Father hath prepared it. When the ten heard it, they murmured against these two brethren. . . . . .

[1] R.V. Cureton.
[2] Bezae. [2] Bezae.

[xx. 25 to xxi. 20 is lost.]

21 The disciples marvelled, and said, How did this fig-
21 tree immediately wither away? Jesus answered and said unto them, Verily I say unto you, If ye have faith, and doubt not, ye shall do not only like what is done unto this fig-tree, but if ye shall say to this mountain, Be thou taken up, and fall into
22 the sea; it shall be so. And all, whatsoever ye shall ask in prayer, believing, ye shall receive.
23 And when he was come into the temple, the chief priests and the elders of the people came near unto him, saying, By what authority doest thou these things? tell us, and who gave thee this authority?
24 Jesus answered and said unto them, And I also will ask you one word, which if ye tell me, I will tell you
25 by what authority I do these things. The baptism of John, whence was it? from heaven, or from men? And they were reasoning with themselves, saying, If we shall say it was from heaven, he will say unto us,
26 Why did ye not believe in him? And if we shall say, It was from men; we fear the multitude; for
27 they all held John as a prophet. And they answered and said to Jesus, We know not. He also[3] said unto them, Neither do I tell you by what authority I do

[3] R.V. Bezae.

these things. But how does it seem to you? A 28
certain man had two sons; he¹ said unto the first, Go,
my son, do the work in the vineyard. He² said unto 29
him, I will not, but afterwards his soul repented, and
he went to the vineyard.³ And he⁴ said to the second 30
likewise, and he answered and said, Yes,⁵ sir, and
went not. Whether of these did the will of his 31
father? They say unto him, *The last.⁶ Jesus
saith unto them, Verily I say unto you, That the
publicans and harlots go into the kingdom of God
before you. For John came unto you in the way of 32
righteousness, and ye believed not in him; but the
publicans and the harlots believed him: and ye, when
ye saw it, at last repented⁷ yourselves, that ye might
believe in him. Hear another parable: a certain 33
man, that was an householder, planted a vineyard,
and made a hedge to it, and digged a [wine] press in
it, and built a tower in it, and delivered it to
husbandmen, and went away⁸: and when it was the 34
season of the fruits, he sent his servants to the
husbandmen, that they might send⁹ him some of the
fruits. And the husbandmen took his servants, and 35
one they beat, and one they killed, and one they
stoned. Again he sent other servants more than the 36
first, and they did unto them in like manner. But 37
last of all he sent unto them his son, saying, Haply¹⁰
they will reverence my son. But the husbandmen, 38
when they saw his son, said, This is the heir; come,
let us kill him, and the inheritance will be ours.¹¹
And they took him, and cast him forth out of the 39
vineyard, and killed him. When therefore the lord 40

¹ Cureton.
² Cureton.
³ Cureton. Bezae.
⁴ Cureton.
⁵ Cureton.
⁶ Cod. Vaticanus. Bezae.
⁷ Bezae.
⁸ Cureton. Bezae.
⁹ Cureton.
¹⁰ Cureton.
¹¹ Cureton.

* v. 31 Codex Bezae, λέγουσιν ὁ αἰσχατος—dicunt novissimus.

of the vineyard shall come, what will he do unto these
41 husbandmen? They say unto him, He will miserably
destroy them,¹ and will give the vineyard to other [1 Cureton. Bezae.]
husbandmen, who will give² the fruits in their season. [2 Cureton.]
42 Jesus saith unto them, Have ye not read in the
scriptures, The stone which the builders rejected, it is
become the head of the corner: this is from the Lord,
43 and it is a marvel in our eyes. Therefore I say unto
you, The kingdom of God shall be taken away from
you, and given to a nation which bringeth forth
45 fruit.³ ⁴But when the chief priests and Pharisees [3 Cureton. 4 Omit v. 44. R.V. marg. Bezae.]
had heard his parables, they knew that he spake
46 against them. And they sought to take him, but
they feared the people, because they took him for a
prophet.

22 Again Jesus answered and spake unto them by
2 parables. The kingdom of heaven is likened unto a
man, a king, which made a marriage feast for his son,
3 and sent his servants to call them that were bidden
4 to the wedding: and they would not come. Again
he sent other servants, saying, Say ye to them which
are bidden, Behold, everything is prepared, come
5 unto⁵ the marriage-feast. But they made light of [5 Syriac— 'the house of.']
it, and there was one who went to his farm, and one
6 who went to his merchandise: and the remnant who
were left laid hold⁶ of his servants, entreated them [6 Cureton.]
7 spitefully, and slew them. And the king⁷ was wroth, [7 Cureton.]
and sent his armies, and they destroyed those mur-
8 derers, and burnt up their city with fire.⁸ Then saith [8 Cureton.]
he to his servants, The wedding-feast is ready, but they
9 which were bidden were not worthy of it. Go ye
therefore into the highways,⁹ and as many as ye [9 Cureton.]
10 shall find, bid to the wedding feast. And those

servants went out into the highways, and gathered together all that they found, bad and good: and the house of the wedding feast was filled with guests. And when the king came in to see the guests, he saw there a man who was not clad in a wedding dress: he saith unto him, Friend, how camest thou in hither not having a wedding garment? And he was speechless. Then said the king to the servants, Seize him by his hands and his feet, and put him out into outer darkness; there shall be weeping and gnashing of teeth. For many are called, but few are chosen.

Then went the Pharisees, and took counsel how they might entangle him in talk. And they sent unto him his disciples, with the servants of Herod, saying to him, Teacher, we know that thou art true, and teachest the way of God in truth, and thou carest not for any man: for thou regardest not the faces of men.[1] How doth it then appear to thee? Is it fitting for us to give tribute unto Caesar, or not? But Jesus knowing their wickedness, said unto them,[2] Ye hypocrites, why tempt ye me? Shew me the coin of the tribute money. And they held out to him a penny. Jesus[3] saith unto them, Whose is this image and inscription? They say unto him, Caesar's. Then saith he unto them, Give what is Caesar's unto Caesar; and what is God's unto God. And when they heard this, they marvelled, and left him, and went their way.

The same day there came to him the Sadducees, saying to him,[4] There is no life of the dead, and asked him, saying, Teacher, Moses said to us,[5] If a man die, leaving no son, his brother shall marry his

---

[1] Bezae.

[2] Cureton.

[3] Cureton.

[4] R.V. marg. Cureton. Bezae.

[5] Cureton.

25 wife. And there were seven brethren: and the first
died, having no son by her, and his wife was married
26 to his brother: Likewise also the second, and also the
27 third, unto the seventh of them. And last of all the
28 woman died. . . . . wife shall she be? for behold,
29 they all had her. Jesus answered and said unto
them, Ye . . . . . . greatly, and ye do not know
30 . . . . . . the dead . . . . . . marry wives, nor are
31 . . . . as touching the resurrection from the dead,
have ye not read the . . . . which God spoke . . . .
32 God of Abraham, and the God of Isaac, and the God
of Jacob? and behold,[1] he is the God, not of the [1 Cureton.]
33 dead, but of the living. And when the multitude
heard these things, they were astonished at his doc-
34 trine. But when the Pharisees saw[2] that he had put [2 Cureton.]
the Sadducees to silence, they gathered themselves
35 together unto him. And one of them asked him,
36 tempting him, and saying to him,[3] Teacher, which [3 Cureton.]
37 commandment is great in the law? Jesus said unto
him, Thou shalt love the Lord thy God with all thy
heart, and with all thy soul, and with all thy strength.[4] [4 Cureton.]
38 This is the great[5] and first commandment. . . . . [5 Cureton. Bezae.]
39 like unto it, thou shalt love thy neighbour . . . .
40
41 On these . . . . hang the law. . . . . And while
the Pharisees were gathered together, ... them,
42 . . . . of the Christ? whose son is he? They say
to unto him, ...
. . . .
45 And if David . . . . him . . . . how . . . . his son?
And they could not give him an answer, neither
durst any man from that hour[6] ask him again. [6 Cureton. Bezae.]
23 Then spake Jesus to the multitude, and to his
2 disciples, On the seat of Moses sit the scribes and

the Pharisees: and all that they tell you, do; but do 3
not ye like unto their works: for they say, and do
not. And¹ they bind heavy burdens² and put them 4
on the shoulders of men; but they do not touch
them. For all things that they do are for to be 5
seen of men: and they make broad the straps of
their phylacteries, and lengthen the fringes of their
garments, and love the chief places at feasts, and 6
the honourable seats in the synagogues, and the
salutations of the marketplaces, and they desire³ 7
that men should call them, Rabbi, Rabbi. But be 8
not ye called Rabbi: one is your teacher,⁴ ⁵and ye all
are brethren. And call no man your father upon the 9
earth: for one is your Father, which is in heaven.
Neither be ye called teachers, for your teacher is the 10
Christ. He who desires among you to be great⁶ 11
shall be your servant. For whosoever shall exalt 12
himself shall be humbled; and whosoever shall
humble himself shall be exalted.

But woe unto you, scribes and Pharisees, hypo- 13
crites! for ye hold the key of the kingdom of
heaven before men: for ye neither enter in yourselves, nor those that are coming do ye suffer them
to enter.

⁷ Woe unto you, scribes and Pharisees, hypocrites! 15
for ye compass sea and land to make one proselyte,
and when he is become one, ye make him the child
of hell twofold more than yourselves.

Woe unto you, ye blind guides, which say, Whoso
shall swear by the temple, it doth not hurt⁸; and 16
whoso shall swear by the gold that is in the temple,
he sins.⁹ Ye fools, and blind, whether is greater,
the gold, or the temple that sanctifieth the gold? 17

Margin notes:
¹ Cureton.
² R.V. marg. Cureton.
³ Cureton.
⁴ R.V.
⁵ R.V. Bezae.
⁶ Cureton.
⁷ Omit r. 14. R.V. Cureton. Bezae.
⁸ Cureton.
⁹ Cureton.

18 And whoso shall swear by the altar, it hurteth not;
but whoso shall swear by the gift that is upon the
19 altar, he sins.[1] Ye blind[2]! whether is greater, the
20 gift, or the altar that sanctifieth the gift? Whoso
therefore shall swear by the altar, sweareth by it, and
21 by all things thereon. And whoso shall swear by
the temple, sweareth by it, and by him that dwelleth
22 therein. And he that shall swear by heaven,
sweareth by the throne of God, and by him that
sitteth thereon.

23 Woe unto you, scribes and Pharisees, hypocrites!
for ye pay tithe of mint and anise and cummin, and
have omitted the weightier matters of the law, judgment, mercy and faith: these ought ye to have done,
24 and those ye ought not to have left. Ye blind
guides, which strain at a gnat, and swallow a camel.
25 Woe unto you, scribes and Pharisees, hypocrites!
for ye make clean the outside of the cup and of the
platter, but within they are full of extortion and all
26 uncleanness. Ye blind Pharisee, cleanse first the
inside of the cup and platter, that the outside of them
may be clean also.
27 Woe unto you, scribes and Pharisees, hypocrites!
for ye are like unto sepulchres, which are whitened
outside, and within are full of dead men's bones, and
of all uncleanness.
28 Even so ye also outwardly appear unto men as
righteous, but within are full of depravity and defor-
29 mity. Woe unto you, scribes and Pharisees, hypocrites!
because ye build the tombs of the prophets, and gar-
30 nish the sepulchres of the righteous, and say, If we
had been in the days of our fathers, we would not have
been partakers with them in the blood of the prophets.

[1] Cureton.
[2] R.V.
Cureton.
Bezae.

Wherefore ye confess that ye are the children of them 31
which killed the prophets. And ye also . . . . the 32
measure of your fathers. Ye serpents, ye generation 33
of vipers, how will ye flee from the judgment[1] of hell[2]?
I send unto you prophets, and wise men and scribes: 34
some of them ye shall kill and crucify; and some of
them shall ye scourge in your synagogues, and persecute them from city to city: that upon you may come 35
all the blood of the righteous, which hath been shed
upon the earth, from the blood of righteous Abel unto
the blood of Zacharia son of Barachia, whom ye slew
between the temple and the altar. Verily I say unto 36
you, All these things shall come upon this generation. O Jerusalem, Jerusalem, thou that killest the 37
prophets, and stonest them that are sent unto thee,
. . . . would I . . . . thy children . . . . as . . . .
gathereth her chickens under her wings, and ye
would not! Behold 38
For I say unto you, Ye shall not see me henceforth, 39
till ye shall say, Blessed is he that cometh in the
name of the Lord.

. . . . Jesus went out from the temple, to go 24
away: and his disciples came showing him the build-
ings of the temple. And he answered[3] and said unto 2
them, See ye all these stones? verily I say unto you,
There shall not be left stone . . . . stone, that shall
not be thrown down. And as he sat upon the mount 3
of Olives, the disciples came saying unto him . . . .
when . . . . the sign of thy coming, and of the end
of the world? Jesus answered and said unto them, 4
. . . . many . . . . in my name, saying, I am the 5
Christ; and shall deceive many . . . . and rumours 6
. . . . and kingdom against kingdom: and there 7

[1] R.V. Bezae.
[2] Gehenna.
[3] R.V. Bezae.

shall be famines¹ and earthquakes in divers places. ¹ R.V. Bezae.
⁸₉ And all these are the beginning of travail. And then shall they deliver you up to afflictions, and shall kill you: and every man shall hate you for my name's
10 sake. Then shall many be offended, and shall betray
11 one another, and shall hate one another. . . . false . . . .
12 shall rise, and shall deceive many. . . . . iniquity
13 . . . . the love of many . . . . endure unto the end,
14 be . . . . this . . . . of the kingdom . . . .
to
18 let him not come down to take out of his house: and he which is in the field, let him not return back to take his clothes.
19 And woe unto them that are with child . . . .
20 who give suck in those days! But pray ye that your flight be not in the winter, neither on the sabbath day:
21 for then shall be great tribulation, ... until this
22 day . . . . shall be. And except . . . . ed those days . . . . be saved . . . . for the elect's sake . . . .
23 days. Then if any man . . . .
24 shall give great signs . . . . possible, they shall de-
25 ceive the very elect. Behold, I have told you before.
26 If they shall say unto you, Behold, he is in the desert; go not forth: or behold, he is in the secret
27 chambers; believe it not. For as the lightning . . . . cast, and is seen² even unto the west; so also shall ² R.V.
28 be the coming of the Son of man. . . . . the body there . . . . eagles.
29 . . . . after the tribulation of those days the sun . . . . and the light of the moon shall not shine, and
30 the stars shall fall from . . . . sign of the Son of man
31 in heaven: . . . . power . . . . his angels with a great³ trumpet, and . . . . his elect from the four ³ R.V. marg.
32 winds, from one end of heaven to the other. Now

learn a parable from the fig-tree; When its branch is tender, and putteth forth leaves, ye know that summer is nigh : so likewise ye, when ye shall see all 33 these things, know that it is near, at the door. Verily 34 I say unto you, This generation[1] shall not pass, till all these things shall be. Heaven and earth shall 35 pass away, and my words shall not pass away.

But of that day and hour knoweth no man, no, 36 not the angels of heaven, but the[2] Father only. For 37 as it was in the days of Noah, so shall be the coming of the Son of man.[3] For as before the 38 flood they were eating and drinking, marrying and giving in marriage, until Noah entered into the ark, ... until came . . . . 39 and carried them all away: . . . . to in an hour that ye think not the Son of man cometh. 44 . . . . his lord over his companions, to give them 45 meat in its season? Blessed is that servant, whom 46 if his lord cometh, he shall find so doing. Verily 47 I say unto you, That he shall make him ruler over all that he hath. But if that evil servant shall 48 say in his heart, My lord delayeth to come; and shall 49 begin to smite his fellow-servants, and to eat and drink with the drunken; the lord of that servant 50 shall come in a day that he doth not expect, and in an hour that he knoweth not. And shall cut him 51 asunder, and appoint him his portion with the hypocrites: and there shall be weeping and gnashing of teeth.

Then shall the kingdom of heaven be likened 25 unto ten virgins, which took their lamps, and went forth to meet the bridegroom and bride.[4] And five 2 of them were foolish, and five were wise. They that 3

---

[1] Or 'tribe.'

[2] R.V. Bezae.

[3] R.V.

[4] Bezae.

were foolish took their lamps, and took no oil with
4 them: but the wise took oil in the vessels with
5 their lamps. While the bridegroom tarried, they all
6 slumbered and slept. And at midnight there was a
cry, Behold, the bridegroom cometh; go ye out to
7 meet him. Then all those virgins arose, and trimmed
8 their lamps. The foolish said unto the wise, Give us
of your oil; for behold, our lamps are going out.
9 These wise ones said unto them, Perhaps it may not
suffice for us and for you: but go ye to them that sell,
10 and buy for yourselves. And while they were going
to buy, the bridegroom came; and they that were
ready went in with him to the marriage: and the
11 door was shut. And afterwards those virgins came,
12 saying Our Lord, open to us. But he answered and
to said, Verily I say unto you, I know you not. . . . . .
37 . . . . didst thirst, and we gave thee drink?
38 And when saw we thee that thou wast a stranger, and
39 took thee in? or thou wast naked . . . .
to
44 . . . . . Our Lord, when saw we thee an hungred, or
athirst, or a stranger, ... or . . . . and did not minister
45 unto thee? Then shall he answer and say unto
them, Verily I say unto you, What ye have not
done to one of these little ones, ... ye have not
46 done it. And these shall go away into everlasting
punishment: but the righteous into life eternal.
26   And it came to pass . . . . his sayings, ... to
2 his disciples, Ye . . . .
to
5 Saying . . . . be . . . . le.
6 And when . . . . house . . . .
to
11 . . . . not at all times with you; me . . . .
12 . . . . hath put this ointment . . . .
13 Verily I say unto you, ... that she hath done

4

.... Then went one of 14
.... thirty pieces of silver. 15
.... passover ? 17 to
He said unto them, Go into the city to such a man, 18
and say unto him, Our Master saith, My time is at
hand; in thy house will I keep the passover with my
disciples. And his disciples did as Jesus had 19
appointed them; and they made ready the passover.
And when it was evening, he sat down with the twelve. 20
And as they did eat, he said unto them, Verily I say 21
unto you, that one of you shall betray me. And they 22
were exceeding sorrowful, and began every one of
them to say,[1] Not I surely, Lord ? He said unto them, 23
He who stretches out his hand with me in the dish,
he shall betray me. And the Son of man goeth as it 24
is written of him: but woe unto that man by whose
hand I am betrayed! it would have been profitable for
him if he had not been born. And Juda, the betrayer, 25
answered and said, Not I surely, Master? He
said unto him, Thou hast said. And as they were 26
eating, Jesus took bread, and blessed it, and brake,
and gave to his disciples, and said, Take, eat; this is
my body. And he took the cup, and gave thanks 27
over it, and gave to them, and said, Take, drink ye
all of it; this is my blood of the new testament, 28
which is shed for many for the remission of sins.
For I say unto you, I will not drink henceforth of 29
this fruit of the vine, until that day when I drink it
new with you in my Father's kingdom. And when 30
they had sung praises, they went out into the
mount of Olives. Then saith Jesus unto them, All 31
ye shall be offended in me this night: for it is
written, I will smite the shepherd, and the sheep

[1] R.V.

32 of his flock shall be scattered abroad. And after I am risen again, I will go before you into Galilee.
33 Simon Cepha answered, and said, If they all shall be offended in thee, yet will I never be offended in
34 thee. Jesus said unto him, Verily I say unto thee, This night, when the cock has not crowed, three
35 times thou shalt deny me. Simon Cepha said unto him, If it should happen to me to die with thee, I will not deny thee. Likewise also said all the
36 disciples. Then Jesus cometh with them unto a place called Gedsemane.[1] He saith to his disciples,
37 Sit ye here, until I go and pray. And he took Simon and the two sons of Zebedee, and began to
38 be sad and to be anxious. Then saith he unto them, Behold, my soul is sorrowful, even unto death:
39 tarry ye here, and watch with me. And he withdrew from them a little, fell on his face, and prayed, saying, O my Father, if it be possible, that this cup pass from me: nevertheless, not my will be done, but
40 thine. And he cometh unto his disciples, and findeth them asleep, and saith unto Simon, Thus, not even
41 one hour could ye watch with me? Watch and pray, that ye enter not into temptation: the spirit is
42 willing, but the flesh is weak. Again the second time he went to pray, saying, O my Father, if this cup may not pass away from me, except I drink it,
43 thy will be done. And he came again, and found them asleep, because their eyes were heavy with
44 sleep. And he left them, and went to pray the third
45 time, and again he spake the same way. Then cometh he to his disciples, and saith unto them. Sleep on now, and take your rest: for behold, the hour is at hand, and the Son of man is betrayed into

[1] Cod.— 'Gusemani.'

the hands of sinners. Rise, let us go hence: he has 46 arrived, he who betrayeth me. And while he yet 47 spake, lo, Juda, one of the twelve, came, and with him a great multitude with swords and staves, from the chief priests and elders of the people. And 48 Juda, the betrayer, gave them a sign, saying, that he . . . . he, take him. . . . . to Jesus . . . . and 49 said to him, Hail, Master. Jesus, ... Then they 50 came near and laid their hands on him, and took Jesus. And behold, one of the disciples of Jesus 51 stretched out his hand, and drew a sword, and struck the servant of the high priest, and took off his ear.

Then said Jesus unto him, Put up again the sword 52 into his place: for all they that take the sword shall perish with the sword. Or thinkest thou that I 53 cannot ask of my Father, and he shall give me more than twelve legions of angels? How shall 54 the scriptures be fulfilled, that thus it must be? In that hour said Jesus . . . . thief have ye come 55 out against me, with swords and staves for to take me? Every day I sat in the temple, teaching, and ye laid no hold on me. But all those things 56 that have happened are that the scriptures of the prophets might be fulfilled.

Then all his disciples forsook him, and fled. And they had laid hold on him and led him away 57 to Caiaphas the high priest, where the scribes and the elders of the people were assembled. But Simon 58 followed him afar off unto the high priest's court, and went in, ... with . . . . end. . . . . witness 59 . . . . and found not . . . . many false witnesses, 60 and they found not . . . . came two oth . . . . false . . . . and said, This one said, I am able to 61

destroy this temple, and in three days I will build it.
62 And the high priest arose, and said unto him, Dost thou not give an answer? What do these witness
63 against thee? But Jesus was silent. The high priest answered and said unto him, I adjure thee by the living God, that thou tell us whether thou be
64 the Christ, the Son of God. He said unto him, Thou hast said: I say unto you, Henceforth[1] ye shall see [1] R.V. Bezae.
65 to 68 the Son of man .... further .... witnesses .... and others smote him on the cheeks, saying, Prophecy unto us, the Christ, who smote thee?
69 Now Simon sat without in the court: and a damsel drew near unto him, saying to him, Thou also
70 wast with Jesus of Galilee. But he denied in the presence[2] of them all, saying, I know not what thou [2] Syriac— 'in the
71 sayest, neither do I understand[3]. And when he eye.' [3] Bezae. had gone out to the door of the court, another (damsel) saw him, and said unto them, This one was
72 with Jesus of Nazareth. And again he denied and
73 swore, I know not this man. And after a little while those who stood by came near, and said to Simon, Surely thou also art one of them; for even
74 thy speech is like[4]. Then began he to curse and to [4] Bezae. swear, I know not this man. And immediately the
75 cock crew. And Simon remembered the word of Jesus, which said unto him, Before the cock crow, thou shalt deny me thrice. And when he went out, he wept bitterly.
27 And when it dawned, all the chief priests and elders of the people took counsel against Jesus to
2 put him to death: And they bound him, and led him away, and delivered him to Pilate the governor.
3 Then when Juda, the betrayer, saw that he was

condemned, he repented, and brought again the thirty pieces of silver to the chief priests and elders, saying, I have sinned in that I have betrayed the blood of the righteous.¹ And they say to him, What is that to us? Thou knowest. And he cast down the silver in the temple, and departed, [and] went and hanged himself, and was strangled. And the chief priests took the silver, and said, It is not lawful to put it into the treasury,² because it is the price of blood. And they took counsel, and bought from it the potter's field, for³ a burial-place for strangers. Wherefore it was called, The field of blood, unto this day. Then was fulfilled that which was spoken by the prophet, who said, I took the thirty pieces of silver, the price of him that was valued, which I was valued at by the children of Israel; and I gave them for the field of the potter, as the Lord commanded me.

And Jesus stood before the governor: and he asked him, saying unto him, Art thou the King of the Jews? Jesus said unto him, Thou hast said. And when the chief priests and Pharisees accused him, he gave them no answer. Then said Pilate unto him, Hearest thou not how many witnesses witness against thee? And he gave him no answer; and greatly did the governor wonder. Now at every feast the governor was wont to release unto the people one prisoner, whom they would. And they had a prisoner, a certain notable man, whose name was Jesus Bar-Abba. He had been thrown into prison because of the evil he had done, and because he was a murderer. And when all the Jews were gathered together, Pilate said unto them, Whom will ye that I release unto you? Jesus Bar-Abba, or

---

¹ R.V. marg.

² Or, 'amongst the offerings.'
³ Literally, 'of a burial place.'

18 Jesus who is called the Christ? For he knew that
19 because of envy they had delivered him unto him. When he was set down on the judgment seat, his wife sent unto him, saying unto him, Have thou nothing to do with that just man, for I have suffered many things this day in my dream because of him.
20 But the chief priests and elders persuaded the people that they should ask for Bar-Abba, and destroy
21 Jesus. The governor answered and said unto them, Whom do ye desire that I should release unto you?
22 They say unto him, Bar-Abba. Pilate saith unto them, And what shall I do unto Jesus, who is called
23 the Christ? They all say, Let him be crucified. He said unto them, Why, what evil hath been done by him? Then they cried out more exceedingly, saying,
24 Let him be crucified. And when Pilate saw that he prevailed nothing, but the more the tumult increased, he took water, and washed his hands in the sight of all the multitude, saying, I am innocent of this
25 blood: ye know. And all the people answered, and said, the blood of this man be on us and on our
26 children. Then released he unto them Bar-Abba, and he scourged Jesus with whips, and delivered him
27 to them to be crucified. Then the soldiers of the governor took Jesus into the Prætorium, and
28 gathered the crowd against him. And they clothed
29 him with a robe of purple and of scarlet.[1] And they [1] Bezae. plaited a crown of thorns, and put it on his head, and they made him hold a reed in his right hand: and they bent their knees before him, and mocked
30 him, saying, Hail to thee, King of the Jews! And they spat in his face, and took up the reed, and smote
31 him on the head. And when they had mocked him,

they stripped him of the garments that he was clothed with, and clothed him with his own garments, and led him away, and went to crucify him. And as ³² they went out, they found a man of Cyrene, whose name was Simon: and they compelled him to bear his cross. And they came to a place which is called ³³ Gogultha.¹ And they gave him to drink wine² ³⁴ mingled with gall: and he tasted it, and would not drink it. And when they had crucified him, they ³⁵ parted his garments,³ casting lots upon them: and ³⁶ they were sitting, and watching there. While they were sitting, they wrote the crime. They set it over ³⁷ his head, Jesus, the King of the Jews.

Then there were crucified with him two male- ³⁸ factors, one on his right hand, and one on his left. And they that passed by blasphemed against him, ³⁹ wagging their heads, and saying, Destroyer of the ⁴⁰ temple, and builder of it in three days, if thou art the Son of God, save thyself, and come down from the cross. And the chief priests also, like the scribes ⁴¹ and Pharisees, were mocking him, and insulting him, and saying, He who saves others, himself he cannot ⁴² save. If he be the King of Israel, let him come down now from the cross, and we will believe in him. He trusted in God; let him deliver him now, if he ⁴³ desireth him: for he said, I am the Son of God. And the malefactors also, which were crucified with ⁴⁴ him, like the rest, insulted him. And from the sixth ⁴⁵ hour there was darkness over all the land until the ninth hour. And at the ninth hour Jesus cried with ⁴⁶ a loud voice, saying, My God, my God, why hast thou forsaken me⁴?

And some of those people who stood there, when ⁴⁷

---

[1] Peshitta.
[2] R.V. Bezae.
[3] Omit latter half of v. 35. R.V. Bezae.
[4] Syriac— 'Elei, Elei, lemana shabactani.'

48 they heard it, said, This one calleth on Elia. And straightway one of them ran, and took a sponge, and dipped it in vinegar, and tied it to a reed, and stretched
49 it out to him to drink. And others said, Let be, let
50 us see whether Elia will come and save him. And Jesus cried with a loud voice, and his spirit went
51 up. And immediately the veil of the sanctuary¹ was ¹ R.V. marg. rent from the very top; and the earth did quake, and
52 the rocks rent; And the graves were opened; and many bodies of the righteous, those which slept,
53 arose, and came out of the graves after his resurrection, and went into the holy city, and appeared unto many.
54 Now the centurion, and they that were watching Jesus with him, when they saw the earthquake, and the things that happened, feared greatly, saying, Truly this was the Son of God.
55 And many women were there beholding afar off, which followed Jesus from Galilee, ministering unto
56 him: Mary Magdalene, and Mary the daughter of James and mother of Joseph, and the mother of the
57 children of Zebedee. And when the even was come, there came a certain rich man of Ramatha, named
58 Joseph, and he also was a disciple of Jesus. He went to Pilate, and asked the body of Jesus; and Pilate
59 commanded it to be given to him. And when Joseph had taken the body, he wrapped it in a new
60 linen cloth, and laid it in his own new-hewn tomb, which he had hewn for himself in the rock: and he rolled a great stone to the door of the sepulchre, and
61 they departed. And there was there Mary Magdalene, and the other Mary, sitting over against the
62 sepulchre. Now the next day that followed the day

of the preparation, the chief priests and Pharisees came together unto Pilate, saying, Sir, we remember 63 that that deceiver said, while he was yet alive, After three days I will rise again. But command that they watch the sepulchre for three days, that his disciples may not come by night and steal him, and say unto the people, He is risen from the dead: and the 64 last error be worse than the first.

Pilate said unto them, Ye have a watch: watch 65 the sepulchre, as ye know. They went and watched 66 his sepulchre, and sealed the stone with the watch.[1]

¹ Bezae.

And on the evening of the sabbath, as the first 28 day of the week dawned, came Mary Magdalene and the other Mary to see the sepulchre. And, behold, 2 there was a great earthquake: for the angel of the Lord descended from heaven and rolled away the stone,[2] and sat above it. And his appearance[2] was 3 like the lightning, and his raiment like the snow: and for fear of him those who were watching did 4 shake, and became as dead men. The angel answered 5 and said unto the women, Fear not ye: for I know that ye seek Jesus, the Nazarene, which was crucified. He is not here: for he is risen as he said unto you. 6 Come, see the place where he was laid. Go quickly, 7 and tell his disciples that he is risen; and behold, he goeth before you into Galilee; there . . . . .

² R.V. Bezae.

[*vv. 8 and following to the end of this Gospel are lost.*]

THE GOSPEL OF MARK

[*vv.* 1 *to* 11 *are lost.*]

1   The spirit driveth him out into the wilderness.
12
13 And he was there forty days, tempted of Satan; and
was with the wild beasts; and the angels were ministering unto him.
14   And after John was delivered up,¹ Jesus came ¹ R.V.
15 into Galilee, and was preaching the gospel of God, Bezae.
The time is fulfilled, and the kingdom of God is
16 come: repent ye, and believe his gospel. And as he
walked by the shore of the lake of Galilee, he saw
Simon and Andrew his brother casting their net into
17 the sea: for they were fishers. And Jesus said unto
them, Follow me, and I will make you fishers of
18 men. And straightway they forsook their nets, and
19 followed him. And when he had walked again a
little further, he saw James the son of Zebedee, and
John his brother, who were also sitting in the ship
20 mending their nets. And straightway he called
them: and they left Zebedee their father with the
hired servants in the ship, and followed him.
21   And he was teaching on the sabbath in the syna-
22 gogue. And they were astonished at his doctrine:
for he taught as one that had authority, and not as
23 their scribes. And there was in their synagogue
a man who had an unclean spirit; and he cried out,
24 and said, What have we to do with thee, Jesus of

Nazareth? thou art come to destroy us. I know thee who thou art, the holy one of God. And Jesus rebuked him, saying, Shut thy mouth, and come out of him. And the unclean spirit threw him down, and when it had cried with a loud voice, it came out of him. And they were all amazed,[1] and were saying one to another, What is this new teaching[2]? he hath authority, and commandeth the unclean spirits, and they do obey him. And his fame went abroad through all the region of Galilee, and many followed him. And he came out of the synagogue, and they came to the house of Simon Cepha and Andrew: and James and John were with him. And Simon's wife's mother was sick of a fever, and they tell him of her. And he came near, and took her, and lifted her up; and immediately the fever left her, and she arose and ministered unto them. And when the sun did set, they brought all that were sick with sore diseases, and all the city were gathered together at his door. And he healed many, and cast out many demons, and suffered them not to speak, because they knew him.

And very early in the morning he went out, and departed into a desert place, and there he prayed. And Simon and they that were with him sought him. And when they had found him, they said unto him, Many men seek thee. He said unto them, Up! Let us go into the nearest villages[3] and towns, that I may preach there also: for therefore I am come. And he preached in all the synagogues of Galilee, and cast out demons. And there came to him a certain leper, and besought him, and fell at his feet, and said unto him, If thou wilt, thou canst make me

---

[1] 'amazement held them all.'
[2] R.V.
[3] Bezae.

41 clean. And Jesus had compassion on him, put out his hand, and touched him, and said to him, I will; be thou clean. ¹And in that hour he became clean. ¹ Omit part of v. 42.
43
44 And he straitly charged him, and saith, See thou . . . . . .

[i. 44 *to* ii. 20 *is lost.*]

2 . . . . a new patch on a worn-out garment: else
21 the new filling-up draws away the weakness of the worn-out one, and the rent becomes worse than
22 before. And no man putteth new wine into worn-out wine-skins: else the wine² doth burst the ² R.V. Bezae. wine-skins, and the wine is spilled, and the wine-skins perish: but they put new wine into new wine-
23 skins. And it came to pass, that he walked on the sabbath-day . . . . and . . . . amongst . . . . were
24 . . . . ears . . . . The Pharisees say unto him, Why
to . . . . on the sabbath-day that which is not . . . .
26 into the house of God,³ and did eat the show-bread, ³ Bezae. which is not lawful to eat but for the priests, and
27 gave also to them which were with him? And he said unto them, The sabbath was created for man.
28 Therefore the Lord of the sabbath is the Son of man.
3 And he entered again into the synagogue; and
2 there was a man . . . . his hand. And they watched him, whether he would heal him on the sabbath day;
3 that they might accuse him. He saith unto the man
to whose hand was withered, Stand up in the midst.
5 . . . . being grieved about the deadness⁴ of their ⁴ Bezae. hearts, and he said unto the man, Stretch forth thy hand. And he stretched it out: and it was restored
6 like its fellow. And straightway the Pharisees went forth with those of the house of Herod, and
7 took counsel how they might destroy him. And

[1] Bezae.

[2] R.V. marg.

Jesus went with his disciples to the sea: and a great multitude from Galilee,[1] and from Judæa, and from Jerusalem, and from beyond Jordan, and from Tyre, and from Sidon, who had heard everything[2] that he did, came unto him. And he spake to his disciples, that they should bring a ship to him because of the multitude, lest they should throng him. For he had healed many; and many were pressing . . . . him, and those that had plagues of unclean spirits upon them fell down before him, and cried, saying, Thou art the Son of God. And he charged them much that they should not make him known.

And he goeth up into a mountain, and calleth unto him whom he would: and they came unto him. And he chose twelve of them, that they should be with him, and that he might send them to preach, and to have power to heal the sick and to cast out demons. And he called Simon Cepha; and James the son of Zebedee, and John his brother: he called them Beni-Ragshi; and Andrew and Philip, and Bartholomew, and Matthew, and Thomas, and James the son of Ḥalfai, and Thaddai, and Simon the Zealot, and Juda Iscariot, the betrayer.

And they went into the house. And the multitude came again to him, so that they could not . . . . . . bread. . . . . . . said, ... can Satan cast out Satan? And if a kingdom be divided against itself, that kingdom cannot stand. And if a house be divided against itself, that house . . . . Satan . . . . against himself, he cannot stand, ... which they blaspheme shall be forgiven . . . . all . . . . who shall blaspheme . . . . eternal . . . . For they said, He hath an unclean spirit.

31 . . . . his mother, ... sent . . . . sat . . . .
to
35 thy mother . . . . without.

4 . . . . And he taught them many things . . . .
3 and while he was speaking . . . . Behold, there went
4 out a sower to sow: and[1] as he sowed, some fell by [1] Bezae.
the wayside, and the fowls[2] came and devoured it. [2] R.V.
5 And some fell on the rock, and sprouted, and because
6 there was no depth of earth below its root, ... the
7 sun was . . . . and it withered. And some fell
to among thorns, ... yielded no . . . . He that
11 . . . ears . . . And he said . . . Unto you he hath
given the mystery of the kingdom of God: but unto
them that are without, all things are done in
12 parables. That seeing they may see, and . . . . not
perceive; lest they should repent, ... to them
13 their sins. And he said unto them, Know ye not
this parable? and how then will ye know all parables?
14 The sower . . . . the word . . . . they by the way-
15 side, they who hear the word . . . . they have heard
16 . . . . and taketh away . . . . they . . . . word
. . . . receive it . . . .

[vv. 17 to 41 are lost.]

41 . . . . obey him?

5 And he came over unto the other side of the sea,
2 into the country of Gergesenes. And when he was
come up out of the ship, there met him a certain man
3 who had an unclean spirit, which [spirit] dwelt among
the tombs; and no man could bind him with chains,
4 because he had broken many fetters and chains, and
5 escaped, and no man could tame him. And always,
night and day, he was crying in the tombs, and in
the mountains, and wounding himself with stones.[3] [3] R.V.

And when he saw Jesus afar off, he ran and worshipped him, and cried with a loud voice, and said, What have I to do with thee, Jesus, thou Son of the Most High God? I adjure thee by God, that thou torment me not. For he said unto him, Come, thou unclean spirit, out of the man. And he asked him, What is thy name? and he said unto him, Our name is Legion: for we are many. And these demons besought him that he would not send them out of the country. Now there was there nigh unto the mountains a great herd of swine feeding. And these demons besought him, Send us into the swine, that we may enter into them. And[1] he gave them leave. And when the unclean spirits went out they entered into the swine: and the herd ran, and fell into the sea, about two thousand, and they were choked in the sea. And they that fed them[2] fled, and told it in the cities, and in the villages. And they went out to see what had come to pass. And they came to . . . . and saw him . . . . was . . . . they . . . . to to him . . . . dismiss him . . . . his disciples in the ship, he that had had the demon prayed him that he might be with him. And he[3] suffered him not, but said unto him, Go home to thy people, and shew them what the Lord hath done unto thee, and hath had mercy on thee. And he went, and began to preach in Decapolis what Jesus had done unto him: and they all did marvel.

And when Jesus had crossed over again unto the other side, a great multitude gathered unto him on the shore of the sea. And there cometh one of the rulers of the synagogue, whose name was Joaras; when he saw him, he fell at his feet, and besought

[1] R.V.

[2] R.V. Bezae.

[3] R.V.

him,[1] saying unto him, My daughter is very sick,   [1] Bezae.
come and lay thy hands on her, and she shall live.
24 And he went with him, and a great multitude
25 followed him, and thronged him. And a certain
26 woman, which had an issue of blood twelve years, and
had suffered many things of many physicians, and
had spent all that she had, and . . . . nothing . . . .

[v. 27 to vi. 5 is lost.]

6
5 . . . there none of the mighty works, save that he
laid his hands upon a few sick folk, and they were
6 healed. And he marvelled at their want of faith.

And he went round about the villages, and
7 taught; and called the twelve disciples,[2] and sent   [2] Bezae.
them by two and two, and gave them power over
8 unclean spirits, and commanded them that they
should take nothing for the way, save a staff only:
9 no scrip, no bread, no money in their purse:[3] but be   [3] MS. 'your purses.'
10 shod with sandals, and not put on two coats. Into
whatsoever house ye enter, there be until ye depart
11 from thence. And whosoever shall not receive you,
nor hear you, when ye depart thence, shake off the
dust of your feet for a testimony unto them.[4]   [4] R.V. Bezae.

12 And they went out, and preached that they
13 should repent. And they cast out many demons,
and anointed many with oil, and healed the sick.
14 And Herod the king heard, (for his fame was well-
known [unto him]:) and he said, He is John the
Baptist; he is risen from the dead, therefore great
15 is his power. And others said, He is Elia. Others
16 said, He is a prophet, like one of the prophets. But
when Herod heard it, he said, This is John, he
17 whose head I cut off, he is risen.[5] For Herod had   [5] R.V. Bezae.

sent and laid hold upon John, and bound him in prison for Herodia's sake, his brother Philip's wife, for he had married her. For John had said unto 18 Herod, It is not lawful for thee to have thy brother's wife. Then Herodia had threatened him, and would 19 have killed him, but she could not. For Herod feared 20 John; for he knew that he was a just man and an holy, and observed him: and many things that he heard from him he did, and heard him gladly. And 21 it happened that on Herod's birthday he made a supper to his lords, and chiliarchs,[1] and the chiefs of Galilee: and the daughter of Herodia came in and 22 danced, and pleased Herod and them that sat with him, and the king said unto the damsel, Ask of me, and I will give thee, even unto the half of my king- 23 dom. And he swore unto her with an oath. And 24 the damsel went forth, and took counsel with her mother, What shall I ask? She said unto her, The head of John the Baptist. And she went in at 25 once to the king, and said unto him, I will that thou give me immediately the head of John the Baptist in a charger. And the king was exceeding 26 sorry, but for the oath's sake, and for their sakes that sat at meat,[2] he could not change. And he sent 27 an executioner, that he should cut off his head and bring it: and he went and cut off his head in the prison, and he brought it in a charger, and gave it 28 to the damsel, and the damsel carried it to her mother. And when his disciples heard of it, they 29 came and took up his corpse, and laid it in a tomb. And the apostles came unto Jesus, and told him what 30 they[3] had done and taught.

And he said unto them, Come, let us go into the 31

---

[1] Or 'military tribunes.'

[2] Or 're-clined.'

[3] MS. 'he.'

desert apart, and rest a little. There were many going
and coming to him, and they had no place not even
32 to eat bread. And they departed into a desert place
33 by ship alone. And many saw them, and knew them,
and followed him by land,[1] from all the cities. And [1] R.V. marg.
34 when they came,[2] and he[2] saw the great multitude, he [2] R.V.
had compassion on them, because they were as sheep
not having a shepherd: and he began to teach them.
35 And when it began to be evening, his disciples came
near, saying unto him, This is a desert place, and the
36 time is passed. Send away these people, that they may
go into the villages that are round about, and buy
37 themselves something to eat.[3] He said unto them, [3] R.V. Bezae.
Give ye them to eat. They say unto him, Shall we
go and buy a hundred pennyworth of bread, and
38 give them to eat? He saith unto them, Go, see how
many loaves ye have. They say unto him, Five
39 loaves and two fishes. And he commanded them all
40 to sit down on the grass. And they sat down by
41 companies, by hundreds, and by fifties. And he took
these five loaves and two fishes, and looked to heaven,
and blessed, and brake the loaves, and gave them to
his disciples to set before them; and the two fishes
42 they divided among them all. And they did all eat,
43 and were filled. And they took up from before them
the fragments, twelve baskets full, the remains of
44 those five loaves and of those two fishes. And they
that did eat of them were five thousand men.

45 And straightway he commanded his disciples to
go up into the ship, and to go before him unto Beth-
46 saida, while he sent away that multitude. And when
he had sent them away, he went to a mountain
47 to pray. But when it was evening, and the ship

[1] Codex—'and he was alone.'

was in the midst of the sea, he[1] was alone on the land. And when he saw them tormented with the fear of the waves, for the wind was against them, he cometh to them walking on the waters, and would have passed by them. When they saw him walking upon the waters, they thought that he was a demon. And when they saw him, they all cried out; and immediately he talked with them, and saith unto them, Be of good courage, it is I, be not afraid. And he went up unto them into the ship, and the wind ceased: and they were sore amazed in themselves[2];

[2] R.V.

for they understood not about the bread, because their heart was blinded. And when they had passed over, they came up to the land of Gennesar. And when he was come up out of the ship, in the hour that they knew him, they ran to the whole region, and brought those that were sick, carrying them on beds. And wheresoever Jesus entered, into cities, or villages, or fields and streets, they placed the beds of the sick, and besought him that they might touch, if it were but the border of his garment: and all who touched him were made whole.

And Pharisees and scribes which came from Jerusalem, came together unto him. And they saw his disciples eating bread when they had not washed their hands. For all the Jews and Pharisees, unless

[3] Bezae.
[4] *when they come is understood.*

they wash their hands, eat not bread,[3] holding the tradition of the elders. And[4] from the market, except they wash, they eat not. And they keep many things which they have received, and the washing of cups and vessels. And after these things the scribes and Pharisees asked him, saying unto him, Why do not thy disciples keep the command-

ments of the ancients, for they wash not their hands
6 and they eat bread? Jesus said unto them, Well hath
Isaia the prophet prophesied of you, as it is written
that he said, This people honoureth me with its
7 lips, but with its heart it is far from me. But in
vain do they worship me, who teach for doctrines the
9 commandments of men. [1] Ye do well, who forsake the
commandments of God, that ye may establish your
10 commandments. For Moses said, Honour thy father and
thy mother: and whoso curseth his father or his mother,
11 let him die the death. But ye say, that if he shall say
to his father and his mother, It is Corban, wherewith
12 thou mightest be profited by me: and ye suffer him
13 not to honour his father or his mother: and ye reject
the word of God because of your commandments.

14 And many such like things do ye. And he
called all the multitude, and said unto them,
15 Hearken, all of you, and obey. There is nothing
from without a man, that entering into him, can
defile him: but what comes out of a man, this is
16 what defiles the man. Who hath ears to hear, let
17 him hear. And when he was entered into the house
from the multitude, his disciples asked him concern-
18 ing the parable. And he saith unto them, Are ye
yet so stubborn? Do ye not understand anything?
that not everything which entereth into a man defileth
19 him, because it entereth not into his heart, but into
20 the belly, and is cast out, and all meat is purged. But
that which cometh out of the man, that defileth the
21 man. For out of the heart proceed the evil thoughts
22 of man, adulteries, fornications, murders, thefts, de-
ceits, wickedness, frauds, lasciviousness, an evil eye,
23 blasphemy, pride, foolishness: all these evil things

[1] Omit v. 8.

coming out from within, and defiling the man. And 24
[1] R.V. marg. he arose, and went to the borders of Tyre,[1] and when
he had entered into a house, he would have no man
know him, but he could not be hid. And when a 25
woman heard it, whose daughter had an unclean spirit,
she came and fell down before him. This woman 26
was a widow, from the borders of Tyre of Phœnicia,
and she besought him that he would cast forth the
spirit out of her daughter. He said unto her, ... 27
First let the children be filled: it is not meet to take
the children's bread, and to cast it to the dogs. The 28
woman saith unto him, Lord, even the dogs eat of
the crumbs which are over from the children's table.
He said unto her, For this saying go thy way, be- 29
hold, the demon is gone out of thy daughter. And 30
when she went to her house, she found her daughter
. . . . from her, and . . . . lying upon the bed. And 31
again . . . . from the borders . . . . Sidon, he came
to the lake of Galilee, amidst the borders of Decapolis.
. . . . a certain deaf stammerer, and they beseech 32
him that he would . . . . lay on him. . . . . from 33
the multitude, and put . . . . into his ears . . . .
And looking up to heaven, he sighed, and said unto 34
him, Be opened. . . . . the string of his tongue, and 35
he spake plain. And he commanded them that they 36
should . . . . no man: and as much . . . . a great
deal more they proclaimed it, ... were greatly 37
astonished, saying, ... all things well: . . . . he
maketh the deaf to hear, and the dumb to speak.

In those days . . . when there was . . . . a **8**
[3] R.V. Bezae. great multitude, and they had nothing to eat, he[2]
called his disciples, and saith unto them, I have com- 2
passion on this multitude, for behold, three days they

3 continue with me, and have nothing to eat: and if I send them away fasting to their home, they will faint in the way: and some of them are come from
4 far. His disciples said unto him, Whence art thou able to satisfy them with bread here in the wilder-
5 ness? And he asked them and said to them, How many loaves have ye? They said unto him, Seven.
6 And he commanded the multitude to sit down on the ground: and he took those seven loaves, and blessed, and brake, and gave to his disciples, that they should set before them: and they set before the multitude.
7 And there were a few fishes: and when he had blessed them also, he told them to set before them.
8 And they did eat, and were filled: and they took up what remained over of the crumbs seven baskets.
9 The people that ate were about four thousand, and
10 he sent them away. And he went up and sat in the boat with his disciples, and they came into the
11 hill of Magdan. And the Pharisees went out, and began seeking from him, and asking of him a sign
12 from heaven, tempting him. And he was troubled in spirit, and saith, Why do this generation[1] seek a sign? verily I say unto you, there shall no sign be
13 given unto this generation.[1] And he left them again, and sat in the ship, and went to the other side of
14 the lake. And they forgot . . . . bread, ... with
15 them in the ship. And he commanded them, saying,
to . . . . beware of . . . . of Herod. . . . .
. . . . ye . . . . . . and do ye not remember?
19 Those five loaves which the five thousand ate of, and how many baskets full of fragments . . . . unto
20 him . . . .
to
22 . . . . and they bring to him a blind man . . . .

[1] Or 'tribe.'

besought . . . . on his eyes, and asked him 23
his hand . . . . to
. . . . neither go thou into the town.   26

And Jesus went out, and his disciples, into the 27
towns of Cesarea Philippi: and he asked his disciples by the way, saying unto them, What do men say
about me, that I am? They say unto him, Some say, 28
He is John the Baptist: and others say, Elia: and
others, One of the prophets. He saith unto them, And 29
ye, whom say ye that I am? Cepha saith unto him,
Thou art the Christ. And he charged them that they 30
should tell no man of him. And he began to teach 31
them that the Son of man must suffer many things,
and be rejected of the elders, and of the chief priests,
and scribes, and they shall kill him, and the third day
he shall rise. And he was speaking the saying openly. 32
Then Simon Cepha, as though he pitied him, said to
him, Be it far from thee. And when he had turned, 33
he looked on his disciples, and he rebuked Cepha, and
said, Get thee behind me, Satan: for thou carest not
for God, but for man.

And he called the multitude with his disciples, 34
and said unto them, Whosoever will come after me,
let him deny himself, and take up his cross, and
come. For whosoever will save his life shall lose it, 35
and whosoever shall lose his life[1] for my gospel's
sake shall save it. For what shall it profit a man, if 36
he shall inherit the whole world, and lose his soul? 37
Or what shall a man give in exchange for his soul?
For whosoever shall be ashamed of me, and of my 38
words in this adulterous and sinful generation, of
him also shall the Son of man be ashamed, when he
cometh in the glory of his Father with the holy angels.

[1] Bezae.

9 He said unto them, Verily I say unto you, that there be some of them that stand here, which shall not taste of death, till they have seen the king-
2 dom of God coming with power. And after six days, Jesus taketh Peter, and James, and John, and leadeth them up into an high mountain apart by themselves: and he was transfigured before them.
3 And he became shining, and his raiment became
4 white like snow: and there appeared unto them
5 Moses and Elia talking with him. Cepha answered and said to Jesus, Master, it is good that we are here, and we may make three tabernacles; one
6 for thee, and one for Moses, and one for Elia. And he wist not what he was saying, for fear had fallen
7 upon him. And a cloud overshadowed him: and a voice came out of the cloud, This is my Son,
8 who is beloved: hear him. And suddenly again when his disciples looked, no man appeared to them, save Jesus only. As they went down from the moun-
9 tain,[1] he charged them that they should tell no man what they had seen, except when the Son of
10 man was risen from the dead. And they kept the saying with themselves, meditating and saying, What is this word that he said? When he is risen from the dead?
11 And they asked him, saying, The scribes say
12 that Elia cometh first. He answered and said unto them, Elia cometh first, that he may restore every thing; and how it is written of the Son of man,
13 must he not suffer much, and be crucified? But I say unto you, That Elia is[2] come, and they have done unto him whatsoever they listed, as it is written of
14 him. When he ca . . . . . . he saw about them

[1] MS. makes a full stop after 'mountain.'
[2] R.V. Bezae.

many . . . . and the scribes questioning with them.
And straightway . . . . were amazed, and ran and 15
saluted him. And he asked them, What question ye 16
with them? And one of the multitude answered 17
and said, ... I have brought . . . . He answered to 19
. . . . to them, O faithless generation, how long, till
when shall I be with you and suffer you? Bring
thy son to me. And he brought him unto him: 20
and when he saw him, the spirit threw him down
straightway, and he fell on the ground, and wallowed
foaming. And he asked . . . . from . . . . He said 21
unto him, Behold, from his childhood. And it hath 22
thrown him often into the fire, and into the water,
to destroy him: but as much as thou canst do, Lord,
help me, and have compassion on me. Jesus said 23
unto him, If thou believest, all things can happen
unto thee. And straightway the father of the child 24
cried out,[1] and said, I believe, Lord, help my want.
When Jesus saw that the people were coming and 25
running, he rebuked the spirit, and said unto it,
I charge thee, thou deaf and dumb spirit, come out
of him, and enter not again into him. And it cried, 26
and vexed him greatly, and came out of him, and
he was like one dead, and many thought that he
was dead. But Jesus took him by his hand, and 27
raised him up, and delivered him to his father.
And when he was come into the house, his disciples 28
asked him privately, Why could not we cast him
out? He said unto them, This kind cometh out by 29
nothing but by fasting and prayer.

And when they had gone forth from thence, they 30
passed through Galilee, and he would not that any
man should know it. And he taught his disciples, 31

[1] R.V.

saying to them, The Son of man shall be delivered up
into the hands of men, and they shall kill him, and
when they have killed him, on the third day he shall
32 rise. And they understood not what he said unto
33 them, and were afraid to ask him. And he came to
Capernaum; and when he had entered into the house,
he asked them, What were ye speaking about one to
34 another on the way? But they held their peace:
for they had reasoned about who should be greatest.
35 And he sat down, and called his twelve, and said
unto them, Whosoever desires to be first, shall be
36 last of all men, and servant of all men. And he
took a certain child, and set him in the midst of
37 them: and looked at him, and said unto them, Whosoever shall receive a child like this in my name,
receiveth me[1]: he receiveth not me, but him that
38 sent me. John answered and said unto him, Our
Master, we saw one casting out demons in thy name,
and we forbade him, because he followed not us.
39 But he[2] said unto them, Forbid him not, for there
is no man who does anything in my name, and is
40 able to speak evil of me. For he who is not against
41 us is with us. For whosoever shall give you a cup of
water to drink in the name that ye are the Christ's,
verily I say unto you, he shall not lose his reward.
42 And whosoever shall offend one of these little ones
that believe on me, it were better for him if a mill-
stone of an ass[3] were cast about his neck, and he
43 were drowned in the sea. If therefore thy hand
cause thee to offend, cut it off from thee: for it is
better for thee that having one hand thou shouldst
enter into life, and not that having two hands thou
45 shouldst go into the unquenchable fire: [4]and if thy

[1] A line has been dropped here.
[2] Bezae.
[3] R.V. marg. Bezae.
[4] Omit v. 44. R.V.

foot cause thee to offend, cut it off: cast it from thee: for it is better for thee that being halt thou shouldst enter into life, and not that having two feet thou shouldst go into Gehenna. ¹If thine eye cause thee 47 to offend, pluck it out from thee: for it is better for thee that having one eye thou shouldst enter into the kingdom of God, and not that having two eyes thou shouldst go into Gehenna: where their 48 worm dieth not, and their fire is not quenched. For 49 every one shall be salted with fire.² Salt is good: 50 but if the salt is seasonless, wherewith will we season it? Have salt³, and be at peace one with another.

And he arose from thence, and came into the 10 borders of Judæa beyond Jordan: and a multitude came together again unto him. As he was wont, he healed and taught them. And⁴ they asked him, 2 tempting him, Is it lawful for a man to leave his wife? And he answered and said unto them, What 3 did Moses command you? They said unto him, 4 Moses suffered us to write a bill of divorcement, and give⁵ it to her, and to put her away. Jesus answered 5 and said unto them, Moses, because of the hardness of your heart allowed you this precept. But from 6 the beginning God .... and female .... For this 7 cause shall a man leave his father and his mother,⁶ and they twain shall be one flesh: thenceforth 8 they are not twain, but one flesh. What therefore 9 God hath joined together, let not man put asunder. And when he had entered into the house, his disci- 10 ples asked him again about this. He said unto them, 11 Any woman who shall leave her husband, and be married to another, committeth adultery. And any 12

---

¹ Omit v. 46. R.V.
² R.V.
³ Or 'let there be salt with you.'
⁴ Bezae.
⁵ Bezae.
⁶ R.V. marg.

man who shall leave his wife, and marry another,
13 committeth adultery. And they brought young children to him, that he should lay his hands on them, and his disciples rebuked those that brought
14 them. When Jesus saw it, he was displeased, and rebuked them, and said unto them, Suffer the children to come unto me, and forbid them not: for those who
15 are like them, theirs is the kingdom of God. Verily I say unto you, Whosoever shall not receive the kingdom of God as a child, he shall not enter therein.
16 And he called them,[1] and laid his hands on them, and blessed them. [1] Bezae.

17 As he journeyed in the way, one ran, and fell on his knees, and said to him, Good Teacher, what shall
18 I do that I may inherit eternal life? Jesus said unto him, Why callest thou me good? there is no
19 one good but one, God. But thou knowest the commandments, Do not kill, Do not commit adultery, Do not steal, Do not bear false witness. Honour thy
20 father and thy mother. He answered and said unto him, Teacher, all these things have I observed, lo,
21 from my youth. . . . . beholding him, ... and said unto him, One . . . . to thee, go, sell all that thou hast, and give to the poor, and thou shalt have treasure in heaven, and take up thy cross, and follow
22 me. And he was grieved about this saying, and
23 went away . . . . . for he had great riches. And Jesus looked at his disciples, and said, How hard it is for them who trust in their riches to enter into the
24 kingdom of God! And his disciples were astonished at his words. But Jesus answereth again, and saith unto them, Children, how hard it is for them who trust in their riches to enter into the kingdom of

God! For it is easier for a camel to enter into the eye of a needle, than for a rich man into the kingdom of heaven. And they were the more astonished among themselves. Who then can be saved? Jesus looked upon them and said, With men this is impossible, except with God: for with God everything is possible. Cepha said unto him, Lo, we have left all, and followed thee. Jesus answered and said, Verily I say unto you, that every man who hath left house, or brethren, or sisters, or mother,[1] or father, or children, or lands, for my sake and my gospel's, but he shall receive an hundredfold in this time, houses, and brethren, and sisters, and mothers, and children, and lands, with persecutions; and in the world to come he shall inherit eternal life. For many are first that shall be last: and last that shall be first.

And while they were going up in the way to Jerusalem, and Jesus was going before them, those who were with him were amazed, being afraid. And he took his twelve, and began to tell them what should happen unto him, Behold, we go up to Jerusalem, and the Son of man shall be delivered unto the chief priests, and unto the scribes: and they shall condemn him to death, and shall deliver him to the people. And they shall mock him, and shall scourge him, and shall spit in his face, and shall kill him, and on the third day he shall rise.

And James and John, the sons of Zebedee, come unto him, saying unto him, Master, we wish that whatsoever we shall ask thee thou wilt do for us. He said unto them, What would ye that I should do for you? They said unto him, Grant unto us that we may sit on thy right hand, and on thy left hand, in

[1] R.V.

38 thy glory. Jesus answered and said unto them, Ye know not what ye ask: can ye drink of the cup that
39 I drink of? or be baptized with the baptism? They say unto him, We are able. Jesus said unto them, Ye may be able to drink of the cup that I drink of: and ye may be able to be baptized with the baptism
40 that I am baptized with: But to sit on my right hand or on my left hand, this is not mine to give,
41 but for others[1] it is prepared. And when the ten heard it, they began to be displeased with James and
42 John. And he called them, and said unto them, Ye
43 know that the chiefs of the nations are their lords. Let it not be so among you: but whosoever will be
44 great among you, let him be your minister: and whosoever of you will be the chiefest, let him be servant
45 of all men. Like as the Son of man came not to be ministered unto, but to minister, and to give his life a ransom for many.
46 And he came to Jericho: and as he went out of Jericho, he and his disciples, and a great multitude, Timai Bar-Timai, a blind man, sat on the
47 highway and begged. And when he heard that it was Jesus of Nazareth, he began to cry out and say,
48 Son of David, have mercy on me. And many charged him that he should hold his peace: and again he cried the more, Son of David, have mercy
49 on me. And Jesus stood still, and said that they should bring him near; and he called the blind man, and they said unto him, Fear not, rise, he calleth thee.
50 And he rose, and took up his garment, and came to
51 Jesus. Jesus answered and said unto him, What wilt thou that I should do unto thee? The blind
52 man said unto him, Lord,[2] that I may see.[3] Jesus

[1] Bezae.
[2] Or 'Rabbuli.'
[3] Bezae.

said unto him, Go, thy faith hath saved thee. And immediately his eyes were opened, and he followed him in the way.

And when they came nigh to Jerusalem, unto 11 Bethphage, unto Bethany, at the mount of Olives, he sendeth two of his disciples, and saith, Go into the 2 village over against you, and as soon as ye be entered into it, ye shall find a colt tied, whereon never man rode, loose him, and bring him. And if 3 any man say anything unto you, say unto him, The Lord hath need of him, and straightway he will send him hither. And they went, and found the 4 colt tied at the door of a court in the street. And as they loosed him, certain of them that stood 5 there said, What do ye, loosing the colt? And they 6 said unto them even as Jesus had said unto them. And they brought the colt to Jesus, and cast their 7 garments on it, and made him ride upon it.

And many spread their garments in the way: and 8 they that went before him, and they that followed him, 9 cried, saying, Osanna, blessed is he that cometh in the name of the Lord. Blessed be the kingdom that 10 cometh of our father David[1]: peace in the highest. And they entered into Jerusalem, and he entered 11 into the temple, and saw all things; and when the eventide was come, he went out unto Bethany with the twelve. And on the morrow, when he went 12 out from Bethany, he was hungry. And he saw a 13 certain fig tree afar off, having leaves, and he came to it, if haply he might find anything thereon, and he came, but found nothing but leaves: it was not the time of figs. He[2] answered and said unto it, 14 Henceforth and for ever let no man eat of thy

[1] R.V. Bezae.
[2] R.V. Bezae.

15 fruit. And his disciples heard it. And when he was come to Jerusalem, and had entered into the temple of God, he began to cast out them that sold and bought in the temple, and the tables of the money changers, and the tables of them that sold
16 doves, and would not suffer any man to carry a
17 vessel within the temple. And he taught, and said, Is it not written thus, My house shall be called a house of prayer for all nations? but ye have made it a
18 den of thieves. And the chief priests and the scribes[1] heard it, and sought how they might destroy him: for they feared him, for all the people were amazed
19 at his doctrine. And when even came, he went
20 out of the city. And when they passed by in the morning, they saw the fig tree dried up from its
21 root. And when Cepha remembered, he said unto him, Master, the fig tree which thou cursedst is dried
22 up. Jesus answered and said unto them, If ye have
23 faith in God,[2] verily I say unto you, that if ye shall say to this mountain, Be thou removed, and cast into the sea; and shall not doubt in his mind, but shall believe that the thing which he saith shall come to
24 pass, it shall come to pass. Therefore I say unto you, What things soever ye pray for, believing that
25 ye shall receive them, ye shall have them. And when ye stand praying, forgive, if ye have ought against any man: that your Father also which is in heaven may forgive you your sins.
27 [3]And he came again to Jerusalem, and he was walking in the temple, and there came to him the chief
28 priests, and the scribes, and the elders, and say unto him, By what authority doest thou these things?
29 and who gave thee this authority? Jesus answered

[1] R.V. Bezae.
[2] Or, 'the faith of God.'
[3] Omit v. 26 R.V.

and said unto them, I will also ask of you one word, which ye shall answer me, and I will tell you by what authority I do these things. The baptism of John, was it from heaven, or of men? Tell me. And they considered, and said, If we shall say, From heaven, he will say unto¹ us, Why did ye not believe him? And if we shall say, Of men, they feared the people: for they all held John, that he was a prophet.² They said unto him, We do not know. Jesus answered and said unto them, Neither do I tell you by what authority I do these things.

And he began to speak in parables. A man³ planted a vineyard, and set a hedge about it, and digged a wine-press in it, and built a tower in it, and let it out to husbandmen, and went abroad.⁴ And he sent his servant at the season of fruit to the husbandmen, that they might send to him of the fruit of the vineyard. And they took him, and beat him, and sent him away empty. ⁵And again he sent to them another servant; and him also they killed: and many others; they beat some, and they killed some. He had one beloved son, he sent him to them, and said, Perhaps they will reverence my son. But those husbandmen said among themselves, This is his son, his heir; come, let us kill him, and the inheritance shall be ours. And they took him, and killed him, and cast him out of the vineyard. When the lord of the vineyard cometh, what will he do? he will destroy these husbandmen, and will give his vineyard to others. And have ye not read the scripture: The stone which the builders rejected is become the head of the corner: this was from the Lord, and it is a marvel in our eyes? And they sought to lay hold on him, and they feared the

---

¹ Bezae.

² R.V.

³ R.V. Bezae.

⁴ Bezae.

⁵ Omit v. 4.

people, for they understood that he had spoken this parable against them: and they left him, and went
13 their way. And they sent unto him certain of the Pharisees and of the house of Herod, that they might
14 catch him in his word. And they began to say unto him, deceitfully, Teacher, we know that thou art true, and carest for no man: for thou regardest not the face of man, but teachest the way of God in truth. Is it lawful to give tribute to Cæsar, or shall we not
15 give? And he knowing their craftiness, said unto them, Why tempt ye me? bring me a penny, that I
16 may see it. And they brought it to him. He saith unto them, Whose is this image and inscription?
17 They say unto him, Cæsar's. Jesus answered and said, Render the things that are Cæsar's to Cæsar, and the things that are God's to God. And they
18 marvelled at him.

And the Sadducees came unto him, those which
19 say there is no resurrection; and they asked him, saying, Teacher, Moses wrote unto us that when . . . die,
to
. . . . thy strength: this is the first commandment.
31 And the second which is like it, Thou shalt love thy neighbour as thyself. There is none other com-
32 mandment greater than these. The scribe said unto him, Well, Master, thou hast spoken with truth[1]: for [1] Bezae.
33 there is one God, and there is none other but he. And that a man should love him from all his heart,[2] and [2] Bezae. from all his soul, and from all his strength, and that he should love his neighbour as himself, is more than
34 all whole burnt offerings and sacrifices. When Jesus saw that he returned him an answer well, he answered[3] [3] Bezae. and said unto him, Thou art not far from the kingdom of God. And no man durst question him again.

Jesus said while he taught in the temple, How 35
say the scribes that the Christ is the Son of David?
and David himself said by the Holy Ghost, The 36
Lord said unto my Lord, Sit on my right hand, until
I place thine enemies beneath thy feet.[1] And if 37
David call him[2] Lord, how was he his son? And all
the multitude heard him gladly. And he said while 38
he was teaching, Keep yourselves from the scribes,
who love to walk in the porches,[3] and love greetings
in the market-places, and the chief seats in the syna- 39
gogues, and the uppermost rooms at feasts: and 40
devour widows' houses, and who for a pretence
lengthen their prayers: these shall receive greater
condemnation.

And while Jesus stood over against the treasury, 41
he beheld many who cast money into the treasury:
and many of the rich who cast in much. And there 42
came a certain poor widow, she threw in two mites,
which make two farthings, which make an eighth.
Jesus called his disciples and said unto them, ... 43
unto you . . . . poor widow hath cast in more than
all men into the treasury: for all men have cast in 44
from what was superfluous to them; but she hath
cast in . . . . all that she had.

And as Jesus went forth out of the temple, one 13
of his disciples said unto him, Master, behold, see
the stones and the great building. Jesus said unto 2
him, See that building? there shall not be left here[4]
stone upon stone that shall not be thrown down.

And as he sat on the mount of Olives, over 3
against the temple, Cepha, and James, and John and
Andrew asked him privately, Tell us when these 4
things shall be, and what is the sign with which

---

[1] R.V. marg Bezae.
[2] Literally, 'our Lord.'
[3] In the Stone.
[4] R.V. Bezae.

5 these things are accomplished? Jesus said unto
6 them, See that no man lead you astray. For many
shall come in my name, and shall say, I am he¹; and ¹ R.V. Bezae.
7 shall lead many astray. But when ye shall hear of
wars and rumours of wars, be not afraid: for it is
8 about to be, but the end till now is not yet. For
nation shall rise against nation, and kingdom against
kingdom: and there shall be earthquakes in divers
places, famines and tumults: these things are the
9 beginning of travail. ²And they shall deliver you up ² Bezae.
to the people, and to councils; and ye shall stand
10 before kings, and ye shall be beaten before governors
for my sake, for a testimony to them and to all
11 nations . . . . for . . . . But when they shall bring
you nigh to deliver you up, ... not what ye shall
speak³: but what shall be given you in that hour, ³ R.V. Bezae.
that speak ye: for it is not ye that speak, but the
12 Holy Ghost. For the brother shall deliver his
brother to death, and the father his son; and the
children shall rise up against the parents, and shall
13 cause them to be put to death. And all men
shall hate you for my name's sake. Whosoever
14 shall endure to the end, he shall be saved. When
ye see the sign of the abomination of desolation
standing where it ought not, (let him that readeth
15 understand), then they that are in Judæa, let them
flee to the mountain: and he that is on the house-
top, let him not come down into the house, and let
16 him not enter to take anything from his house: and
he that is in the field, let him not return back to
17 take his clothes. But woe to them that are with
child, and to them that give suck in those days!
18
19 And pray ye that it be⁴ not in the winter. For there ⁴ R.V. Bezae

shall be tribulation in those days, such as there hath not been the like of it, since the days when God created the world until this day, and never again shall be. And except these days had been shortened, 20 no flesh would have been saved: but for the elect's sake, whom he chose, the days are shortened. And 21 then if any man shall say unto you, Lo, here is the Christ; lo, he is there; believe it not: for there shall 22 arise false Christs, and prophets of lies, and shall give signs and wonders, so that, if possible, they may lead astray even the elect. But look ye, I have fore- 23 told you all things. But in those days, after that 24 tribulation, the sun shall be darkened, and the moon shall not shew her light, and the stars shall fall from[1] 25 heaven, ... the powers of heaven . . . . And 26 then shall they see the Son of man coming on the clouds with great power and with glory. And then 27 shall he send his angels, and shall gather together his elect from the four winds, from the uttermost part of the earth to the uttermost part of heaven. Now 28 learn a parable from the fig tree: When her branches are tender, and put forth her leaves, ye know that summer is nigh: so also ye, when ye shall see these 29 things come to pass, know that it is nigh, at the doors. Verily I say unto you, that this generation[2] 30 shall not pass, till all these things shall be.[3] Heaven 31 and earth shall pass away: and my words shall not pass away. But of that day and of that hour knoweth 32 no man, no, not the angels which are in heaven, nor even the Son, but the Father. Watch ye then 33 and pray: for ye know not the time. For like[4] 34 as a man who took a journey, and left his house, giving . . . . to his servants, to every man his work,

[1] R.V.

[2] Or 'tribe.'
[3] Bezae.

[4] R.V.

35 and commanded the porter to watch: watch ye therefore: for ye know not when the master of the
36 house cometh, if at even, or at mid [night], or at the dawn, or in the morning: lest coming suddenly he
37 find you sleeping. And what I say unto you I say unto all of you, Watch.

14 Two days before there was the unleavened bread of the passover the chief priests and the scribes sought how they might take him by craft, and put
2 him to death. For they said, Not on the feast-
3 day, lest there be an uproar of the people. And being in Bethany, in the house of Simon the leper, as he sat at meat, there came a certain woman, carrying an alabaster box of spikenard, very pure[1] and of great price; and she broke it, and poured it on his
4 head. And there were some that had indignation
5 within themselves, and said, Why . . . . for this might have been sold for three hundred pence, and have been given to the poor. And they murmured
6 against her in their teeth. Then said Jesus unto them, Let her alone; why trouble ye her? for she
7 hath wrought a good work on me. For ye have the poor with you always, and whensoever ye will ye may deal with them: but I am not with you always.
8 For that which she hath done, behold, as if for my burying she hath done it, and hath anointed my
9 body beforehand. Verily I say unto you, That when the gospel shall be preached throughout the whole world, there will be a memorial of what she hath done.
10 And Juda Iscariot, one of the twelve, went unto
11 the chief priests, so that he might betray him. And they, when they heard it, were glad, and promised to

[1] Syriac keeps πιστικός.

give him silver. And he sought for a way in which he might betray him. On the first day of unleavened 12 bread, when they . . . . the passover, his disciples said unto him, Where wilt thou that we go and prepare that thou mayest eat the p . . . . r? . . . . two 13 . . . . . and saith unto them, Go ye into the city; lo, there shall meet you a certain man bearing a pitcher of water: follow him whithersoever he shall 14 go in. And say ye to the goodman of the house, The Master saith, My time is come. Where is the guest-chamber, where I shall eat the passover with my disciples? And behold, he will shew you a large 15 upper room, strewn, and prepared: there . . . . And 16 his disciples went as . . . . and came to the city, and found as he had said unto them: and they made ready the passover. And when it was evening he 17 cometh with his twelve. And as they sat and did 18 eat, Jesus said unto them, Verily, verily, I say unto you, that one of you which eateth with me, he shall betray me. And they began to be sorrowful, and to 19 say unto him one by one, Not I, surely[1]? And[2] he said 20 unto them, One of the twelve who stretcheth out his hand with me in the dish. And the Son of man 21 goeth, as it is written of him: but woe to that man . . . . the Son of man is betrayed! good were it for him if he had not been born. . . . . and as they did 22 eat, ... bread, ... brake, gave to his disciples, and said unto them, Take,[3] this is my body. And he took the cup, and blessed it, and gave to 23 them: and they drank of it. And he said unto 24 them, This is my blood of the new testament, which is shed for many. Verily I say unto you, I will drink 25 no more of the fruit of the vine, until that day that

[1] R.V.
[2] R.V. Bezae.

[3] R.V. Bezae.

I drink it with you anew in the kingdom of God.
26 And they sung praises, and went out to the mount
27 of Olives. Jesus saith unto them, All ye shall be
offended because of me: for it is written, I will smite
28 the shepherd, and the sheep shall be scattered. But
when I am risen, I will go before you into Galilee.
29 Cepha answered and said unto him, If all shall be
30 offended, I will not. Jesus saith unto him, Verily,
verily, I say unto thee, that this day, in this night,
the cock shall not crow twice, until thou shalt deny
31 me thrice. And Simon spake the more vehemently,
If I should die with thee, I will not deny thee.[1] [1] R.V.
32 Likewise also said they all. And they came to a
place which was called Gedsemane: and he saith to
33 his disciples, Sit ye here, until I pray.[2] And he [2] Bezae.
took C[epha], and James and John, and began to be
34 very sad, and sore troubled, and he saith unto them,
35 My soul is sorrowful, even unto death. And he
went away a little, and fell on his face[3] on the ground, [3] Bezae.
and prayed that, if it were possible, the hour might
36 pass from him. And he said, My Father, all things
are possible in thy hands; let this cup pass from
37 me: but not my will be done, but thine. And he
cometh, and findeth them sleeping, and saith unto
Cepha, Simon, sleepest thou? couldest thou not
38 watch one hour? Watch and pray, that ye enter not
into temptation: the spirit is willing, but the body
39 is weak. And he went away again, and prayed, say-
40 ing the same word. And he came and found them
again sleeping, for their eyes were carrying sleep,
and they wist not what they should say unto him.
41 And he cometh the third time, and saith unto them,
Sleep, and take your rest: the hour is come, the end

is at hand; behold, the Son of man is betrayed into the hands of sinners. Arise, let us be going: behold, he 42 that betrayeth me is at hand. And¹ while he yet 43 spake, cometh Juda, one of the twelve, and with him a great multitude, carrying swords and staves, from the chief priests and scribes and elders. And he that 44 betrayed him had given them a sign, saying, He whom I shall kiss, that is he; take him cautiously, and lead him away. And straightway he cometh to him, say- 45 ing unto him, Rabbi; and kisseth him. And they laid 46 hands on him, and took him. But one of those that 47 stood by drew a sword, and smote the servant of the high priest, and took² off his ear. Jesus answered 48 and said unto them, As against a thief are ye come out with swords and staves to seize me? I was daily 49 with you in the temple teaching, and ye took me not: but that the scripture might³ be fulfilled. And 50 all his disciples left him, and fled. And a certain 51 young man came, ... wrapped . . . . . . and 52 they laid hold on him; . . . . left the garment in their hands, ... to the chief priests: . . . . all 53 the people were . . . . And Cepha followed them 54 afar off, as far as the house of the high priest: and he was sitting with . . . . fire. . . . . and all . . . . 55 were seeking witness against Jesus to put him to death; and found it not. . . . . false . . . . he . . . . 56 57 saying, We heard him say, I will destroy the⁴ temple 58 that is made with hands, and in three days I will make another not made with hands. And not even 59 so did their witness agree. And the high priest 60 stood up in the midst, and asked Jesus, saying unto him, Dost thou not return an answer? What do these witness against thee? But he held his peace, and 61

¹ Bezae.

² Bezae.

³ Bezae.

⁴ Bezae.

replied nothing. And again the high priest asked
him the second time, saying unto him, Art thou the
62 Christ, the Son of the Blessed? Jesus answered and
said unto him,¹ I am: .... ye shall see the Son of [1] Bezae.
man sitting on the right hand of power, and when
63 he comes on the clouds of heaven. And then the
high priest rent his clothes, and saith, What there-
64 fore? For behold, ye all have heard the blasphemy:
what think ye? And they all condemned him to be
65 guilty of death. And some began to spit on him,
and to b .... saying, Prophecy unto us now: and
the servants did strike him on the cheek. ....
66 Cepha .... in the court of the high priest, a certain maid servant of the high priest saw him as he
67 was warming himself, and said unto him, And thou
68 also wast with Jesus of Nazareth. But he denied,
saying, I know not, neither understand I what thou
69 sayest. And he went out to the outer² court; and³ [2] R.V. marg. Bezae.
the maid saw him again, and began to say to them that [3] R.V. marg.
70 stood by, This also⁴ is one of them. And he denied [4] Bezae.
it again. And again,⁵ a little after, they that stood [5] R.V. marg.
by said to Cepha, Surely thou art one of them: for
71 thou art a Galilean.⁶ And he cursed and swore, I [6] R.V. Bezae.
72 know not this man .... you .... And the cock
crew the second time. And Cepha called to mind
the word that Jesus had said unto him, The cock
..... not crow twice, thou shalt deny me thrice.
And he began to weep.⁷ [7] R.V. marg. Bezae.
15 And in the morning the chief priests held a con-
sultation, and the elders and scribes, and all the
people, and bound Jesus, and carried him away, and
2 delivered him to Pilate. And Pilate asked him, Art
thou the King of the Jews? He answered and said

unto him, Thou sayest. And the chief priests accused 3
him of many things: but he gave no answer. And 4
again Pilate said unto him, Dost thou not reply? to
.... was a man .... who had done wrong and
committed murder. And the people cried, and began 8
to ask that he should do it unto them. Pilate answered 9
and said unto them, Will ye that I release unto you
the King of the Jews? For he .... had delivered 10
him ... And the chief priests persuaded the people 11,
that he should ask him to release unto them Bar-abba.
.... answered .... crucified. 12
And the soldiers .... into .... Prætorium; .... to 16
And they clothed him with purple, and platted a 17
crown of thorns, and put it on him.¹ And they 18
began to salute him, Hail, King of the Jews! And 19
they smote him on the head with a reed, and did
spit in his face, and fell on their knees, and worshipped him. And when they had mocked 20
they stripped him of his purple robe, and put his own
clothes on him, and led him out to crucify him.
And they compelled Simon a Cyrenian man, who 21
passed by, coming out of the country, the father of
Alexander and Rufus, to bear his cross. And they 22
bring him unto the place which is called Gogoltha,
which is, interpreted, a skull. And they gave him 23
wine sweetened with spice: but he received it not.
And they crucified him, and parted his garments 24
amongst them, and cast lots upon them.² And it 25
was the third hour, and they crucified him. And 26
the inscription of his accusation was, This is³ the
King of the Jews. And with him they crucify two 27
thieves; the one on his right hand, and the other on
his left. ⁴And they blasphemed against him, wagging 29

¹ R.V.

² Bezae.

³ Bezae.

⁴ Omit v. 28.
R.V.
Bezae.

their heads, and saying, Ah, thou that destroyest the
30 temple, and buildest it in three days, save thyself,
31 and come down from the cross. And again also the
chief priests, mocking among themselves with the
scribes, said, He saved others; himself he cannot
32 save; the Christ the King of Israel! let him descend
from the cross, that we may see and believe. And
they also that were crucified with him reviled him.
33 And when it was the sixth hour, there was dark-
34 ness until the ninth hour. And at the ninth hour
he[1] cried with a loud voice, My God, my God, why
35 hast thou forsaken me[2]? And some of them that
36 stood by heard it, and said, He calleth Elia. And
one ran, filled a sponge with vinegar, and put it
on a reed, and gave him to drink. And they said,
Let alone; let us see if Elia cometh to take him
37 down. And Jesus, when he had cried with a loud
voice, expired.
38 And the veil of the temple was rent in twain,
39 from the top to the bottom. And when the centurion,
who was standing beside him, saw him crying out
and expiring,[3] he said, Truly this was the Son of God.
40 And there were women who were standing afar off
and looking on: Mary Magdalene, and Mary the
daughter of James the Less, the mother of Joseph,
41 and Salome; those who came with him from Galilee,
and many others who were ministering unto him,
42 who had come up with him to Jerusalem. And
43 it was on the sabbath. And Joseph came from
Ramatha, an honourable man, a counsellor, and who
also looked for the kingdom of heaven; and he
was bold, and went in unto Pilate, and craved the
44 body of Jesus. And Pilate marvelled that he were

[1] Bezae.
[2] Syriac—'Alah(i), Alah(i), lemana shabactani.'
[3] Bezae.

already dead: and he sent and called the centurion, and asked him if he were dead. And when he learned it of the centurion, he gave the body to Joseph. And he bought fine linen, and brought it, and wrapped him in the linen, and laid him in a sepulchre which was hewn out of a rock, and rolling a stone, placed it against the door of the sepulchre. And Mary Magdalene and Mary the daughter of James beheld where he was laid.

And when the sabbath was passed, Mary Magdalene, and Mary the daughter of James, and Salome, had bought oil and spices, that they might come and anoint him. And in the morning, the first day of the week, they came unto the sepulchre, when the sun was rising. And they said among themselves, But who shall roll us away the stone of the sepulchre? for it was very great.[1] And they went, and saw that this stone was rolled away. And they entered into the sepulchre, and saw a young man sitting on their right side,[2] clothed in a white garment; and they were affrighted. And he saith unto them, Be not affrighted: ye seek Jesus of Nazareth, which was crucified: he is risen; he is not here: behold the place where he was laid. But go your way, tell his disciples and Cepha that behold, he goeth before you into Galilee: there shall ye see him, as he said unto you. And when they had heard . . . . they went out; and went, and said nothing to any man, for they were afraid.

[1] Bezae.
[2] Or 'on their right hand.'

HERE ENDETH THE GOSPEL OF MARK.

THE GOSPEL OF LUKE

1 Forasmuch as many have desired to write and to relate about those things that have been fulfilled 2 amongst us, even as they have transmitted them to us, who from the beginning were eye-witnesses, 3 and ministers of the word: it seemed good to me also, who have investigated all these things from the beginning, to write of them one by one carefully unto 4 thee,[1] noble Theophilus, that thou mayest know the certainty of the words wherein thou hast been instructed.

5 There was in the days of Herod, king of Judæa, a certain priest named Zacharia, of the division of the house of Abiam: and his wife was of the daughters 6 of Aaron, her name was Elisabeth. And they were both righteous before God, walking in all the com-7 mandments and righteousness of the Lord, and they were blameless in all their manner of life. And they had no child, because Elisabeth was barren, and 8 they were both now well on in days. And it came to pass, that while he was ministering in the priest's 9 order before God, according to the custom of the priest's ministry, his lot was to offer incense. And 10 when he went into the temple, a crowd of the people were standing and praying at the time of incense. 11 And there appeared to Zacharia an angel of the Lord standing on the right side of the altar of incense. 12 And he was troubled, and shook when he saw the

[1] Or, 'who have investigated all these things carefully one by one, from the beginning, to write of them unto thee.'

angel, and fear fell upon him. The angel said unto him, Fear not, Zacharia: for behold, God has heard the voice of thy prayer, and thy wife Elisabeth shall bear thee a son, and thou shalt call his name John. And thou shalt have joy and glory; and many shall rejoice at his birth. For[1] he shall be great before the Lord, and shall drink neither wine nor strong drink; and he shall be filled with the Holy Ghost, while he is still in the womb of his mother. And many of . . . . the angel from her. And Mary arose in those days, and went up with care to the hill country, to a city of Juda; and entered into the house of Zacharia, and saluted Elisabeth. And it came to pass, that, when Elisabeth heard the salutation[2] of Mary, the babe leaped in her womb; and Elisabeth was filled with the Holy Ghost; and she cried with a loud voice, and said to Mary, Blessed art thou among women, and blessed is the fruit of thy womb. And whence is this to me, that the mother of my Lord should come to me? For lo, when the voice of thy salutation fell on mine ear, with great joy did the babe leap in my womb. And blessed is she that believed that there is a fulfilment of those things which were told her from the Lord. And Mary said, My soul doth magnify the Lord, and my spirit hath rejoiced in God the Saviour, who hath regarded the lowliness of his handmaiden. For from henceforth all generations shall call me blessed. For he hath done to me great things; he who by name is glorious and holy, whose mercy is on the generation and on the tribe to those who fear him. He hath shewed strength with his arm; and hath scattered

---

[1] Bezae.

[2] Or, 'when Elisabeth saluted Mary.'

52 the imagination of the hearts of the proud ones. He
hath put down the mighty from their seats, and hath
53 exalted the humble. And he hath filled the poor
with his good things; and the rich he hath despised[1] [1] Or, 'thrust out.'
54 when in want.[2] He hath cared for his son Israel, [2] Syriac— probably ܣܒܠܐ
55 and hath remembered his mercy; as he spake to our
56 fathers, to Abraham, and to his seed for ever. And
Mary abode with Elisabeth about three months, and
57 returned to her house. And when Elisabeth's time of
58 her delivery was fulfilled, she brought forth a son. And
her neighbours and her cousins heard that the Lord
had multiplied mercy towards her; and they rejoiced
59 with her. And it came to pass, that on the eighth
day they came to circumcise the child; and they
60 called him by the name of his father, Zacharia. And
his mother said, Not so;[3] but he shall be called John. [3] R.V.
61 And they said unto her, There is none of thy kindred
62 that is called by this name John. And they spake
also to his father, as to how he desired that he should
63 be called. And he asked for a writing tablet, and
64 wrote on it, John is his name. And immediately[4] [4] Bezae.
the string of his tongue was loosened, and he blessed
65 God. And they marvelled all. And fear was upon
all their neighbours, and in all the hill-country of
66 Judæa these things were talked about. And they hid
them up in their heart, saying, What will this
child become? for[5] the hand of the Lord is with [5] R.V. Bezae.
67 him. And his father Zacharia was filled with the
68 Holy Ghost, and prophesied, saying, Blessed be the
God of Israel; for he hath visited his people, and
69 hath wrought[6] redemption for them, and hath raised [6] R.V. Bezae.
up an horn of salvation for us in the house of David
70 his servant;[7] as also he spake by the mouth of his [7] Bezae.

holy prophets, which have been from everlasting:[1] and hath saved us[2] from the hands[3] of our enemies, and all that hate us; to perform mercy with our[4] fathers, and to remember his holy covenant; the oath which he sware to Abraham, our father, that he would grant unto us, that without fear we should be delivered out of the hand of our enemies, that we might serve before him in uprightness and righteousness all the days of our life. And thou, child, shalt be called the prophet of the Highest: thou shalt go before the face of the Lord to prepare his ways; that he may give knowledge of salvation unto his people by the remission of their sins, through the tender mercy of our God; whereby the dayspring from on high will visit us, to give light to them that sit in' darkness and in the shadow of death, to guide our feet into the way of peace. And the child grew, and waxed strong in spirit, and . . . . in the desert until the day of his shewing unto Israel.

And it came to pass in those days, Augustus Cæsar commanded that all the land should be enrolled. And this was the first enrolment[5] . . . . governor of Syria. And every man . . . . also from . . . . went . . . . that he might be enrolled there. And Joseph also . . . . Joseph . . . . from Nazareth, a city of Galilee, to Judæa, to the city of David, which is called Bethlehem, he, and Mary his wife, being great with child; that there they might be enrolled, because they were both of the house of David. And while they were there, the days were accomplished for the delivery. And she brought forth her first-born son, and wrapped him in swaddling clothes, and laid him in a manger; because there

---

[1] Bezae.
[2] Literally 'brought to salvation.'
[3] Bezae.
[4] Bezae.
[5] R.V.

8 was for them . . . . place . . . . There . . . .
9 watching . . . . when . . . . and they . . . .
10 great fear. . . . . great . . . . which shall be to all the
11 world. For there is born . . . . Saviour, ... the
12 Lord, the Christ, in the city of David. . . . . to you
a sign; ye shall find the babe wrapped in swaddling
13 clothes, and laid in a manger. And suddenly there was
14 seen with him . . . . praising God, and saying, Glory
to God in the highest, and peace upon earth, and
15 good-will to men. . . . [Beth]lehem . . . that which
16
17 . . . . with haste . . . . lying . . . . and related
what had been spoken to them concerning the child.
18 And all men who heard from the shepherds, as they
told what they had seen and heard, wondered and
19 were astonished. But Mary kept everything in her
20 heart, and pondered them in her mind. And the
shepherds returned, glorifying God, and talking about
the things which they had seen and heard, as it was
told unto them.

21   And when eight days were fulfilled, the child was
circumcised, and his name was called Jesus, which
was so named of the angel before he was conceived
22 in the womb. And the days of her purification were
accomplished, according as it is written in the law of
Moses. Then they brought him up to Jerusalem, to
23 present him before the Lord; (as it is written in the
law of the Lord, Every male that openeth the womb
24 shall be called holy to the Lord;) and to offer a sacrifice according as it is written in the law of the Lord,
A pair of turtledoves, or two young ones of a dove.

25   And there was a certain man in Jerusalem, whose
name was Simeon; righteous he was and just, awaiting the desire of Israel: and the Holy Ghost

was upon him. And it was said unto him by the 26
Holy Ghost, that he should not see death before he
had seen the Lord's Christ. And he came by the 27
Spirit into the temple: and when the parents brought
in the child Jesus, to do to him according as it is
commanded in the law, he, Simeon, received him on 28
his arms, and blessed God, and said, Now lettest thou 29
thy servant, Lord, depart in peace, according as thou
hast said: for behold, mine eyes have seen thy mercy, 30
which thou hast prepared before the face of all nations; 31
a light for the revelation[1] of the Gentiles, and the glory 32
of thy people Israel. And his father[2] and his mother 33
marvelled at those things which were spoken of him.
And Simeon blessed them, and said unto Mary his 34
mother, Behold, this one is set in Israel for the falling
and rising of many, and for the sign of contention
which is spoken of. And through thine own soul 35
a spear shall pass, that the thoughts of the hearts
of many may be revealed. And also Hanna the pro- 36
phetess,[3] the daughter of Phanuel, of the tribe of
Asher: and she also was [aged] many days, and
seven days only was she with her husband after her
virginity; and the rest of her life she was in widow- 37
hood, eighty and four years; she went not out from
the temple, and with fasting and prayer and entreaty
was serving day and night. And she also rose[4] in 38
that instant, and gave thanks to the Lord, and spake
of him to all them that looked for the redemption of
Jerusalem. And Joseph and Mary, when they had 39
fulfilled in the temple on the first-born all that is
written in the law, returned into Galilee, to Nazareth
their city.

And the child grew, and waxed strong,[5] filled 40

[1] R.V. marg.
[2] R.V. Bezae.
[3] Bezae.
[4] Bezae.
[5] Bezae.

with wisdom: and the grace of God was upon him.
41 And his parents¹ went every year to Jerusalem at the
42 feast of unleavened bread of the passover. And
when he was twelve years old, they went up as was
43 their wont to the feast. And when they had fulfilled
. . . . the boy Jesus tarried . . . . in Jerusalem; and
44 his parents¹ ² knew it not, for they supposed that he
was with . . . . one day; they sought for Jesus
45 among . . . . and among . . . . not . . . . . to Jerusalem,
46 and there they sought him. And after three days
they found him in the temple, sitting in the midst of
47 the doctors, ... them, and asking them. And all
they that heard him were amazed at him, and won-
48 dered at his wisdom and his answers. And when
his parents found him, they were amazed: and his
mother said unto him, Son, why hast thou done thus
to us? behold, thy father and I were seeking thee
49 with much anxiety. He said unto them, Why were
ye seeking me? wist ye not that I must be with my
50 Father? And they understood not the word which
51 he spake to them. And he went down with them,
and came to Nazareth, and he was subject unto
52 them: but his mother kept all these sayings. And
Jesus grew in stature, and increased in wisdom, and
in favour with God and with man.

3 Now in the fifteenth year, in the reign of Tiberius
Cæsar, in the government of Pontius Pilate in Judæa,
while Herod was tetrarch in Galilee, and Philip his
brother tetrarch in the region of Iturea, and in the
country of Trachonitis, and Lysanias tetrarch in the
region of Habilene, in the high-priesthood of Hannan
2 and of Caiaphas, came the word of God upon John the
son of Zacharia, and he was preaching in the wilder-

¹ Or, 'his relatives.'
² R.V. Bezae.

ness, and in all the region round about Jordan, the 3
baptism of repentance unto remission of sins; as it 4
is written in the prophecy[1] of Isaiah the prophet,
The voice of one crying in the wilderness, Make ye
ready a way for the Lord, and make straight in the
plain a path for our[2] God. All the valleys shall be filled, 5
the mountains and the hills shall be brought low;
the rough shall become smooth, and the difficult
places [shall be] plains; and the glory of the Lord 6
shall be revealed, and all flesh shall see it together.[3]

And he said to the multitudes that went to him 7
to be baptized, O generation of vipers, who hath
shewed you to flee from the wrath to come? Bring 8
forth therefore fruits meet for repentance, and begin
not to say, Our father is Abraham: for I say unto you,
That God is able of these stones to raise up children
unto Abraham. And behold, the axe hath reached 9
unto the root of the trees[4]: every tree therefore
which bringeth not forth good fruit is hewn down,
and cast into the fire. And the multitude asked 10
him, What shall we do? He[5] saith unto them, He 11
that hath two coats, let him give one[6] to him that hath
none; and he that hath meat, let him do likewise.
And the publicans also came to be baptized, and 12
said unto him,[7] What shall we do? And he said unto 13
them, Do not steal anything beyond what is appointed
unto you. And the soldiers likewise demanded of him, 14
saying, What shall we do, we also? He said unto them,
Do violence to no man, and do injury to no man[8];
let your wages suffice for you. And the people who 15
heard him were reasoning in their heart about John,
and saying, Is this then[9] perhaps the Christ? He[10] 16
answered to every man, and said unto them, Behold

---

[1] Cureton.

[2] Cureton.

[3] Cureton.

[4] Cureton.

[5] Cureton.
[6] Cureton.

[7] Cureton.

[8] Cureton.

[9] Cureton.
[10] Bezae.

16 I baptize you with water; but there cometh . . . . mightier than I, the latchets of whose shoes I am not worthy to unloose: he shall baptize you with fire and
17 with the Holy Ghost: he who holds a fan in his hand, and he will cleanse his floor, and will gather the wheat into his garner; but the chaff he will burn
18 with fire unquenchable. Also many other things,
19 exhorting, he preached to the people. But Herod the tetrarch, because John had reproved him on account of Herodia, the wife of the brother of Herod, and
20 for all the evils which he had done, Herod[1] added [1] Bezae. yet this above all, that he shut up John in prison.

21 And when all the people were baptized, Jesus also was baptized, and while he prayed, the heavens were
22 opened, and the Holy Ghost descended upon him in the likeness of the body[2] of a dove, and a voice was [2] R.V. heard from heaven,[3] Thou art my Son, and my be- [3] R.V. Bezae.
23 loved; in whom I am well pleased. And Jesus when he was about thirty years old, as he was called the
24 son of Joseph . . . son of Matthat, son . . . .
25 to Janna, ... son of Matt . . . . son . . . . son of
28 Eldum, son of Er, son of Jesu, son of Elie . . . .
29 30 son of Simeon, son of Juda, son of Joseph, son of
31 Jonam, son of Eliakim, son of Melia, son of Men,
32 son of Mattatha, son of Nathan, son of David, son of Jesse, son of Jobel,[4] son of Boash, son of Shela, son [4] Bezae.
33 of Nahson, son of A . . . . son . . . . son of Hesrun,[5] [5] R.V.
34 son of Phares, son of Juda, son of Jacob, son of Isaac,
35 son of Abraham, son of Tharah, son of Nachor, son of Serug, son of Argau, son of Peleg, son of Heber, son of
36 Shalah, son of Helam, son of Ar . . . , son of Shem,
37 son of Noah, son of Lamech, son of Methusalah, son of Henuch, son of Jared, son of Mahalalail, son of

Cainan, son of Enosh, son of Sheth, son of Adam, 38 son of God.

And Jesus being full of the Holy Ghost returned 4 from Jordan, and the Holy Spirit led him, and took him out to the wilderness, that he might be tempted 2 of Satan, and he was there forty days. And after forty days that he had fasted, he hungered. And the 3 devil said unto him, If thou be the Son of God, say to this stone that it become bread. Jesus said to him, It 4 is written, That man shall not live by bread alone.¹ And Satan led him and took him up into an high 5 mountain, shewed unto him all the kingdoms of the earth in a little time, and said unto him, All these 6 kingdoms and their glory which are committed to me I will give to thee, all this power and glory, because that to me he gave it; and to whom I will I give it. If thou wilt worship before me, all shall be 7 thine. Jesus answered and said unto him,² It is 8 written, Thou shalt worship³ the Lord thy God, and him only shalt thou serve. And he brought him to 9 Jerusalem, and set him on a pinnacle of the temple, and said unto him, If thou be the Son of God, cast thyself from hence: for it is written, He shall com- 10 mand his angels concerning thee, that they may keep thee: and in their hands they shall bear thee up, 11 lest thou shouldest strike on a stone. Jesus answered 12 and said unto him, Thou shalt not tempt the Lord thy God. And when Satan had ended his tempta- 13 tions, he departed from him for a season.⁴

And Jesus returned in the power of the Spirit 14 into Galilee: and there went out a fame about him in all that region. And he taught in their synagogues, 15 and he was glorified of all. And he came to Naza- 16

¹ R.V.

² R.V. Bezae.
³ Literally 'it is written to worship.'

⁴ Or, 'until the time.'

16 reth, where he had been brought up: and he entered into the synagogue on the sabbath-day, as he was
17 accustomed. And they gave¹ unto him the book of Isaia the prophet, and he stood up for to read. When he had opened the book, he found the place that is
18 written, The Spirit of the Lord is upon thee, because that he hath anointed thee to preach the gospel to the poor, and sent me to preach deliverance to the
19 captives, and to the blind sight,² to assure the contrite of forgiveness, and to preach the acceptable year of
20 the Lord. And he rolled up the book,³ and gave it to the minister, and sat down. And they were all gazing
21 on him. And he began to say unto them, This day
22 is this scripture fulfilled in your ears. And all bare him witness, and wondered at the gracious words which proceeded out of his mouth. And they said,
23 Is not this Joseph's son? He said unto them, Perhaps ye will say unto me this proverb, Physician, heal thyself: and the things which ye have heard that I have done in Capernaum, ye will say to me, Do also here in
24 thy city. He said unto them, Verily I say unto you,
25 There is no prophet who is accepted in his city. But I tell you of a truth, many widows were in Israel in the days of Elia the prophet, when the heaven was shut up three years and six months, when great famine was
26 throughout all the land; but unto none of them was Elia sent, save unto Sarepta⁴ of Sidon, unto a woman,
27 a widow. And many lepers were in Israel in the time
28 of Elisha .... in the synagogue .... heard these
29 things. were filled with wrath, and thrust him out of the city, and led him to the brow of the hill whereon their city was built, so that they might hang⁵ him.
30
31 And he passed even amongst them, and came down

¹ Cod.—'he gave.'
² Bezae.
³ Bezae.
⁴ Bezae.
⁵ The Syriac translator has mistaken κρημνίσαι for κρεμάσαι.

to Capernaum, a city of Galilee, and taught them on 31
the sabbath days. And they were astonished at his 32
doctrine: for his word was with power. And there 33
was in their synagogue a man which had the spirit
of a demon, ... what have we to do with thee, 34
Jesus of Nazareth? art thou come to destroy us?
.... Shut thy mouth ... of him. And the demon 35
threw him in the midst, and came out of him, not
having hurt him at all. And amazement, ... to all 36
of them ... one to ... saying, What then is this
word, which with authority and power commandeth
these unclean spirits, and they come out. And the 37
fame of him went out in all the country round about
them. And when he rose from the synagogue, he 38
entered into Simon's house. And Simon's wife's
mother was taken with a great fever; and he rebuked 39
the fever; and it left her: and immediately she arose
and ministered unto them. Now when the sun was 40
setting, all they that had any sick with sore diseases
brought them unto him; and on each of them he
[1 R.V. marg. Bezae.] laid his hand, and healed them all. And demons[1] 41
came out of many, crying out, and saying, Thou art
[2 R.V. Bezae.] the[2] Son of God. And he rebuked them, and suffered
them not to speak, because they knew him, that he
was the Christ. And at the dawn of day he went 42
out, and went to a desert place: and a multitude
.... sought him, and came unto him, ... that
he should not depart from them. And he said unto 43
them, I must also preach the kingdom of God in
other cities. And he preached in the synagogues of 44
[3 R.V. marg.] Judæa.[3]

And it came to pass, the multitude .... was that 5
they might hear .... the word of God, and he was

1 standing on the shore of the lake¹ of Gennesar and he
2 saw . . . . two ships standing on the shore of the lake:
. . . and its fishermen . . . their nets; and one of them
3 was Simon's . . . And Jesus went up and sat down
in it, and said, Take it from the dry land a little way
on the water. And he sat down, and taught the multi-
4 tude from the ship. And when he had ceased from
speaking . . . he said unto Simon, Launch out into the
5 deep, and throw your nets for fishing. Simon answered
and said unto him, Master, we have toiled all the night,
and have found nothing: but now at thy word we
6 will guide the net. And when they cast their nets,
they enclosed many fishes: and their nets were broken.
7 And they beckoned unto their partners, which were
in other ships, that they should come and help
them. And when they came, they brought up fish,
and filled both the ships, and they were nearly sinking
8 from the weight of them. When Simon Peter saw
it, he fell on his face before the feet of Jesus, saying
to him, O Lord, depart from me, for I am a sinful
9 man. For amazement had taken hold of him, and
of all who were with him, at the draught of the
10 fishes which they had taken: and so was also James,
and John, the sons of Zebedee, because they were
partners of Simon. And Jesus said unto Simon,
Fear not; from henceforth thou shalt be catching
11 men to life. And they brought these ships to land,
and forsook all, and followed him.
12   And when he was in one of the cities, a certain
man came who was full of leprosy. He saw Jesus,
and fell on his face, and besought him, and said to
him, Lord, if thou wilt, thou art able to cleanse me.
13 And he put forth his hand, and touched him, and

¹ Cod.—probably ܝܡܐ

said to him, I will: be thou clean. And immediately 13
his leprosy departed from him. And Jesus charged 14
him that he should tell no man: but go, and shew
thyself to the priest, and offer for thy cleansing,
according as Moses commanded, that it may be a
testimony to them. And so much the more went 15
there a fame abroad of him: and great multitudes
came together to hear from him, and to be healed[1] of
their infirmities. And he withdrew himself into the 16
wilderness, and prayed. And it came to pass on one 17
of the days .... Pharisees .... the law ....
every to[wn] .... of Judæa .... and the power
.... brought .... and they sought .... to lay 18
him .... his bed 19
reason ye ....: ...... to 22
unto him, Come .... to 27
, ... all 28

[1] R.V. Bezae.

[v. 29 *to* vi. 11 *is lost.*]

.... in those days, ... to a mountain 6
continued all night .... in prayer to God. And 12 / 13
when it dawned, he called .... and chose ....
..... Cepha, ... Zebedee, and Philip and 14
Bartholomew, and Matthew and Thomas, and James 15
the son of Ḥalfai, and Simon who was called ....
and Juda the son of James, and Juda Iscariot, he 16
who was the betrayer. And he came down with them 17
to the plain, and stood, he and the multitude of his
disciples, and a multitude of the crowd of people,
who came from all Judæa and from Jerusalem, and
from the sea-coast, and from Tyre and from Sidon,
which came to hear him, and to be healed of all their
diseases; and they that were vexed with unclean 18

19 spirits, that they might be healed. All sought to
touch him: for there went virtue out of him, and
20 healed them all. And he lifted up his eyes on his
disciples, and said,

Blessed are the poor: for theirs is the kingdom
of heaven.
21 Blessed are they that hunger now: for they shall
be satisfied.

Blessed are they that weep now: for they shall laugh.
22 Blessed are ye, when men shall hate you, and
separate you, and shall reproach and cast upon
you the name of evil, for the Son of man's sake.
23 . . . . ye . . . . and leap: for your reward is great
24 in heaven: for in like manner did their fathers unto
25 the prophets. . . . . Woe unto you that laugh now!
26 for ye shall weep and lament. Woe unto you when
27 men shall speak well of you! for so did . . . . But
unto you which hear, I say, Love your enemies, do
28 good to them which hate you, bless them that curse
you, and pray for them which despitefully use you.
29 And unto him that smiteth thee on the cheek, offer
to him the other; and him that taketh away thy
30 cloke or thy coat, forbid him not. Give to every
man that asketh of thee; and of him that taketh
31 away what is thine do not a . . . . to them . . . .
32
33 And if . . . . And if . . . . good . . . . which good
34 . . . . that ye shall receive, ... your thanks . . . .
35 for others lend to sinners, ... But yet love your
enemies, and do good to them, and lend, and do not
cease hope of men[1]; and your reward shall be great
in heaven, and ye shall be sons of the Most High:
36 for he is kind to the evil and to the unthankful. Be
37 ye[2] merciful, even as your Father is merciful. Judge

[1] R.V. marg. Or, 'do not cut off the hope of any.'
[2] R.V. Bezae.

not, that ye be not judged: condemn not, that ye be not condemned[1]: release, and ye shall be released: give, and it shall be given unto you; with good measure, and running over, shall they cast into your bosom. For with what measure ye mete it shall be measured to you. And he spake this parable unto them, Can the blind guide the blind? and shall not both fall into a pit? The disciple is not perfect as his master in teaching. And why beholdest thou the mote that is in thy brother's eye, and the beam that is in thine eye is not seen by thee? How canst thou say to thy brother, Brother, let me cast the mote out of thine eye; and behold, in thine own eye a beam is lying?[2] Thou hypocrite, cast out first the beam from thine eye, and then thou[3] shalt see to cast the mote out of thy brother's eye. For there is no good tree that bringeth forth corrupt fruit; neither a corrupt tree that bringeth forth good fruit. Every tree is known by his fruit. For they do not gather thorns of figs, neither of brambles do they gather grapes. A good man out of the good treasure which is in his heart bringeth forth good things; and an evil man from the evil treasure that is in his heart bringeth forth evil things: for from the abundance of the heart the mouth speaketh. And why call ye me Lord, Lord, and what I say unto you ye do not? For every man that cometh unto me and heareth my words, and doeth them, I will shew you to whom he is like: A man who built a house, and digged and went deep, and laid a foundation upon the rock: and when there were floods, and the rivers were full, they beat upon that house, and could not shake it. But he that heareth, and doeth not, is like a man that built

[1] R.V. Bezae.
[2] Bezae.
[3] 'it shall be seen by thee.'

a house upon the earth, without a foundation; and the stream beat upon it, and immediately threw it down; and the fall of that house was great.

7 And when he had ended all these sayings in the hearing of the people, he entered into Capernaum. 2 And the servant of a certain centurion was very sick, and he was dear unto his lord, and was at the point of 3 death. And he heard concerning Jesus, and sent unto him the elders of the Jews, beseeching him that 4 he would come and save his servant. And they came to Jesus, beseeching him earnestly, and saying, He is 5 worthy that thou shouldest do this to him: for he loveth our nation, and hath also built us a synagogue. 6 And Jesus went with them. And when he was near, a little way from the house, behold, the centurion sent his friends to him, and bid him, Lord, trouble not thyself: for I am not worthy that thou shouldest 7 enter under my roof: but speak with a word, and 8 my boy shall be healed. For I also am a man subject to authority, and soldiers are under[1] me, and I say to this one, Go, and he goeth; and to another, Come, and he cometh; and to my servant, Do this, and he 9 doeth it. And when Jesus heard these things, he marvelled at him, and turned him about, and said unto the crowd that followed him, I say unto you, that not even in Israel have I found faith such as 10 this. And they that were sent, returned to the 11 house, and found the servant whole.[2] And after- wards they went to a city, whose name was Nain; and his[3] disciples went with him, and a great multi- 12 tude. He came nigh to the gate of the city, ... was of his mother, and she was a widow: and there was with her a great multitude of the people of the

[1] Syriac—'under my hand.'
[2] R.V.
[3] R.V. Beza?.

city. Jesus saw her, and had compassion on her, 13
and said unto her, Weep not. . . . . came near 14
and they that bare him stood. He said, Young man,
I say unto thee, Arise. And he that was dead arose, 15
and sat up . . . . to speak . . . . to his mother. And 16
fear took hold of them all : . . . . God, saying, That
a great prophet is risen up among us ; . . . . God
. . . . his people. . . . . went forth about him 17
in all the region of Judæa, and in all the region 18
. . . . And John called two of his disciples, and sent 19
to Jesus, saying, Art thou he that should come? or
look we for another? And they came to him, and 20
said unto him, John Baptist hath sent us unto thee,
saying, Art thou he that should come? or . . . . for
another? . . . . infirmities, and of plagues, and of 21
spirits . . . . said . . . . tell . . . . and the lame 22
. . . . and the lepers . . . . the dead . . . . whoso- 23
ever shall not be offended in me. And when the 24
disciples of John were departed, he began to speak
unto the multitude concerning John, What went ye
out for to s . . e? A reed shaken with the wind?
But what went ye out for to see? A man clothed 25
in soft raiment? Behold, they which are gorgeously
apparalled, and live delicately, are amongst kings.
But what went ye out for to see? A prophet? Yea, 26
I say unto you, he was more than a prophet. This 27
is he, of whom it is written, Behold, I send my messenger . . . . the way before thee. I say unto you, 28
That there is not a prophet amongst them that are
born of women . . . . is greater than he. And all the 29
people and the publicans that heard him justified
themselves to God, who were baptized with the
baptism of John. But the scribes and Pharisees 30

rejected for themselves the will of God, who were not
31 baptized of him. ¹Whereunto then shall I liken the [1 R.V. Bezae.]
men of this generation? and to what are they like?
32 They are like unto children who sit in the marketplace, and send to their companions, We have piped
unto you, and ye have not danced; and we have
33 mourned unto you, and ye have not wept. For John
the Baptist came unto you neither eating² nor drink- [2 Bezae.]
34 ing;² and ye say, He hath a demon. And the Son of
man is come eating and drinking; and ye say, Behold
a gluttonous man, and a wine-bibber, a friend of
35 publicans and of sinners! And wisdom is justified
of all her children.

36 And there came a certain Pharisee, desiring him
that he would eat with him. And he went into the
37 Pharisee's house. While he was sitting at meat,³ a⁴ [3 Syriac— 'reclining.' 4 Cureton.]
certain woman, a sinner, was in that city, and when she [5 R.V. Cureton.]
knew that he⁵ was sitting at meat⁶ in the house of that [6 Syriac— 'reclining.']
Pharisee, she took an alabaster box of sweet ointment,⁷ [7 Cureton.]
38 and stood behind him at his feet and wept, and bathed⁸ [8 Cureton. Bezae.]
his feet with her tears, and wiped them with the
hairs of her head, and kissed his feet, and anointed
39 them with the ointment. Now when the Pharisee
which had bidden him saw it, he considered within
himself, and said, This man, if he were a prophet,
would have known who this sinful woman is who
hath come near to him, and what is her reputation.⁹ [9 Cureton.]
40 Jesus¹⁰ said unto him, Simon, I have somewhat [10 Cureton.]
to say unto thee. He said unto him, Our Lord,
41 say on. Jesus said unto him, There was a man, a
money-lender,¹¹ who had two debtors: one owed him [11 R.V. Bezae.]
42 fifty pence, and one five hundred pence. And
when they had nothing to pay, he¹² forgave them [12 R.V. Cureton. Bezae.]

8

both.¹ Which of them will love him most? Simon said to him, I suppose that he to whom much was forgiven. Jesus said unto him, Thou hast judged well.² And he turned to the woman, and said unto Simon, Seest thou this woman? I entered into thy house, and thou gavest me no water for my feet: but this one hath bathed them with her tears, and wiped them with the hairs of her head. Thou hast not kissed me: but she, since she³ came in, hath not ceased to kiss my feet. Thou didst not anoint me:⁴ but she⁵ hath anointed my feet with sweet ointment.⁶ Wherefore I say, Her many sins are forgiven her; for she loved much: for he to whom little is forgiven, loveth little. And he said unto her, Thy sins are forgiven thee. And they that sat at meat began to say within themselves, Who is this who forgiveth sins also? And he said to that woman, Thy faith hath saved thee; go in peace.

After⁷ these things, he went about amongst the villages and the cities, and his twelve were with him, preaching the kingdom of God,⁸ and these women who had been healed of evil spirits and of infirmities, Mary who was called Magdalene, out of whom had gone seven devils, and Joanna the wife of Chuza, Herod's steward, and Susan, and many others, who ministered unto them of their substance. And when great multitudes were gathered together, and those from the⁹ cities came to him, he began to speak to them by a parable: Behold,¹⁰ a sower went out to sow: and as he was sowing, some fell by the way¹¹ side; and it was trodden down, and the fowls¹² devoured it. And some fell upon a rock;¹³ and because there was no moisture it shrank and dried up. And

¹ R. V. Cureton. Bezae.
² Cureton.
³ Or, 'since I came in.'
⁴ Cureton.
⁵ R. V.
Cureton. Bezae.
⁶ Cureton.
⁷ Cureton.
⁸ Cureton.
⁹ Cureton.
¹⁰ Cureton.
¹¹ Syriac— 'by the hand of the path.'
¹² Cureton. Bezae.
¹³ Cureton.

8 some fell among thorns; and they choked it. And some fell on good ground; and it sprouted, and bare fruit an hundredfold. And when he said these things,
9 he spoke with a loud voice,[1] .... ears .... And [1] Cureton.
10 his disciples asked him, What .... It is given to know .... of the kingdom of God: but to those without, it is not given to them to know because .... in parables I speak[2] .... to them; that [2] Cureton. whilst they see, they may not see, and whilst they
11 hear, they may not understand. .... Now the parable .... The seed is the word of God. And
12 those who are by the way-side .... hear .... and cometh the enemy, ... the word from their heart, lest they should believe and be saved. ....
13 rock, are they which, when they hear the word, receive it hastily[3] with joy; .... they have no root, ... [3] Cureton. for a while they believe, ... temptation ....
14 they hear, and with the cares .... and with the
15 pleasures .... are choked, and bear no fruit.[4] That [4] Cureton. then .... on good ground .... those who with a .... and good heart hear the word and keep it,
16 and bear fruit with patience. .... lighteth .... and covereth it with a vessel, or putteth it under a bed; but setteth it upon a ..... that whoso-
17 ever entereth in may see its light. For there is nothing covered that shall not be revealed; and there is nothing hidden, that shall not be made known and
18 come abroad. Take heed[5] what ye have heard: for [5] Cureton. whoso hath, to him shall be given; and whoso hath not, even that which he thinketh[6] he hath shall be [6] R. V. Cureton. taken from him.
19   And his mother and his brethren came to him, and could not come at him because of the crowd.[7] [7] R. V. Bezae.

And they said to him,[1] Thy mother and thy brethren are standing without, desiring to see thee. And he answered and said unto them, My mother and my brethren are those which hear the word of God, and do it. And on a certain day he went up, and sat in a ship, he and his disciples with him[2]: and he said unto them, Let us go over unto the other side of the lake.[3] And as they were going he slept: and there was a storm of wind on the lake; and their ship was filled, and they were nearly sinking. And they came near[4] and awoke him, saying, Master, master, we perish. And he arose, and rebuked the wind and the tempest of the lake: and there was a calm. And he said unto them, Where is your faith? And they being afraid wondered, saying one to another, Who then is this? who commandeth even the wind and the sea,[5] and they obey him. And they went to the country of the Gadarenes, which is over against Galilee. And when he went up to the land, there met him a certain man out of the city which had a demon a long time, and ware no clothes, neither abode in any house, but in the tombs. When he saw Jesus, he cried out, and falling down, worshipped him,[6] and with a loud voice said, What have I to do with thee, Jesus, thou Son of God most high? I beseech thee, torment me not. He had commanded the unclean spirit to come out of the man. For oft-times it had fastened on him: and he was bound with chains and with fetters, to keep him: and he brake his bonds, and cut them,[7] and was led by the [demon] into the wilderness. And Jesus asked him, saying, What is thy name? He said unto him, Legion: for we are many in[8] him.

20

21

22

23

24

25

26

27

28

29

30

[1] Cureton.

[2] Cureton.

[3] Cureton.

[4] Cureton. Bezae.

[5] Cureton.

[6] Cureton.

[7] Cureton.

[8] Cureton.

31 And they besought him that he would not command
32 them to go into the deep. And there was there on
the mountain a herd of many swine feeding: and
those demons besought him that he would suffer
them to go into the swine: and he suffered them.
33 And the demons went out of the man, and entered
into the swine: and all the herd went straight[1] to [1 Cureton.]
the rock, and they fell[2] into the sea, and were choked. [2 Cureton.]
34 And when they that fed them saw what had happened,
they fled, and related it in the city and in the villages.[3] [3 Cureton.]
35 And the people went out and saw what had happened;[4] [4 Cureton.]
and they came to Jesus, and found the man, out of
whom those devils were departed, clothed, and sober,
sitting at the feet of Jesus: and they were afraid.
36 [5]And they related to them how the man[6] was saved. [5 Cureton. 6 Cureton.]
37 And the whole multitude of the Gadarenes[7] be- [7 Cureton. Bezae.]
sought him to depart from them; for fear had
seized on them: and he went up into the ship, and
38 departed from them. Then he from whom the
demons had gone out besought him that he might
39 be with him: but Jesus sent him away, saying, Return to thy house, and relate[8] the things that God [8 Cureton.]
hath done to thee. And he went, and published in
40 the whole city what[9] Jesus had done unto him. And[10] [9 Cureton. 10 R.V. Cureton.]
when our Lord was returning, a great multitude received him: for they were looking for him. And[11] [11 Cureton. Bezae.]
41 there came a certain man named Joarish, and he
was a ruler of the synagogue: and he fell down at
Jesus' feet, and besought that he would come into his
42 house: for he had one only daughter, and she was
about twelve years of age, and she lay a-dying. But
43 as he went, the people thronged him. And a certain
woman who had an issue of blood twelve years,[12] and [12 R.V. marg. Bezae.]

could not be healed of any one, came near behind 44
him, and took hold of the border of his garment: and
the fountain of her issue of blood stanched. And 45
Jesus said, Who touched me? And when all denied,
Cepha[1] said unto him, Our Master, the multitude
throng and press thee, and sayest thou, Who touched 46
me? Jesus answered and said unto him, Somebody
hath touched me: for I know that strength is gone
out of me. And when the woman saw that even this 47
did not escape him,[2] she came trembling, and falling
down, worshipped him.[3] And she said[4] in the sight
of all the people, for what cause she had touched
[him], and how she was healed immediately. And he 48
answered and said unto her, Daughter, thy faith hath
saved thee; go in peace.

While he yet spake, they[5] came from the house 49
of the ruler of the synagogue, saying to him, Thy
daughter is dead; trouble not the Teacher. But 50
when Jesus heard it, he answered and said unto him,
Fear not: only believe, and she shall live. And when 51
he came to the house of that man,[6] he suffered no
man to go in, save Cepha, and James, and John, and
the father and the mother of the maiden. And all 52
men wept, and bewailed her: but he said unto them,
Weep not; for she is not dead, she sleepeth. And 53
they laughed at him,[7] knowing that she was dead.
And[8] he took her by her hand, and called her, saying, 54
Maid, arise. And her spirit returned, and straight- 55
way she arose: and he commanded to give her to
eat.[9] And her parents were astonished: and he 56
charged them that they should tell no man what had
happened.[10]

Then he called his twelve disciples, and gave 9

1 them power and authority over all demons, and to
2 cure diseases. And he sent them to preach the
3 kingdom of God, and to heal.¹ And he said unto   ¹ R.V. marg.
them, Carry nothing for the way, neither staves, nor
scrip, neither bread, neither silver; neither have
4 two coats. And whatsoever house ye enter into,
5 there abide, and thence depart. And those who will
not receive you, when ye go out of that city, shake
off the very dust of your feet, that it may be a testi-
6 mony to you. And when his apostles had departed
they went about among the villages and the cities,
preaching,² and healing everywhere.   ² Cureton.
7   And Herod the tetrarch heard of all that had
happened:³ and he marvelled, because they⁴ said that   ³ Cureton.
⁴ Cureton.
8 John was risen from the dead; and others said⁵ that   ⁵ Cureton.
Elia had appeared; and others said that one of the
9 old prophets was risen. And Herod said, ...
10 I hear concerning him? and he desired . . . . that
11 they had done. . . . privately . . . [Beth]saida. . . .
12 came his twelve, and said to him, We are in the
desert; send these multitudes away, that they may
go into these villages⁶ round about, and to the   ⁶ Cureton.
hamlets, and lodge, or that they may find them-
13 selves victuals. He said . . . . to him . . . .
to
22 . . . . elders and priests and scribes, and be slain,
. . . . days shall rise.
23   And he said,⁷ Whosoever desires to come after   ⁷ Cureton.
me, let him deny himself, and take up his cross, and
24 follow me. For whoso will save . . . .
to
27 . . . .
28 the kingdom of God. And it came to pass after
these sayings, about eight days, that he took Cepha
and James and John, and went up into a mountain

to pray. And as he was praying, the look of his 29
countenance was changed, and his raiment was white
and dazzling.¹ And, behold, two men were talking 30
with him, Moses and Elijah: and they appeared in 31
glory, and spake about his decease which was about
to be accomplished² at Jerusalem. And Cepha and 32
they that were with him were heavy with sleep: and
when they awoke, they saw his glory, and these two
men who were standing with him. And when they 33
began to depart from him, Cepha³ said unto Jesus,
Our Master, it is good that we are here: and let us
make three tabernacles; one for thee, and one for
Moses, and one for Elijah: and he knew not what he
was saying. And while he said these things, there 34
came a cloud and overshadowed them: and when
they saw those who⁴ were⁵ entering into the cloud,
they feared. And a voice was heard from the cloud, 35
This is my Son⁶ the chosen, hear ye him. And when 36
there was the voice, Jesus was found alone. And
they held their peace, and in the sight of men they
told nothing of what they had seen in those days.⁷

And⁸ in that day when they were come down 37
from the mountain, a great multitude⁹ met them.
And¹⁰ a certain man from the multitude cried, saying, 38
Teacher, I beseech thee, look upon my son: for he is
mine only one. And a spirit cometh to him sud- 39
denly, and it throweth him down, and chastiseth
him; and he foameth, and it hardly departeth
from him, when it hath bruised him. And I be- 40
sought thy disciples that they should cast it out;
and they were not able to deliver him. Jesus 41
answered and said, O perverse¹¹ and faithless generation, how long shall I be with you, and suffer you?

¹ Or, 'like lightning.'
² Or, 'that he was about to be betrayed.'
³ Cureton.
⁴ Cureton.
⁵ Or, 'when they saw that they were entering.'
⁶ R.V.
⁷ Cureton.
⁸ Cureton.
⁹ Cureton.
¹⁰ Cureton.
¹¹ Cureton.

42 bring hither thy son. And as he was coming near, the demon threw him down, and chastised him. And Jesus rebuked that unclean spirit, and healed the
43 boy, and delivered him to his father. And they were all astonished at the greatness of God. And while all men were marvelling at all which he[1] did, he said unto [1 R.V. Cureton.]
44 his disciples, Put[2] these sayings in your ears: for the Son of man is about to be delivered into the hands of [2 Bezae. Bezae. Cureton.]
45 men. But they understood not this saying, because[3] it was hid from them, that they should not perceive [3 Cureton.]
46 it: and they were afraid about this saying. And there arose amongst them a reasoning, which should
47 be greatest amongst them. But when Jesus knew the reasoning of their heart, he took a child, and set
48 him beside them, and said,[4] Whoso shall receive this child in my name receiveth me: and whoso receiveth me receiveth him that sent me: for he that is small [4 Cureton. Bezae.]
49 and is a child to you, that one is great. John answered and said unto him,[5] Our Master, we saw one who was casting out demons in thy name; and we [5 Cureton.]
50 forbad him, because he goeth not with us. Jesus said unto him, Forbid [him] not: for he that is not against you is for you.[6] [6 R.V. Cureton.]
51 And when the days of his going up[7] were [7 Bezae. Cureton.]
52 fulfilled, he set[8] his face to go to Jerusalem, and sent messengers before his face: and they went, and entered into a village of the Samaritans, to [8 Cureton.]
53 make ready for him. And they did not receive him, because his face was set to go to Jerusalem.
54 And when his disciples James and John saw this, they said unto him,[9] Our Lord, wilt thou that we command fire to come down from heaven, [9 Cureton.]
55 and consume them?[10] And he rebuked them,[11] [10 R.V. Cureton. 11 R.V.]

[1] R.V. Cureton.	And they went to another village. And[1] as they 56
[2] Bezae.	went in the way, a man said unto him,[2] I will 57
	follow thee whithersoever thou goest. Jesus said 58
	unto him, Verily the foxes have holes, and the birds of
[3] R.V. Cureton.	the heaven[3] have nests; but the Son of man hath
	not where to lean his head. And he said unto another, 59
[4] Bezae.	Follow me. He said unto him,[4] Suffer me first to go
[5] R.V. Bezae.	and bury my father. He[5] said unto him, Let the 60
	dead bury their dead: but go thou and preach the
[6] Cureton.	kingdom of God. Another[6] said to him, Lord, I will 61
	follow thee; but first let me go and tell it to them
[7] Cureton.	of my house, and I will come.[7] Jesus saith unto 62
	him, No man putting his hand on the ploughshare,
	and looking back, is fit for the kingdom of God.
	And after these things he appointed of his dis- 10
[8] R.V. marg. Cureton.	ciples other seventy-two,[8] and sent them two and
[9] Cureton. Bezae.	two before his face to every place and city,[9] . . . . to
	come. . . . . harvest . . . . Lord of the harvest, ... 2
	labourers . . . . Go: behold, I send you like lambs 3
	. . . . wolves. . . . . not . . . . purses for yourselves, ... 4
	scrip, ... and salute not . . . . by the way. And 5
[10] Cureton.	into whatsoever house ye enter first,[10] say to it, Peace
	in the house. And if the son of peace be there, shall 6
	rest . . . . upon you . . . . and . . . . not . . . . to 7
	its neighbour. And into whatsoever city ye enter, 8
	that they receive you, eat . . . . And behold even to 11
	the dust . . . . we . . . . this, ... the kingdom
	of God . . . . I say unto you, It shall be much more 12
	tolerable for Sodom in the day of judgment, than
	for that city. Woe unto thee, Chorazin! woe unto 13
	thee, Bethsaida! for if the mighty works that have
[11] Cureton. [12] Cureton. Bezae. [13] Cureton.	been in you had been in Tyre and Sidon, perhaps[11] they had[12] repented[13] in sackcloth and ashes. Never- 14

14 theless it shall be more tolerable for Tyre and for
15 Sidon in that day than for you. And thou, Capernaum,
to
18 . . . . unto heaven, ... beheld Satan . . . . who fell
19 like lightning from heaven. Behold, I give unto you
power to tread on serpents and scorpions . . . . and
all the . . . of the enemy: and nothing shall hurt you.
20 Notwithstanding, in this rejoice not, that the demons
are subject unto you; but¹ rejoice in² your names, that [1] R.V. Cureton. [2] Bezae. Cureton.
21 they are written in heaven. And in that hour . . . . .
in spirit, ... O Father, Lord . . . . and of earth,
22 . . . . and who knoweth the Son, except the Father?
and who knoweth the Father, except the Son, and
23 he to whom the Son will reveal him? And he turned
him unto his disciples, and said unto them,³ Blessed [3] Cureton. Bezae.
24 are the eyes which see what ye see: for I tell you, that
many prophets and kings have desired to see what
ye see, and have not seen it; and to hear what ye hear,
25 and have not heard it. While he said these things,⁴ [4] Cureton.
a certain teacher of the law, who was standing⁵ . . . . [5] Cureton.
26 came near, saying unto him, ... eternal. Jesus⁶ said [6] Cureton.
unto him, In the law, how is it written? and how readest
27 thou? Then he answered and said unto him, Thou
shalt love the Lord thy God from⁷ all thy heart, and [7] Cureton.
from all thy soul, and from all thy strength, and from
all thy mind; and thy neighbour as thyself. Jesus⁸ said [8] Cureton.
28 unto him, Thou hast said rightly: do these things,
29 and thou shalt live. But he, willing to justify himself,
said unto Jesus, And who is my neighbour? He
30 said unto him, A certain man went down from Jerusalem to Jericho, and thieves fell, and stripped
him, and beat him, and left him between death
31 and life, and went their way. And a certain priest
happened to come down that way: and he saw him,

[1] Cureton.	and passed him by.[1] And likewise also a Levite, 32 when he reached that place, saw him and passed
[2] Cureton.	him by.[2] But a certain Samaritan, as he was 33
[3] Cureton.	journeying on his way, came near him,[3] saw him, and had compassion on him, and coming near, bound up 34 his wounds, and poured on them oil and wine, and set him on his ass, and brought him to an inn, and took care of him. And at the dawn of the day he 35 took out two pence, and gave them to the host, and said, Take care of him: and when I return again, whatsoever thou hast spent on him, I will repay thee. Which of these three, doth it seem to thee, was 36
[4] Cureton.	neighbour unto him that fell into the hands[4] of the thieves? He said unto him, He that shewed mercy 37 on him. Jesus said unto him, Go and do thou also likewise.
[5] R.V. Cureton.	And[5] as they were going in the way, ... and 38 a woman . . . . Martha received him into her house. And she had a sister called Mary, and she came and 39 sat at Jesus' feet, and heard his word. But Martha 40 was cumbered with service, and she came saying unto him, Lord, dost thou not care about me, that my sister hath left me alone to serve? bid her that she help me. Jesus answered and said unto her, 41
[6] Bezae.	Martha, Martha, Mary[6] hath chosen for herself the 42 good part, which shall not be taken away from her.
[7] Cureton.	And[7] while he was praying, ... after he had 11 ceased from his prayer, said . . . . of his disciples
[8] Cureton.	. . . . . . to pray, as John[8] taught his disciples.
[9] R.V.	And he said, When ye are praying, say, Father,[9] 2
[10] R.V. Cureton.	Hallowed be thy name, and thy kingdom come.[10]
[11] Cureton.	And give us the continual bread of every day.[11] 3 And forgive us our sins; and we also, we forgive every 4

4 one who is indebted to us. And lead us not into
temptation.¹ 　　　　　　　　　　　　　　　　¹ R.V.
5 　And Jesus² said unto them, Which of you who ² Cureton.
has a friend, shall go unto him at midnight, and
shall say unto him, My³ friend, lend me three loaves; ³ Cureton.
6 because a friend is come to me from the way, and I
7 have nothing to set before him? And he . . . .
within . . . . to him . . . . Trouble me not: because⁴ ⁴ Cureton.
the door is shut, and the children are with me in
8 bed; . . . I can[not] rise and give thee. I say unto
you, If he will not give to him for the sake of friend-
ship, yet because of importunity he will rise and
9 give to him as much as he needeth. And I also say
unto you, Ask, and it shall be given unto you; seek,
and ye shall find; knock, and it shall be opened unto
10 you. For every one that asketh, receiveth; . . . he that
seeketh . . . and to every one that knocketh it shall
11 be opened. Which . . . of you,⁵ if his son shall ask ⁵ R.V. marg.
of him a fish, will he perhaps instead of a fish give a
12 serpent? If he shall ask an egg, will he perhaps
13 offer him a scorpion? And if ye . . . know how to
give good gifts to your children: how much more
to shall the Father who is in heaven give good things
24 to those . . . man . . . find . . . I will return . . .
25 whence I came out. When it cometh, . . . swept
26 and garnished. Then it goeth, taking seven . . . .
27
28 the last . . . man . . . the first. . . . of God, and
29 keep it. And when multitudes were gathered together,
he began to say, This generation . . . generation . . .
30 sign. . . . not be given . . . Jona. . . . . unto the
31 Ninevites, so . . . . of the Son . . . . of the south . . . .
32 in the judgment with . . . . . at the preaching of
Jona; and, behold, a greater than Jona is here.

No man lighteth a lamp, and putteth it in a secret 33
place, but he putteth it above a candlestick, that they
who come in may see its light. For the lamp of the 34
body is the eye: therefore when thine eye is single, all
thy body also is shining;[1] but if thine eye be evil, thy
body also is dark.[2] Take heed therefore, lest the light 35
that is in thee be darkness. Therefore also thy body, 36
when there is in it no lamp that hath shone, is dark;
thus while thy lamp is shining, it gives light to thee.

And[3] a certain Pharisee besought him to dine 37
with him: and when he had sat down to meat,
he[4] marvelled why he had not washed before dinner. 38
Jesus said unto him, Ye Pharisees make clean the 39
outside of the cup and the platter; and your inward
part is full of ravening and wickedness. Ye devoid 40
of understanding,[5] did not he that made that which
is without make that which is within also? But 41
what is within you[6], give it in alms; and, behold,
all things are clean unto you. But woe unto 42
you, Pharisees! for ye tithe mint and rue and
all herbs, and pass over judgment and the love of
God: these ought to have been done, and those
also not left.

Woe unto you, Pharisees! for ye love the 43
honoured[7] seats in the synagogues, and greetings
in the markets. Woe unto you![8] for ye are graves 44
which ye see not, and men walk above them, and
ye do not know. And one of the scribes answered, 45
Teacher, thus saying thou reproachest us also. He
said unto him, Woe unto you also, ye scribes! for 46
ye lade men with heavy burdens, and ye do not
touch them with one of your fingers. Woe unto 47
you! for ye build the sepulchres of the prophets, whom

---

[1] Cureton. Bezae.
[2] Bezae.
[3] Cureton. Bezae.
[4] Bezae.
[5] Cureton.
[6] R.V. Cureton.
[7] Cureton.
[8] R.V. Cureton.

48 your fathers killed. So¹ ye are witnesses, and confess ¹ R.V. Cureton.
to the deeds of your fathers, that they² killed them, ² R.V.
49 and ye build.³ Therefore⁴ said the wisdom of God, ³ Bezae. ⁴ Cureton.
I will send them prophets and apostles, and some of
50 them they shall slay and persecute: that the blood
of all the prophets, which has been shed since the
world was created, until this generation, may be
51 required; from the blood of Habel unto the blood of
Zacharia, who was slain between the altar and the
temple⁵: verily I say unto you, It shall be required ⁵ Bezae.
52 from the hands of this generation. Woe unto you,
scribes! for ye have hidden⁶ the keys of knowledge: ⁶ Cureton. Bezae.
ye entered not in, and them that were entering in
53 ye hindered. And as he said these things against
them in the sight⁷ of all the people, he began to be ⁷ Syriac— 'in the eye.'
displeasing to the scribes and to the Pharisees; and
they were disputing⁸ with him about many things⁹: ⁸ Cureton. ⁹ Cureton.
54 and were seeking to lay hold of an accusation¹⁰ against ¹⁰ Bezae.
him.

12 And¹¹ when a great multitude were gathered to- ¹¹ Cureton. Bezae.
gether to him, insomuch that they trode one upon
another, he began to say to his disciples, Beware of
2 the leaven of the Pharisees, which is hypocrisy. For
there is nothing covered that shall not be revealed;
3 neither hid that shall not be known. For the things
that ye have spoken in darkness shall be heard in
the light; and that which ye have whispered¹² in the ¹² Cureton.
ear in closets shall be proclaimed upon the house-
4 tops. And I say unto you my friends, Be not afraid
of them that kill the body, and after that find no
5 more that they can do. But I will shew¹³ you whom ¹³ Cureton. Bezae.
ye shall fear: Fear him, which after he hath killed
hath power to cast into hell; yea, I say unto you, He

is to be feared. For five sparrows are sold for two 6
farthings, and not one of them is forgotten before
God. For even the very hairs of the hair of your 7
head are numbered. Fear not therefore: because[1] ye
are better than many sparrows.[2] For I say unto you, 8
Whosoever shall confess me before men, him shall
the Son of man also confess before the angels of
God. [3]And whosoever shall speak a word against 10
the Son of man, it shall be forgiven him: but unto
him that blasphemeth against the Holy Ghost it
shall not be forgiven. And when they bring you 11
into the synagogues, before magistrates, and powers,
take ye no thought how ye shall answer[4] for yourselves, or what ye shall say: for the . . . . Ghost 12
. . . . what ye shall say.
    . . . . a certain man . . . . company . . . . Teacher, 13
. . . . to my brother, ... divide . . . . Man, ... 14
not . . . . in the abundance of the goods 15

And he spake this[5] parable unto them,[6] The 16
ground of a certain rich man brought to him much 17
produce:[7] and he thought within himself, saying,
What shall I do, because I have no room where to 18
bestow my produce? But it is fitting for me that I
should pull down my barns, and build, and enlarge 19
them, and I will gather in them my produce. And
I will say to my soul, Behold, much goods are
laid up for thee for[8] years; . . . . eat, drink, and be 20
merry. But God said unto him, O devoid of understanding,[9] this night do they require thy soul of thee:
then whose shall these things be, which thou hast pro- 21
vided? So . . . . treasures, and is not rich with God.

And he said unto his disciples, Therefore I say unto 22
you, Take no thought for the[10] life,[11] what ye shall eat;

---

[1] Cureton.
[2] Or, 'because ye are much better than.'
[3] Omit v. 9.
[4] Or— 'apologise.' Cureton. Bezae.
[5] Cureton.
[6] Cureton.
[7] Cureton.
[8] Cureton.
[9] Cureton. Bezae.
[10] Bezae.
[11] Literally, 'soul.'

23 neither for the body, what ye shall put on. For¹ the life [¹ R.V. Cureton. Bezae.]
is more than meat, and the body than raiment. Con-
24 sider the ravens: for they neither sow nor reap; which
neither have storehouses nor barns; and God feedeth
them: how much therefore are ye more than the fowls?
25
26 Which of you . . . add to his stature one cubit? . . .
27 least, . . . ye . . . rest? Consider the lilies: how they spin
not, and weave not²; and³ I say unto you, that even Solo- [² Cureton. Bezae. ³ Cureton. Bezae.]
28 mon in all his glory was not arrayed like them. If then
the grass which is to-day in the fields, and to-morrow is
cast into the oven, God clothes, how much more you, O
29 ye of little faith? Therefore do not . . . what ye shall
30 eat . . . drink . . . require . . . therefore seek . . .
31
32 of God; . . . . shall be added unto you. Fear not,
little flock; for your Father is well pleased to give you
33 the kingdom. Sell all that ye have, and give alms;
and make to yourselves purses which wax not old,
and a treasure that faileth not in the heavens, where
34 no thieves steal, and no moth corrupts. And where
35 your treasure is, there will your heart be also. Let
your loins be girded about, and your lamps burning.
36 And be like unto men that wait for their lord, when
he goeth away from the wedding; that when he
cometh and knocketh, they may open unto him
37 immediately. Blessed are those servants, whom the
lord when he cometh shall find watching: verily I
say unto you, that he shall gird his loins,⁴ and make [⁴ Cureton.]
them sit down to meat, and will pass by⁵ and serve [⁵ Bezae.]
38 them. And if he shall come in the second watch,
or the third, and shall find them so, blessed are
39 they.⁶ But this know, that if the lord of the [⁶ R.V. Cureton. Bezae.]
house knew at what hour the thief would come,⁷ he [⁷ Cureton.]
40 would not suffer his house to be broken into. Be ye

therefore ready also: for the Son of man cometh at 40
an hour when ye think not. Cepha said unto him, 41
Lord, speakest thou this parable unto us, or even to
all? Jesus said unto him, Who is that faithful 42
steward, whom his lord shall set over his companions,¹ to give them meat in its season? Blessed is 43
he, whom his lord when he cometh shall find so
doing. Of a truth I say unto you, that he will make 44
him ruler over all that he hath. But² if that servant 45
say in his heart, My lord delayeth to come; and
shall begin to beat the menservants and maidens,
and to eat and drink, and to be drunken; the lord 46
of that servant will come in a day when he thinketh
not, and at an hour when he is not aware, and will
cut him to pieces, and will place him with the un-
believers. The servant who knew the will of his lord, 47
and did not prepare himself according to his will,³
shall be beaten⁴ with many stripes. But he that 48
knew not, and did commit what is worthy of stripes,
shall be beaten⁴ with few stripes. For unto whomsoever much is given, at his hand shall much be
required: and to whom they⁵ have committed much,
of him will they require the more. For I am come to 49
cast fire on the earth; and what will I, if it be
already kindled? I have a baptism to be baptized 50
with; and how am I straitened till it be finished!⁶
Suppose ye that I am come to give peace on earth? 51
I tell you, Nay; but⁷ division. For from henceforth 52
there shall be five in one house; they shall be divided,
three against two, and two against three. ... his⁸ son 53
... against his⁹ father; ... her¹⁰ mother; ... her¹¹
daughter-in-law ... mother-in-law ... ye see ... out of 54
the west, ... ye say, ... it is rain;¹² ... so it is. And 55

¹ Cureton.

² R.V.
Cureton.
Bezae.

³ Cureton.
⁴ Syriac—
'shall swal-
low' conf.
Modern
[Egyptian—
'eat sticks.'

⁵ R.V.
Cureton.
Bezae.

⁶ Cureton.
Bezae.

⁷ Cureton.
Bezae.
⁸ Cureton.
⁹ Cureton.
Bezae.
¹⁰ R.V.
Cureton.
¹¹ R.V.
Cureton.
Bezae.
¹² Cureton.

55 when ... the south ... ye ... and it cometh to pass.
56 .... crites, ... of the heaven and of the earth
ye know how to try:¹ this time and its signs ye do
57 not search to prove. Why of yourselves do ye not
58 judge the truth?² When thou goest with thine adversary to the magistrate, as thou art in the way, give him trouble,³ and be delivered from him; lest he hale thee to the judge, and the judge deliver thee to the officer, and the officer cast thee into prison.
59 I tell thee, thou shalt not depart thence, till thou hast paid the last farthing.

¹ R.V. marg. Cureton. Bezae.
² Cureton.
³ Or, 'give him his works.' Bezae.

13 And at that time came some who told him of the Galileans, those whose blood Pilate had mingled with
2 their sacrifices. Jesus answered and said unto them, Suppose ye that these Galileans were sinners more than
3 all the Galileans, that thus it happened unto them? I tell you, Nay: but ye also, except ye repent, ... all
4 likewise perish. Or those eighteen, upon whom the tower in Shiloaḥ fell, and slew them, think ye that they were sinners more than all the men that dwell in Jeru-
5 salem? I tell you, Nay: but ye also ... likewise perish.
6
7 ... parable; A certain man had ... planted ... and
8 he came ... And he said unto him, Lord, let it alone
9 this year also, until ... dung it: ... And if ... fruit, ... and if not, next year thou shalt cut it down.
10 And while he was teaching on the sabbath in one
11 of the synagogues, there⁴ was a certain woman who had a spirit ..... eighteen years, and was bowed down, and could not stretch herself out completely.⁵
12
to ... said ... of you ... from the stall, and go to
15
16 give him water? and a daughter of Abraham, ... she ... be loosed from this bond ... on the ... day
17 ... rejoiced ... were ... by his hands.⁶

⁴ Cureton.
⁵ Cureton.
⁶ Cureton.

He said, Unto what is the kingdom of God like? 18
and whereunto shall I resemble it? It is like a grain 19
of mustard seed, which a man took, and cast into his
garden; .... tree; and the fowls of the heaven
lodged .... Again 20
in the villages and in the cities, and he was teaching.[1] to 22

[1] Cureton.

And[2] whilst he was going to Jerusalem, a certain 23
man came, asking him, and said to him, Lord, are
there few that be saved? Jesus[3] said unto him,
Strive to enter in at the strait gate: for I say unto 24
you, that many will seek to enter in by it, and shall
not be able; for when once the master of the house 25
will rise, and will shut to the door, and ye are
standing[4] without, and knocking at the door, and
saying, Our Lord, open to us; and he shall answer
and say unto you, I know you not whence ye are:
then shall ye begin to say, We have eaten and 26
drunk before[5] thee, and thou hast taught in our
streets. And he shall say, Verily I say unto you, I 27
know you not, whence ye are; depart from me, for
ye are all workers of falsehood. There shall be 28
weeping and gnashing of teeth, when ye shall see
Abraham, and Isaac, and Jacob, and all the prophets,
in the kingdom of God. And they shall come from 29
the east, and from the west, and from the north, and
from the south, and shall sit down in the kingdom of
God. And behold, there are last which shall be first, 30
and first last.

[2] Cureton.
[3] Cureton.
[4] Cureton.
[5] Cureton. Bezae.

And in these[6] days there came men of the Phari- 31
sees, saying unto him, Get thee out, depart hence:
for Herod seeketh to kill thee. He said unto them, 32
Go [tell] that fox, Behold, I cast out demons, and I
accomplish my cures to-day and to-morrow, and on the

[6] Cureton.

33 third I shall be perfected.¹ Nevertheless I must go
34 to-day and to-morrow, and the day following: for it cannot be that a prophet perish out of Jerusalem.

Jerusalem, Jerusalem, who hast killed the prophets, and hast stoned them who were sent unto thee; how often would I have gathered thy children together, as a hen that gathereth² her brood under
35 her wings, and ye would not! Behold, your house is forsaken! And³ I say unto you, Ye shall not see me, till it come⁴ that ye shall say, Blessed is he that cometh in the name of the Lord.

14 And⁵ when he went into the house of one of the chief Pharisees to eat bread on the sabbath day,
2 they watched what he would do.⁶ And⁷ a man
3 who had the dropsy was before him. Jesus answered and said unto the scribes and Pharisees,⁸ Is
4 it lawful to heal on the sabbath day? And they held their peace. And he took him, and healed him,
5 and let him go; and he said⁹ unto them, Which of you, whose ox or whose ass shall fall into a pit on the sabbath day, and will not pull him, drawing him up?
6 And they could not give¹⁰ him an answer about these
7 things. And he spake this¹¹ parable unto those which were bidden, and were¹² choosing the chief places;
8 saying unto them, When thou art bidden to a wedding, sit not down in the honourable place,¹³ lest a more honourable man than thou be bidden there;
9 and he that bade thee and him come and say to thee, Give this man place; when thou shalt sit down
10 ashamed¹⁴ in the lowest place. But when thou art bidden, go and sit down in the lowest place; that when he that bade thee cometh, he may say unto thee, Friend, go up higher; and thou shalt have

¹ Or, 'betrayed.'
² Cureton.
³ R.V. Cureton. Bezae.
⁴ Bezae.
⁵ Cureton.
⁶ Cureton.
⁷ Cureton.
⁸ Cureton. Bezae.
⁹ R.V. Cureton. Bezae.
¹⁰ Cureton.
¹¹ Cureton.
¹² Cureton.
¹³ Cureton.
¹⁴ Cureton.

glory¹ in the sight² of them that sit at meat. For 11 whosoever exalteth himself shall be humbled; and whosoever humbleth himself shall be exalted. And 12 he said also to the lord of the supper,³ When thou makest a supper, call not thy friends, nor thy brethren, neither thy kinsmen, nor thy rich neighbours; lest they also bid thee, and there be this recompence unto thee. But when thou makest a 13 supper, call the poor, and the blind, and the lame, and the maimed, and the despised, and many others: and thou shalt be blessed; for they have nothing to 14 recompence thee: and thy recompence⁴ shall be at the resurrection of the just.

And when one of them that sat⁵ at meat⁶ heard 15 these things, he said unto them, Blessed is he that shall eat meat in the kingdom of God. Jesus said unto him, 16 A certain man made a great supper, and bade many: and sent his servant at supper time to say to those 17 that were bidden, that they should come; behold,⁷ everything is ready. And they all began immediately⁸ 18 to make excuse.⁹ The first said unto him, I have bought a piece of ground, and I must needs go out¹⁰ and see it: I pray thee have me excused. And another 19 said, I have bought five yoke of oxen, and I go to prove them: I pray thee have me excused. And another 20 said, I have married a wife, and therefore I cannot come. And that servant came, and¹¹ told these things 21 to his lord. Then the master of the house became angry, and said to his servant, Go out quickly into the streets and lanes of the city, and bring in hither the poor, and the lame, and the afflicted,¹² and the blind. And the servant said, Lord, behold what thou hast 22 commanded is done, and yet there is room at the

---

¹ R. V. Cureton. Bezae.
² Syriac— 'in the eye.'
³ Cureton.
⁴ Cureton.
⁵ Or, 'reclined.'
⁶ Cureton.
⁷ Cureton.
⁸ Cureton.
⁹ Or, 'beg off.'
¹⁰ R. V. Cureton. Bezae.
¹¹ R. V. Cureton.
¹² Cureton.

23 feast.¹ He said to his servant, Go out to the high-   [1] Cureton.
ways and hedges, and make² them come in, that my   [2] Cureton.
24 house may be filled. For I say unto you, That none
of those men which were bidden shall taste of the
supper.

25   And when there went with him great multitudes:
26 he turned, and said unto them, He who cometh unto
me, and hateth not his father, and his mother, and
his brothers, and his sisters, and his wife, and his
children, and his own life also, cannot be my disciple.
28 ³For which of you, desiring to build a tower, doth   [3] Omit v. 27.
not first sit down, and count the cost, whether he
29 have sufficient to finish it? Lest⁴ if he hath laid   [4] Cureton.
a foundation, and is not able to finish, all that
30 behold should⁵ mock him, saying, This man began to   [5] Cureton.
31 build, and was not able to finish. Or what king,
who goeth to fight with another king, doth not first
consider whether he is able with ten thousand to
meet him that cometh against him with twenty
32 thousand? Or else, while he is far off, he sendeth
ambassadors and asketh him concerning⁶ peace.   [6] Cureton. Bezae.
33 Thus every one of you that forsaketh not all his
34 substance, cannot be my disciple. Salt is good: but
if the salt be savourless, wherewith shall it be
35 salted? Neither for the land nor for the dunghill is
it fit; but it is cast out. He who hath ears to hear,
let him hear.

15   And the publicans and the sinners were drawing
2 near unto him to hear him. And the scribes and
the Pharisees were murmuring, and saying, This man
3 receiveth sinners, and eateth with them. He spake
4 unto them this parable.⁷ Which of you having an   [7] Cureton.
hundred sheep, and having lost one of them, doth not

leave the ninety and nine in the wilderness, and goeth 4
seeking¹ that which is lost, until he find it? And 5
when he hath found it, he lifteth it on his shoulders,
and rejoiceth. And he cometh to his² house, and 6
calleth his friends and his neighbours, saying, Rejoice
with me, for I have found my sheep which was lost.
I say unto you, that likewise there shall be joy in 7
heaven over one sinner that repenteth, [more] than
over ninety and nine just persons which do not need
repentance. Or what woman, who has ten drachmas, 8
and loses one of them, doth not light a lamp, and
sweep the house, and seek diligently till she find it?
And when she hath found it, she calleth her friends 9
and her neighbours, saying to them, Rejoice with me;
for I have found my drachma which was³ lost. I say 10
that likewise there shall be joy before all⁴ the angels
of God over one sinner that repenteth.

He said unto them,⁵ A certain man had two sons: 11
the younger said to his father, Give me the portion 12
that cometh to me of thy substance. And he divided
unto the . . . And after a few⁶ days the younger son 13
gathered all that came to him and went into a far country, and there squandered his substance, because he
was living wastefully with harlots.⁷ And when he had 14
spent all that was his, and there was a famine in that
land,⁸ he went and joined himself to one of the 15
people of that country; and he sent him into his
field to feed swine. He was longing for those husks 16
that the swine did eat, to fill his belly: and no man
gave unto him. When he came to himself, he said, 17
How many hired servants there are now⁹ in my
father's house, who have plenty of bread, and I
perish here with hunger! But I will arise and go to 18

¹ Cureton.
² Cureton.
³ Cureton.
⁴ Cureton.
⁵ Cureton.
⁶ Cureton.
⁷ Cureton.
⁸ Cureton.
⁹ Cureton.

18 my father, and will say unto him, Father, I have
19 sinned against heaven, and before thee, and am no
more worthy to be called thy son: make me as one
20 of thy hired servants. And he arose, and came to
his father. But when he was yet a great way off,
his father saw him, and had compassion on him, and
21 ran, and fell on his neck, and kissed him. And his
son said unto him, Father, I have sinned against
heaven, and before[1] thee: henceforth I am not worthy
22 to be called thy son. His father said unto his servants, Bring forth quickly[2] the best robe, and put it
on him; and put a ring on his hand, and shoe him
23 with shoes: and bring and kill the calf, the one that
24 is fattened; let us eat and be merry: for this my
son was dead, and is alive; he was lost, and is
25 found. And they began to be merry. And his elder
son was in the field: and as he came and drew nigh
to the house, he heard the sound of piping and music.[3]
26 And he called one of the servants, and asked him
27 What is this? He said unto him, Thy brother
is come; and thy father hath killed the fatted calf,
28 because he hath received him in health.[4] And
he was angry and would not go in: and[5] his
29 father came out, and entreated him. He answered
and said to his father, Lo, how many years do
I thee service, and I have not transgressed
thy commandments: and never hast thou given
me one kid, that I might make merry with my
30 friends: and this thy son, when he hath wasted
thy goods with harlots, thou hast killed for him
31 that fatted calf. He said unto him, Son, thou art
32 ever with me, and all that I have is thine. But it
was meet that we should make merry, and be

[1] Cureton. Bezae.
[2] R. V. Bezae.
[3] Or, 'symphony.'
[4] Or, 'whole.' Bezae.
[5] R. V. Bezae.

glad: for this thy brother was dead, and is alive; 32
and was lost, and is found.

And he said again to his disciples, There was a **16**
certain rich man, which had a steward; and he was
accused before him, as if he had spoiled his goods.
And his lord called him, and said unto him, What 2
is this that I hear against thee? Come, give an
account of thy authority; for thou canst not be
again my steward.[1] The steward said within him- 3
self, What shall I do? for my lord taketh away from
me the stewardship: I cannot dig; to beg I am
ashamed. I know[2] what I shall do, that when I have 4
gone out of the stewardship, they may receive me
into their houses. And he called one of the debtors, 5
. . . . . to the first, how much . . . . . to my lord?
He said, ... an hundred measures o . . . . . Sit 6
down quickly, write . . . . . fifty. . . . . . said he to 7
another, And thou, how much owest thou to him?
He said unto him, An hundred measures of wheat.
And he sat down immediately, and wrote them four-
score. And the lord commended the unjust[3] steward, 8
because he had done wisely: for the children of this
world are wiser in their generation . . . . . than the
children of light. And I also say unto you, Make to 9
yourselves friends of the mammon of unrighteousness;
that when it[4] fails, they may receive you into their everlasting habitations. For he that is faithful in little 10
is faithful also in much: and he that is unjust in
little is unjust . . . . If . . . . in the mammon of 11
unrighteousness, not . . . . faithful . . . who will
commit to you the true?[5] And if in what is not your 12
own . . . . faithful, who will give you your own? For 13
there is no servant who can serve two masters: . . .

[1] Or, 'lord of my house.'

[2] 'it is known to me.' Bezae.

[3] 'the steward of injustice.'

[4] R. V. Bezae.

[5] Bezae.

13 he will hate the one, and love the other; or he will bear with the one, and despise the other. Ye cannot serve God and mammon.

14 And it came to pass, when the Pharisees heard all these things, they derided him, because they loved[1] [1 Bezae.]
15 silver. He said unto them, Ye are they which justify yourselves in the sight[2] of men; but God knoweth [2 R. V.] your hearts: for that which is great amongst men is abominable before God.

16 The law and the prophets were until John: since then the kingdom of God is preached and every man
17 presseth into it. But it is easier for heaven and earth to pass, than one letter of the law to pass.
18 Whosoever putteth away his wife, and marrieth another, committeth adultery: and whosoever marrieth her that is put away committeth adultery.

19 A certain man, who was rich, was clothed in purple and a fine robe, and fared sumptuously
20 every day: and there was a certain poor man[3] named [3 Bezae.] Lazar, who was laid at his gate, and desiring to fill his belly with what fell from the table of that rich
21 man: and the dogs also came and licked his sores.
22 And it came to pass, that the poor man died, and the angels carried him into Abraham's bosom: and the
23 rich man died, and was buried; and being cast into Sheol, he lifted up his eyes, being in torments, and seeth Abraham afar off, and Lazar in his bosom.
24 And he cried and said, Father Abraham, have mercy on me, and send Lazar, that he may dip the tip of his finger in water, and cool my tongue; for lo, I
25 am tormented in this flame. Abraham said unto him, Remember, nevertheless, that thou in thy lifetime receivedst thy good things, and likewise also Lazar

¹ παρακαλεῖ seems to represent both the Hebrew נָחַם and נִחַם see R.V. marg. Gen. v. 29.

evil things: but now he is at rest¹ here, and thou 25 art tormented. And besides all this, there is a great 26 gulf fixed between us and you: so that they that would cross from hence to you cannot; neither from thence can they cross to us. He said, Therefore I 27 pray thee, father, that thou wouldst send him to my father's house: for I have five brethren; that he may 28 testify unto them, lest they also come into this place of torment. Abraham saith, They have Moses and 29 the prophets; let them hear them. He said unto 30 him, Nay, father Abraham: but if one go unto them from the dead, they will repent. He said unto him, 31 If they hear not Moses and the prophets, neither, though one went from the dead, will they believe him.

And he said unto his disciples, It is impossible 17 that offences should not come: nevertheless, woe unto him by whose hand they come! It were better 2 for him if the millstone of an ass were hanged about his neck, and he were cast into the sea, than that he should offend one of these little ones. Take heed to 3

² R.V.

yourselves: If thy brother sin,² rebuke him; if he repent, forgive him. And if he sin seven times in a 4 day, and these seven times turn to thee, saying, I repent; forgive him.

And his apostles say unto Jesus, Increase 5 our faith. He answered and said unto them, If 6 ye had faith like a grain of mustard seed ye might say unto this sycamine tree, Be thou plucked up by the root from hence, and be thou planted in the sea; and it should obey you. But which 7 of you, having a servant plowing or feeding sheep, and when he is come in from the field, will say unto him straightway, Go and sit down to meat?

8 but will say unto him, Make ready for me wherewith
I may sup, and gird thy loins, and serve me, until I
shall eat and drink; and afterward thou also shalt
9 eat and drink? Doth . . . . . that servant himself
perhaps receive thanks because he did the things
10 that were commanded him?¹ So likewise ye, when ¹ R. V.
ye shall have done all those things which are commanded you, say ye, We are servants: what was our
duty to do, we have done.
11 And as he went to Jerusalem, and passed between
12 Samaria and Galilee, and as he entered into a certain
village, behold, ten men that were lepers were standing
13 afar off: and they lifted up their voices, and said unto
14 him, Jesus, our Master, have mercy on us. And when
he saw them, he said unto them, Go shew yourselves
15 unto the priests. When . . . . . one of them . . . .
that he was cleansed,² turned back to him, and with a ² Bezae.
16 loud voice glorified God, and fell down on his face
before his feet, ... and gave thanks: . . . . and
17 he, this one . . . . was . . . . Jesus . . . . ten . . . .
18 where . . . . . there is not found one of them . . . .
19 returned to give . . . . who . . . . He said . . . .
20 thy faith . . . . . And the Pharisees asked him and
said, ... of God . . . . should come . . . . unto them.
The kingdom of God cometh not with observation:
21 . . . . . neither here it is! . . . . . there it is! for
22 behold, the kingdom of God is amongst you. And
he said to his disciples, The days will come, when ye
shall desire to see one of the days of the Son of man,
23 and ye shall not see it. And if they shall say to you,
24 Lo, there!³ or lo, here! run not, and go not. For as ³ R. V.
the lightning lighteneth from end to end of heaven,
25 so shall be the day of the Son of man. But first

must he suffer many things, and be rejected of 25
this generation. And as it was in the days of Noah, 26
so shall it be also in the days of the Son of man.
For they were eating and drinking, and marrying 27
wives, and giving in marriage,[1] until the day that
Noah entered into the ark, and the flood came, and
carried[2] them all away. And as it was in the days 28
of Lot; they were eating, and drinking, and buying
and selling; and in the day that Lot went out of 29
Sodom he made it rain fire and brimstone from heaven,
and destroyed them all. So shall it be in the day 30
when the Son of man is revealed. But in that hour,[3] 31
he who is on the house-top,[4] let him not come down
to carry away his stuff from the house: and he that
is in the field, let him not return back. And re- 32
member Lot's wife. He who seeketh to save his life 33
shall lose it; and he who loseth his life shall save it.
I tell you, in that night there shall be two in one 34
bed; the one shall be taken, and one[5] shall be left.
Two women shall be grinding at one mill; the one 35
shall be taken, and one[5] shall be left. And two 36
shall be in the field; one shall be taken, and one[5]
shall be left. They say unto him, Where, our Lord? 37
He said unto them, Wheresoever the body is, thither
will the eagles be gathered together.

Again also he spake this[6] parable, that they **18**
should be praying at all times, and that it should
not weary them.[7] There was in a city a judge, 2
which feared not God, neither regarded man: and 3
there was a widow in that city; and she came unto
him, saying unto him, Avenge me of mine adversary;
and he would not.[8] Afterward he said within him- 4
self, If[9] I fear not God, nor regard man; and this 5

---

[1] Syriac—'giving to men.'
[2] Cureton.
[3] Cureton.
[4] Cureton.
[5] Cureton.
[6] Cureton.
[7] Cureton.
[8] Cureton.
[9] Cureton. Bezae.

5 widow who thus troubles me, I will avenge her, lest at
6 the last she should come and take hold of me. Jesus
7 said, Hear what the unjust[1] judge saith. God therefore, shall he not rather take vengeance[2] for his own elect ones, who cry unto him day and night, and he
8 bears long with them? I tell you, he will take vengeance[3] for them speedily. Nevertheless shall the Son of man come,[4] and find faith on the earth?
9 And he spake this parable against men who trusted in themselves that they were righteous, and despised
10 the many:[5] Two men went up into the temple to pray; the one a Pharisee, and the other a publican.
11 The Pharisee stood by himself[6] praying, I thank thee God, that I am not like the rest[7] of men, extortioners, nor oppressors, nor adulterers, nor like
12 this publican. But[8] I fast twice in the week, I give
13 tithes of all that I possess. But the publican stood[9] afar off, and would not lift up so much as his eyes unto heaven, but smote upon his breast, saying,
14 God be merciful to me a sinner. I tell you, this man went down to his house justified more than that[10] [man]: for every one that exalteth himself shall be humbled; and he that humbleth himself shall be
15 exalted. And they brought unto him also infants, that he would lay his hand on them: and his dis-
16 ciples rebuked them. Jesus said unto them, Suffer the children to come unto me, and forbid them not: for those who are like[11] them, theirs is the kingdom
17 of heaven. Verily I say unto you, That whoso shall not receive the kingdom of heaven as a child shall not enter therein.
18 And one of the rulers asked him, saying unto him, Good Teacher,[12] what shall I do that I may

[1] Or, 'Judge of iniquity.'
[2] Cureton. Bezae.
[3] Cureton. Bezae.
[4] Cureton. Bezae.
[5] Cureton.
[6] Or, 'stood praying by himself.' R.V. Cureton. Bezae.
[7] Cureton.
[8] Cureton.
[9] Cureton.
[10] Cureton.
[11] Cureton.
[12] R.V. marg. Cureton. Bezae.

inherit eternal life? Jesus said unto him, Why 19
callest thou me good? there is none good, save one,
God. But thou knowest the commandments, Thou 20
shalt not kill, and thou shalt not commit adultery,
thou shalt not steal, and thou shalt not bear false
witness, Honour thy father and thy mother. He 21
said, All these things, lo, I have kept them from
my youth up. When Jesus heard it, he said unto 22
him, One thing yet thou lackest: sell all that thou
hast, and give to the poor, and thou shalt have treasure in heaven: and come, follow me. But when he 23
heard these things, he became exceeding sorrowful:
for he was very rich. When Jesus saw that he was 24
sorrowful, he said, How hardly shall they that have
riches enter into the kingdom of God! For it is 25
easier for a camel to pass through the eye of a
needle, than for a rich man into the kingdom of
God. And they that heard it said, Who[1] can be 26
saved? He said to them, The things that with 27
men are impossible with God are possible. Cepha 28
said unto him, Lo, we have left all that we have, and
have followed thee. Jesus saith unto him, Verily I 29
say unto thee, There is none that have left house, or
parents, or brethren, or wife, or children, for the
kingdom of God's sake, who shall not receive a 30
hundredfold[2] more in this time, and in the world to
come shall inherit[3] life eternal.

And he took his[4] twelve, and said unto them, 31
Behold, we go up to Jerusalem, and all the things
that are written by the prophets concerning the Son
of man shall be accomplished. For he shall be de- 32
livered up to the peoples, ... and they shall mock
him, and shall spit in his face, and shall scourge 33

[1] Cureton.
[2] Cureton.
[3] Cureton.
[4] Cureton.

33 him, and shall kill him, and on the third day he
34 shall rise. And they understood not one of these things: but the saying was hid from them, and they perceived not the things that were said to
35 them. And¹ as he drew nigh to Jericho, a certain ¹ Cureton.
36 blind man sat by the wayside and begged: and when he heard the voice² of the multitude passing ² Cureton.
37 by, he asked who it was.³ They say to him, ³ Cureton.
38 Jesus of Nazareth passeth by. And he cried, saying,
39 Jesus, Son of David, have mercy on me. And they that went before Jesus⁴ rebuked him, that he ⁴ Cureton.
should hold his peace: and he cried so much the more, saying, Son of David, have mercy on me.
40 And .... stood .... and commanded them to bring⁵ him: and when he was come to him, he asked ⁵ Cureton.
him, saying to him, What wilt thou that I shall do
41 unto thee? He said unto him, Lord, that I may see.
42 Jesus said unto him, See⁶: thy faith hath saved thee. ⁶ Cureton.
43 And immediately he saw,⁷ and followed him, glori- ⁷ Cureton.
fying God: and all the people saw it, and gave praise unto God.

19 And when he had entered and passed through
2 Jericho,⁸ a certain man named Zachai, ... was a pub- ⁸ Cureton.
3 lican, and he was rich, and he sought to see Jesus who he was; and could not because of the crowd, for he was
4 little of stature. And he ran before him, and climbed
5 into a sycamore tree .... because .... was ....
said to him, Make haste, come down, Zachai, for
6 to-day I must be in thy house. And Zachai made
7 haste, came down, and received him joyfully. And when they saw it, ... they murmured, saying, That he had gone in to dwell with a man that is a
8 sinner. And Zachai stood, and said to Jesus, Behold,

10

Lord, the half of my goods I give to the poor; and 8
every one that I have defrauded,¹ I restore four-
fold. Jesus said, This day . . . . . forasmuch as 9
also . . . he is a son of Abraham. . . . . he added 10 11
and spake a parable, because he was nigh to Jerusalem, and they thought that the kingdom of God
was about to be revealed in that hour. He said to 12
them, A certain man, the son of a great family,²
went into a far country to receive a kingdom, and to
return. And he called his ten servants, and gave 13
them ten pounds, and said to them, Trade³ ye . . . .
come. . . . . hated . . . . ambassador . . . . to him 14
not . . . to reign . . . to him . . . to whom he had 15
given . . . . . Then came the first, saying, Lord, thy 16
pound hath gained ten pounds. He said unto him, 17
Well, good servant: thou hast been found faithful in
little, have thou authority over ten cities. And the 18
second came, saying unto him, Lord, thy pound hath
made⁴ five pounds. And he said also to him, 19
Have thou authority also over five cities. And the 20
last one came, saying, Lord, behold, thy pound which
has been⁵ with me, laid up in a napkin: for I feared 21
thee . . . . because thou art a hard man: . . . . .
who takest up what thou layedst not down, and
reapest . . . . didst not sow. And . . . . said unto 22
him, ... faithless . . . . Thou knewest me that I
am a hard man, and I take up what I laid not down,
and I reap what I did not sow. Wherefore didst 23
thou not put my silver into the bank,⁶ and then
I would have come and sought mine own with its
usury? And he said unto them that stood by him, 24
Take from him the pound, and give it to him that
hath ten pounds. ⁷For I say unto you, That unto 26

---

¹ Cureton.
² Cureton.
³ R.V. Cureton. Bezae.
⁴ R.V. Cureton. Bezae.
⁵ Cureton.
⁶ Syriac—'on the table.' Cureton. Bezae.
⁷ Omit v. 25.

26 every one which hath shall be added;[1] and from him   [1] Bezae.
that hath not, even that he hath shall be taken
27 away from him. But nevertheless bring hither mine
enemies, those who would not that I should be king
28 over them, and slay them before me. And when he
had said these things, they went out from there.
29 And as he was going up to Jerusalem, and had
reached Bethphage and Bethany, and . . . . Olives,
30 he sent two of his disciples, ... to them, Go ye
into the village over against us; and when ye enter,
behold, ye shall find a colt tied, on which man never
31 rode: loose him, and bring him hither. And if any
man ask you, Why loose ye him? say thus unto
32 his[2] master, ... And they that were sent went   [2] Cureton.
33 and found even as he had said unto them. And
34 as they were loosing the colt, they said unto them,
35 For its Lord it is required. And they brought the
colt[3] to Jesus: and they cast their garments upon it,   [3] Cureton.
36 and they set Jesus thereon. And as he journeyed
and came, they spread their clothes in the way.
37 When they came near to the descent of the Mount of
Olives, all the crowd of the disciples began to rejoice
and to praise God with a loud voice for all[4] that they   [4] Cureton. Bezae.
38 had seen; and they were saying, Blessed be the
King that cometh in the name of the Lord: peace
39 in heaven, and glory in the highest. And some of the
people from amongst the crowd said unto him, Good
Teacher, rebuke thy disciples, that they shout not.[5]   [5] Cureton.
40 He answered and said unto them, Verily I say unto
you, If these should hold their peace, the stones
41 would cry out. And when he was come near, and
42 saw the city, he wept over it, and said, If even in this
thy day thou hadst known thy peace! but it is

hid from thine eyes. But the days shall come, that 43
thine enemies shall compass thee round, and press
[1 Cureton.] thee in on every side,[1] and shall throw thee down 44
on the ground, and thy children within thee; and
they shall not leave in thee stone upon stone;
[2 Cureton.] because thou knewest not the day[2] of thy visitation.

And when he went into the temple, and began 45
to cast out them that sold therein, and said, My house
. . . the house of prayer: ye have made it a den . . . 46
taught . . . in the temple . . . and the scribes . . .
of the people sought to destroy him, and did not 47
find what they might do to him: for all the people 48
[3 R.V. Cureton. Bezae.] hung[3] upon him to hear him.

. . . of days . . as he taught in the temple, . . . and 20
preached, and the chief priests and the scribes and
[4 Cureton.] the elders stood up[4] against him, saying unto him, 2
By what authority doest thou these things? or who
is he that gave thee this authority? He answered 3
and said unto them, I also will ask you a word, tell
me: The baptism of John, was it from heaven, 4
or . . . . of men? And they reasoned, saying, If 5
we shall say, From heaven; he will say to us, Why
believed ye him not? And if . . . . for the people: 6 to 8
. . . . authority . . . . these things.

And he began to speak to them this parable: A 9
certain man planted . . . . and surrounded it . . . .
and committed it to . . . . for a long time. And at 10
[5 Cureton.] one[5] of the seasons he sent his servant to the husbandmen, that they should give him of the fruit . . . . .
[6 Syriac— 'he added and sent.'] and beat him, ... empty. And he sent yet[6] 11
his other servant: and him also they beat, and sent
. . . . . and they struck him . . . . . from . . . . . 12 to 16
unto them? . . . . . vineyard. They said . . . . .

16 shall destroy the husbandmen, and shall give the
17 vineyard to others. When they heard these things, they knew certainly that he spake this parable about them. And he beheld them, and said, What is this then that is written, The stone which the builders
18 rejected, it is become the head of the corner? For whosoever shall fall upon that stone shall be broken; but on whomsoever it shall fall, it will grind him.
19 And the chief priests and the scribes sought . . . . on him . . . . . in that hour; and they feared
20 the people. And afterwards they sent . . . . . with a word, and they should deliver him to the
21 judgment and to the authority of the governor. And . . . . saying unto him, Teacher, we know that thou sayest and teachest rightly, neither acceptest thou the faces of man, but teachest the word of God in
22 truth: Is it lawful for us to give tribute unto Cæsar,
23 or no? But he perceived their malice, and said unto
24 them, Why tempt ye me? Shew me a penny. The image with the inscription, whose is on it? And they
25 shewed it to him, saying, Cæsar's. He said unto them, Give what is Cæsar's unto Cæsar, and what
26 is God's unto God. And they could not take hold of his word before the people: and they marvelled at his answer, and held their peace.
27 Then came near certain of the Sadducees, those which say there is no[1] resurrection; and they asked
28 him, saying unto him, Teacher,[2] Moses wrote unto us, If any man's brother die, having no children, and leave a wife, that his brother should take his
29 wife, and raise up seed unto his brother. There were seven brethren amongst[3] us: the first took
30 a wife, and died without children. And the second

[1] R.V. Cureton.
[2] Bezae. Cureton. Bezae.
[3] Bezae.

took the woman, and he also died childless. And the 31
third also took her; and in like manner the seven
took her: and they died, and left no children. And¹ 32
the woman died also. In the resurrection, whose 33
wife of them shall she be? for behold, she was wife
to these seven. Jesus answered and said, The 34
children of this world are begotten² and beget³: and
marry and are given in marriage: but those who are 35
worthy of that world, and of that resurrection from
the dead, do not become the wives of men: neither 36
can they die: for they are equal unto the angels, as
the children of the resurrection. But about the dead, 37
that they rise, even Moses shewed, when God spake
with him from the bush, and said, The Lord, the God
of Abraham, the God of Isaac, and the God of Jacob.
And behold, he is not a God of the dead, but of the 38
living; for all live unto him. Certain of the scribes 39
said unto him, Teacher, thou hast well said. And 40
they durst not ask him anything again.

And he said unto them, How say the scribes con- 41
cerning the Christ, that he is David's son? And David 42
himself saith in the book of his Psalms, The Lord
said to my Lord, Sit thou on my right hand, till I 43
make thine enemies the stool beneath thy feet. If 44
David therefore calleth him Lord, how is he his
son?

And when the people were all listening,⁴ he said 45
unto his disciples, Beware of the scribes, which desire 46
to walk in the porches,⁵ and love greetings in the
markets, and the honoured⁶ seats in the synagogues,
and the chief places at feasts; and devour the houses 47
of widows, on pretence⁷ that they make long their
prayers: they shall receive greater condemnation.

---

¹ Cureton.

² Syriac—probably
³ Cureton. Bezae.

⁴ Cureton. Bezae.
⁵ Or, Stoae. Cureton.
⁶ Cureton.
⁷ Cureton.

21	And he lifted his eyes,¹ and saw the rich who	¹ Cureton.
2	were casting their gifts into the treasury. And he saw	
	also a certain poor widow, and she cast in two mites.	
3	He said, Of a truth I say unto you, that this poor	
4	widow hath cast in more than they all: for they of	
	their abundance have cast in unto the offerings²: but	² Cureton.
	she of what was lacking³ to her hath cast in all that	³ Cureton.
	she possessed.	

5 And as some spake of the temple, how it was
6 adorned with goodly stones and gifts, he said to them, See ye these stones? the days will come, that there shall not be left stone upon stone in it, that shall
7 not be thrown down. And they asked him, saying, Teacher, when shall these things be? and what shall
8 be the sign when these things begin⁴ to be? And ⁴ Cureton.
he said unto them, Look,⁵ lest ye be deceived: for ⁵ Cureton. Bezae.
many shall come in my name, and shall say, I am he; and, The time draweth near: go ye not after them.
9 And when ye hear of wars and tumults, be not afraid: for these things must first come to pass; but
10 the end hath not yet arrived.⁶ For nation shall rise ⁶ Cureton.
11 against nation, and kingdom against kingdom: and great earthquakes [shall be] in divers places, and pestilences in divers places, and famines; and there shall be fearful things from heaven, and great signs
12 shall be seen. But before all these, they shall lay their hands on you, and persecute you, and deliver you up to the synagogues, and into prison, and they shall bring you before kings and rulers for my name's
13 sake. And let it be to you a testimony. And set⁷ it ⁷ Cureton.
14
15 selves⁸: for I will give you a mouth, and such wisdom ⁸ Or— 'apologise.' Cureton. Bezae.
that all your adversaries shall not be able to stand

against you. For your brethren shall betray you, and your relatives, and your kinsfolk, and your friends; and they shall put to death some of you. And ye shall be hated of all men for my name's sake. And one hair of the hair of your head shall not perish. For in patience ye shall[1] possess your souls. And when ye shall see Jerusalem compassed with armies, know that her desolation cometh nigh unto her.[2] And they that are in Judæa, let them flee to the mountains; and they that are within her let them depart from her; and they that are in the villages, let them not enter her. For these be the days of vengeance, that all which is written may be fulfilled.

But woe unto them that are with child, and to them that give suck, in those days! for there shall be great distress, and wrath upon this people. And they shall fall by the edge of the sword, and shall be led away captive to every place: and Jerusalem shall be trodden down of all the nations, until the times of the nations be fulfilled. And there shall be signs in the sun, and in the moon, and in the stars; and distress upon the earth, and weakness of the hands of the nations; and the voice of the sea, and shaking; and men's souls shall go out for fear of what is about to come on the earth: and the powers of heaven shall be shaken. And then shall they see the Son of man coming in clouds with great[3] power and glory. When these things begin to come to pass, look up, and lift up your heads; for your redemption draweth nigh.

And he spake to them this[4] parable; Behold the fig tree, and all the trees; when they begin to shoot forth and yield their fruit,[5] ye understand that summer is coming nigh. So likewise ye, when ye see

---

[1] Cureton.

[2] Cureton.

[3] Cureton. Bezae.

[4] Cureton.

[5] Cureton.

31 these things come to pass, know ye that the kingdom
32 of God is nigh at hand. Verily I say unto you, this
generation¹ shall not pass, till all these things come
33 to pass. Heaven and earth shall pass away: and
34 my words shall not pass away. But take heed to
yourselves, lest .... your hearts .... of flesh,²
of wine,³ .... of the world, ... upon you the
35 day .... suddenly .... for it shall come : ...
36 all them ... face .... therefore, ... pray ...
37
38 and all .... came early .... to the temple, ...
22 .... was the feast of unleavened bread, which
2 is called the passover. And the chief priests and
scribes sought how they might kill him; for they
3 feared the people. Then entered Satan into Juda
surnamed Scariot, being of the number of the twelve.
4 And he went and talked with the chief .... how
5 .... unto them. .... silver. .... multitude.
6
7 And when the day of the passover arrived, on
8 which it was the custom to kill the passover, he sent
Cepha and John, and said unto them, Go, prepare
9 us the passover, that we may eat. They say unto
10 him, Where wilt thou that we prepare? He said
unto them, Behold, when ye enter into the city,
there shall a man meet you, bearing a pitcher of
water; follow him into the house where he entereth
11 in. And say to the master of the house, Our⁴ Master
saith, Where is the guest-chamber, where I shall eat
12 the passover, I and my disciples? Behold,⁵ he shall
shew you a large upper room, strewn:⁶ there make
13 ready for us. And they went, and found as he had
said unto them: and they made ready the passover.
14 And when it was⁷ the hour, he sat down, he and his
15 disciples with him. He said unto them, With desire

¹ Or 'race.'
² Cureton.
³ Cureton.
⁴ Cureton.
⁵ Cureton.
⁶ Cureton. Bezae.
⁷ Bezae.

I have desired to eat the passover with you before I 15
suffer: for I say unto you, I will not any more eat 16
thereof, until the kingdom of God be perfected.
And he took bread, and gave thanks over it, and brake, 19
and gave unto them, saying, This is my body which
I give for you: thus do in remembrance of me. And 20
after they had supped, he took the cup, and gave 17
thanks over it, and said, Take this, share it among
yourselves. This is my blood, the new testament. 20
For I say unto you, that henceforth I will not drink 18
of this fruit, until the kingdom of God shall come.
But nevertheless, behold, the hand of my[1] betrayer 21
is with me on the table. And[2] the Son of man goeth, 22
as it is determined: but nevertheless,[3] woe unto him
by whose hand[4] he is betrayed! And they began to 23
enquire among themselves, which of them it was that
should do this thing.

And there was[5] a strife amongst them, who 24
amongst them was great. He said unto them, 25
The kings of the nations are their lords; and they
that have authority over them and do good[6] are
called benefactors. But ye are not so: but he that 26
is greatest among you, let him be as the younger;
and he that is chief, as he that doth serve. For 27
whether is greater, he that sitteth at meat, or he
that serveth? is not he that sitteth at meat? I am
as one who serveth among you. And ye are they 28
which have continued with me in my temptations.
And I promise[7] unto you, as my Father hath pro- 29
mised[7] unto me, a kingdom; that ye may eat and 30
drink with me at my own table in my kingdom, and
sit on twelve[8] thrones, judging the twelve tribes of
the house of Israel.

[1] Cureton.
[2] Cureton.
[3] Cureton. Bezae.
[4] Cureton.
[5] Cureton.
[6] Cureton.
[7] Cureton.
[8] Cureton. Bezae.

31 ¹Simon, Simon, behold, Satan hath desired² that ¹ R.V. ² Cureton.
32 he may sift you as wheat: but I have prayed for thee, that thy faith fail not: and thou also be³ ³ Bezae.
33 converted in time, and establish thy brethren. He said unto him, Lord, I am ready to go with thee,
34 both into prison, and to death. He said unto him, I say unto thee, Cepha, that when the cock has not yet crowed this day, three times thou shalt deny me that thou knowest me.

35 He said unto them, When I sent you without purse, and without scrip, and without shoes, lacked ye
36 anything? They said unto him, Nothing at all.⁴ He ⁴ Cureton. said unto them, Henceforth he that hath a purse, or⁵ ⁵ Cureton. a scrip, let him take it: and he that hath none,⁶ let ⁶ R.V. Bezae.
37 him sell his garment, and buy himself a sword. For I say unto you, that this also which is written is about to be fulfilled in me, He was numbered with the transgressors: and that which concerneth
38 me is to be accomplished.⁷ And they said to Jesus, ⁷ R.V. Behold, here are two swords. He said unto them, They are enough for you.

39 And he came out, and went, as he was wont, to the mount which is called of Beth⁸ Zaita, and his dis- ⁸ i.e. 'the house of Olives.' Cureton.
40 ciples were with him. And when he reached the place, he said unto them, Pray that ye enter not into
41 temptation. And he withdrew from them about a stone's cast, and he kneeled down, and prayed, say-
42 ing, Father, if thou be willing, let this cup pass from
45 me: but not my will be done, but thine.⁹ And he ⁹ Omit vv. 43 44. rose from his prayer, and came to his disciples, and
46 found them sleeping for their sorrow, and said unto them, Why sleep ye? rise, pray, that ye enter not into temptation.

While he yet spake, there appeared a great mul- 47 titude, and he that was called Juda, one of the twelve, came before them, and he drew near to kiss Jesus. Jesus said unto him, Juda, dost thou betray 48 the Son of man with a kiss? And when his dis- 49 ciples saw what was going to happen, they said unto him, Our Lord, shall we smite them with the sword? And one of them smote the servant of the high 50 priest, and took[1] off his right ear. Jesus answered 51 and said, It is enough[2] thus far. And he touched his ear, and healed him. And he said to those who 52 came against him, the chief priests, and the soldiers, and the elders, As against a thief are ye come out against me, with swords and staves? Every day that 53 I was with you in the temple, ye stretched not forth hands against me: but this is your hour, and your power of darkness. And they seized him, and 54 brought him to the house of the high priest.

But Cepha was following him afar off. And a fire 55 was laid[3] in the midst of the court, and they were sitting round it, and Cepha was sitting amongst them. And a certain maid saw him as he sat by 56 the fire, and looked at him, and said, This one also was with him. And he denied, saying, Woman, I know 57 him not. And after a little while, another also saw 58 him, and said unto him, Thou also art one of them. And he said unto him, Let [me] alone, man, I know him not. And it came to pass that about an hour after, another 59 confidently affirmed, saying, Of a truth this fellow was also with him; for he also is a Galilæan. Cepha 60 said, Man, I understand not what thou sayest. And immediately[4] the cock crew. And Jesus[5] turned, and 61 looked upon Cepha. And Cepha remembered the

---

[1] Cureton. Bezae.
[2] Cureton.
[3] Cureton.
[4] Cureton.
[5] Bezae.

61 word of Jesus, how he had said unto him, Before the cock has crowed this day, thou shalt deny me thrice.
62 And he went out, and wept bitterly. And the men
63
64 that held him¹ mocked him, and smote him. And they blindfolded him, saying unto him,² Prophesy, who is it
65 that smote thee? And again many other things they
66 blasphemed and spake against him. And when it was day, the elders of the people and the chief priests and the scribes came together, and led him up into
67 their council, saying, If thou art the Christ, tell us. He said unto them, If I tell you, ye will not believe me:
68 and if I ask you, ye will not give me an answer, nor
69 let me go. For henceforth shall the Son of man sit
70 on the right hand of God. They all said, Art thou then the Son of God? He said unto them, Ye say
71 that I am he. They said, What need have we of witness? for lo, we have heard from his mouth.

¹ R.V. marg. Bezae.
² R.V. Cureton. Bezae.

23 And the whole multitude arose, and brought him
2 unto Pilate. And they began to accuse him, saying, We found this fellow perverting our nation, and forbidding us to give tribute to Cæsar, saying about
3 himself, that he is the king, the Christ. Pilate saith unto him, Art thou then the King of the Jews? He answered and said to him, Thou sayest that I am.
4 Pilate said to the chief priests and to the multitude,
5 I find no accusation against this man. But they cried, saying, He has stirred up the people, teaching through-
6 out all Jewry, beginning from Galilee unto this place.
7 When Pilate heard them say that he was of Galilee, and when he heard that he was under the jurisdiction of Herod, he sent him to Herod, because Herod himself
8 also was at Jerusalem in those days. Now when Herod saw Jesus, he rejoiced exceedingly: for he

had been desirous to see him for a long time, because 8
he had heard of him; and he hoped to see some
sign¹ done by him. Then he questioned with him in 9
cunning² words; but Jesus returned him no answer.
³Then Pilate called the chief priests, and the rulers, 13
and all the people, and said unto them, Ye brought 14
this man unto me, and ye said that he stirreth
up your people: and I have examined him in your
presence, and have found nothing against⁴ him of the
things whereof ye accuse him: no, nor yet Herod: for 15
I sent him⁵ to him⁶; nothing that is worthy of death
did he find against⁴ him, nor has anything worthy of
death been done by him.⁷ I will therefore chastise 16
him, and release him. And all the people⁸ cried 18
out,⁹ saying, Take¹⁰ away this man, and release Bar-
Abba: he who because of wicked deeds and murder 19
was cast into prison. And Pilate¹¹ was wont to release 17
one prisoner unto them at the feast. And again¹² 20
Pilate called them, and said unto them, because he
was willing to release Jesus, Whom will ye that I
release unto you? But they cried, Crucify him, 21
crucify him. Then he said unto them the third time, 22
Why, what evil hath he done? I find nothing worthy
of death against⁴ him: I will therefore chastise him,
and let him go. And they were instant with loud 23
voices, saying unto him that he might be crucified.
And their voices prevailed, and the chief priests
were with them. And Pilate commanded that their 24
will should be done. And he released unto them 25
him who for murder and wicked deeds was cast into
prison, as they had requested: and he delivered Jesus
to their will. And as they led him away, they laid 26
hold upon one Simon, a Cyrenian, coming out of the

---

¹ Cureton.
  Bezae.
² Cureton.
³ Omit vv. 10,
  11, 12.
⁴ Literally,
  'behind
  him.'
⁵ Cureton.
⁶ Cureton.
  Bezae.
⁷ Cureton.
⁸ Transpose
  v. 17.
  Cureton.
⁹ Or, 'gave
  voice.'
  Cureton.
¹⁰ Cureton.
  Bezae.
¹¹ Cureton.
¹² Cureton.

26 country, that he might bear the cross, and follow
27 Jesus. And there followed him a great company of people, and of women, who lamented about him, and wailed.
28 And Jesus turned unto them, and said unto them, Daughters of Jerusalem, weep not for me, but weep
29 for yourselves, and for your children. For, behold, the days are coming, in the which they shall say. Blessed are the barren, and the wombs that have not
30 borne, and the paps that have not[1] given suck. And then shall they begin to say to the mountains, Fall
31 on us; and to the hills, Cover us. [They] who do these things in the moist tree, what shall they do in the
32 dry? And there came[2] with him two malefactors to
33 be put to death. And when they were come to the place, which is called a Skull,[3] they crucified him there, and those malefactors, one on the right hand,
34 and the other on the left. And[4] they parted his
35 garments, and cast lots on them. And the people stood beholding. And the rulers also with them derided him, saying, He saved others; let him save
36 himself, if he be the Christ, the chosen of God. And the soldiers also mocked him, and they were coming
37 near[5] him, saying, Hail to thee![6] If thou be the king of the Jews, save thyself. And they placed also on
38 his head a crown of thorns.[7] And an inscription was written and placed over him,[8] This is the King of
39 the Jews. And one of the malefactors which were crucified, blasphemed[9] against him, saying to him, Art not thou the Christ[10]? save thyself, and us also.
40 And his other companion[11] rebuked him, saying, Dost thou not fear God? for behold, we also are in the
41 condemnation. And behold,[12] we are recompensed

[1] Cureton. Bezae.
[2] Cureton.
[3] Syriac—'carcafta.'
[4] R.V. marg. Bezae.
[5] Cureton.
[6] Cureton.
[7] Cureton. Bezae.
[8] R.V. Cureton.
[9] Cureton. Bezae.
[10] R.V. Cureton.
[11] Cureton.
[12] Cureton.

as we are worthy, and as we have done: but this 41
man, nothing that is hateful¹ hath been done by
him. And he said unto Jesus, Lord, remember me 42
when thou comest into² thy kingdom. Jesus said 43
unto him, Verily I say unto thee, To day shalt thou
be with me in paradise. And it was about the sixth 44
hour, and there was a darkness over all the earth
until the ninth hour. And the sun was darkened, 45
and the veil of the temple was rent in the midst.

And Jesus cried with a loud voice, and said, 46
Father, into thy hands I place³ my spirit: and he
expired.⁴ And when the centurion saw what had hap- 47
pened, he glorified God, saying, Certainly this was a
righteous man. And all those who had ventured there, 48
and saw what happened, smote upon their breasts,
saying, Woe to us, what hath befallen us! woe to
us for our sins⁵! And all the acquaintances of Jesus 49
were standing afar off, and the women who came
with him from Galilee, beholding these things. And 50
a certain man whose name was Joseph, he was a
counsellor, a just man, and a good,⁶ from Ramtha,
a village of Judæa, and he was looking for the king- 51
dom of heaven. This man 52
. . . . to
  54
had dawned. And the women who came with him 55
from Galilee, went to the sepulchre in their footsteps,⁷ and saw the body while they brought it in
there,⁸ and returned, and prepared spices and sweet⁹ 56
ointment; and rested on the sabbath according as
is commanded.¹⁰

Now upon the first day of the week, very early **24**
in the morning, they came unto the sepulchre,
and they brought what¹¹ they had prepared, and

Margin notes:
¹ Cureton.
² Or, 'with.'
³ Cureton.
⁴ Or, 'ended.'
⁵ Cureton.
⁶ Cureton.
⁷ Cureton.
⁸ Cureton.
⁹ Cureton.
¹⁰ Cureton.
¹¹ Cureton. Bezae.

2 other women came with them. And they found the
3 stone rolled away from the sepulchre. And they
4 entered in, and found not the body of[1] Jesus. And
as they were grieved[2] about this, there appeared two
men standing above them, and their garments were
5 dazzling: and they were afraid, and bowed their
heads,[3] and looked on the ground for their fear.[4] These
men[5] said unto them, Why seek ye the living among
6 the dead? He is not here, but is risen: remember
what[6] he spake unto you when he was yet in Galilee,
7 and said to you,[7] The Son of man must be delivered
into the hands of sinful men, and be crucified,
8 and in three days rise. And they remembered
9 these[8] words, and returned from the sepulchre, and
told these things unto the eleven, and the rest of
10 the disciples.[9] Mary Magdalene, and Joanna, and
Mary the daughter[10] of James, and the rest who were
11 with them, they told the apostles. And they appeared
in their eyes as if they had spoken these words from
12 their wonder,[11] and they believed them not. Then
arose Simon, and ran unto the sepulchre; and he
stooped down and saw the linen clothes only,[12] and he
went home, and wondered what had come to pass.
13 And[13] he appeared unto two of them the same
day as they were going to a village called Emmaus,
which was distant from Jerusalem threescore fur-
14 longs. And they talked together of all these things
15 which had happened. And while they were talking
and enquiring, Jesus came and made up[14] to them,
16 and walked with them. And their eyes were holden
17 that they should not perceive him. He said unto
them, What are these words which ye talk of whilst ye
18 are sad[15]? One of them, whose name was Cleopa, said

[1] Cureton.
[2] Cureton.
[3] Cureton.
[4] Cureton.
[5] Cureton.
[6] Cureton. Bezae.
[7] Cureton.
[8] Cureton.
[9] Cureton.
[10] Cureton.
[11] Cureton.
[12] Cureton.
[13] Cureton.
[14] Cureton.
[15] Cureton.

unto him, Art thou then a stranger from Jerusalem, who 18 hast not known what is come to pass there? He said 19 unto them, What? They said unto him, Concerning Jesus the Nazarene, which was a man,[1] a prophet, and he was able in power, and in deed and in word before God and before all the people: and the chief priests 20 and elders delivered him to the judgment of death, 21 and crucified him. And we supposed that it was he who was to have redeemed Israel: and behold,[2] it is three days since all these things happened. And 22 certain women also of us, went to the sepulchre, where he had been laid[3]; and when they found not 23 his body, they came, saying to us, that they had seen angels there,[4] and they were amazed,[5] and said about him that he was alive. And also some[6] of us went 24 to the sepulchre, and found it even so as the women had said: but him they saw not.

Then said Jesus unto them, O devoid[7] of under- 25 standing, and heavy[8] of heart to believe from all the things that the prophets have spoken! Ought not 26 Christ to have suffered these things, and to enter into his glory? And he began to speak to them from 27 Moses, and from all the prophets, and expounded unto them concerning himself from all the scriptures. And 28 they drew nigh to the village whither they went: and he appeared to them as if he would have gone to a further place. And they began to entreat him that he 29 would be with them, because it was nearly dark.[9] And he went in with them as if he would tarry with them. And[10] as he sat at meat, he took bread, and blessed, 30 and brake, and gave to them. And immediately[11] their 31 eyes were opened, and they knew him; and he was lifted[12] away from them. And they said one to another, 32

[1] Cureton. Bezae.

[2] Cureton.

[3] Cureton.

[4] Cureton.
[5] Cureton.
[6] Cureton.

[7] Cureton.
[8] Cureton.

[9] Cureton.

[10] Cureton.
[11] Cureton.

[12] Cureton.

32 Was not our heart heavy[1] by the way, while he ex-
33 pounded to us the scriptures? And they rose up the
   same hour, and returned to Jerusalem, and found the
   eleven gathered together, and them that were with
34 them. And they came, saying, Our Lord is risen
35 indeed, and hath appeared to Simon. And they also
   told what things had happened in the way, and how
   he was known as he brake bread.

36   And while they thus spake, he was found stand-
     ing[2] amongst them, and said unto them, Peace
37 be with you. But they were shaken[3] and terri-
   fied, and supposed that they had seen a spirit.
38 Then Jesus[4] said unto them, Why are ye shaken,
39 and why do thoughts arise in your hearts? Behold,
   see my hands and my feet, and feel and see that it is
   I: for a spirit . . . flesh and bones, ... as . . . .
40
41 see me . . . . . When . . . . . not . . . . . . were.
   Again he said unto them, Have ye here anything to
42 eat? And they gave unto him a piece of a broiled
43 fish.[5] And when he had taken it, he ate before
44 their eyes.[6] He said unto them, These words I spake
   unto you, while I was with you, that all things might
   be fulfilled, which are written concerning me in the
   law of Moses, and in the prophets, and in the psalms.
45 And then he opened their understanding, that they
46 might understand the scriptures, and said unto
   them, Lo, thus it behoved . . . . the Christ . . . .
47 from the dead in three days: and that repentance
   and remission of sins should be preached in my
   name, among all nations, beginning at Jerusalem.
48
49 And ye are witnesses of these things. And[7] I send
   upon you the promise of my Father: tarry ye in the
   city, until ye be clothed with power from on high.

[1] Cureton. 'heavy,' or 'burning' —only the difference of a dot.
[2] Cureton.
[3] Cureton.
[4] Cureton.
[5] R.V. Bezae.
[6] Cureton.
[7] Bezae.

And he led them out as far as to Bethany, and he 50 lifted up his hands, and blessed them. And while 51 he blessed them, he was lifted up from them. And 52 they[1] returned to Jerusalem with great joy: and 53 were continually blessing[2] God in the temple.

[1] Bezae.
[2] R.V.

HERE ENDETH THE GOSPEL OF LUKE.

THE GOSPEL OF JOHN

[i. 1—24 *is lost.*]

1 .... baptizest thou then, if thou art not the
25
26 Christ, nor even Elia, nor even a prophet? John
said unto them, I baptize with water: but among
27 you standeth he whom ye know not; he who
cometh after me,[1] he, whose shoe's latchet I am   [1] R.V. Cureton.
28 not worthy to unloose. These things he spake in
Beth 'Abara beyond Jordan, where John was bap-
29 tizing. And the .... day .... unto him, ...
30 This is he of whom I said, A man cometh after me,
and he was before me: because he existed before me.
31 And I knew him not; but that he should be made
known[2] to Israel, I am come to baptize with water.   [2] Cureton.
32 And John bare record, ... the Spirit .....
descending from heaven, and it abode upon him.
33 And I knew him not: but he that sent me to baptize
.... said unto me, ... whom thou .....
descending, ... and remaining on him, he it is
34 which baptizeth with the .... Ghost. And I ....
that this is the chosen[3] one of God.   [3] Cureton.
35   Again the next day after John stood, and two of
36 his disciples with him; and he looked upon Jesus
as he walked, and said, Behold .... the Lamb of
37 God! And when those disciples heard John speak,
38 they followed him. And our Lord turned, and said
unto them, What seek ye? They say unto him, Our

Master,[1] where art thou[2]? He saith unto them, 39 Come and ye shall[3] see. And they followed him, and saw where he was,[4] and they were with him that day: and it was about the tenth hour. And the 40 name of one of these disciples of John was Andrew, the brother of Simon. And Andrew saw Simon his 41 brother on that day, and saith unto him, My brother, we have found the Messiah.[5] And he led him and 42 he came to our Lord. And our Lord beheld him, and said unto him, Thou art Simon the son of Jona: thou shalt be called Cepha, which is being interpreted into Greek, Peter.

The day following, he would go forth into Galilee, 43 and findeth Philip, and our Lord saith unto him, Follow me. Now Philip was by his family of Beth 44 Saida, of the city of Andrew and Simon. And 45 Philip findeth Nathanael, and Philip saith unto Nathanael, He of whom Moses wrote, and the prophets, we have found him, that he is Jesus the son of Joseph of Nazareth. Nathanael said unto him, 46 Can there any good thing come out of Nazareth? Philip saith unto him, Come, and thou shalt see. And . . . . saw him 47

[47 *to* ii. 15 *is lost.*]

And said unto them that sold doves, Take these 2 things hence; and make not my Father's house an 16 house of merchandise. When he did these things 17 his disciples remembered that it was written, The zeal of thine house hath eaten me up. The Jews say 18 unto him, ... sign . . . . shewest thou unto us, that thou doest these things? Our Lord answered 19 and said unto them, Destroy the temple, and in three

---

[1] Or, 'Rabban.' Cureton.
[2] Cureton.
[3] R.V. Cureton.
[4] Cureton.
[5] Or, 'the Christ.'

20 days . . . . In forty and six years . . . . the temple
21 . . . . . in three days thou wilt build it? But he
22 spake of the temple of his body. And when he was risen from the dead, his disciples remembered that he had said this; and they believed the scripture, and the word which our Lord had said.
23 And when he was in Jerusalem, in the days of the feast of unleavened bread . . . . . were . . . . .
24 which he did to them. But our Lord did not trust
25 himself to them, and . . . . not . . . . that any man should testify about the work of man: for he knew the heart in man . . . .

3 And there was there a man of the Pharisees, named Nicodemus, and this man was a ruler of the
2 Jews. He came to our Lord by night, and said unto him, Rabbi, we know that thou art sent to us from God, a teacher: because no man can do these signs,
3 except he whom God is with. Our Lord said unto him, Verily, verily, I say unto thee, that if a man be not born again,[1] he cannot see the kingdom of God.   [1] Syriac—'from the beginning.'
4 Nicodemus saith unto him, How can an old man be born? can he perhaps enter again into the womb of his
5 mother, and be born again? Our Lord said unto him, Verily, verily, I say unto thee, that if a man be not born of the Spirit and water, he cannot enter the
6 kingdom of God. That which is born of the flesh is flesh; and that which is born of the Spirit is spirit;
7 because God is a living Spirit. And marvel not that
8 I told you to be born. The wind bloweth where it listeth, and thou hearest the sound thereof, but thou knowest[2] not whence it cometh, nor whither it   [2] Cureton. goeth: so are they which are born of water[3] and the   [3] Cureton.
9 Spirit. Nicodemus said unto him, How can this[4] be?   [4] Cureton.

Our Lord said unto him, Art thou a teacher of Israel, and knowest not these things? Verily I say unto thee, that what we know we speak,[1] and what we have seen we testify[2]; and ye receive not our witness. If I have told you of things on the earth, and ye believe not, how, if I tell you of things that are in heaven, will ye believe me[3]? . . . . . hath ascended up to heaven, ... but he . . . . heaven, ... the Son of man which is from heaven. And as Moses lifted up the serpent in the wilderness, even so . . . . . whosoever believeth in him should not perish, but have eternal life. . . . . the world, ... that whosoever believeth in him . . . . not . . . . For God sent [not] his Son into the world to judge the world; but that the world through him might be saved. He that believeth on him is not condemned: and he that believeth not in him is condemned, because he hath not believed in the name of the only Son. This is condemnation, that light is come . . . . wrought in God.

And after these things our Lord and his disciples came to Judæa; and there he baptized, and dwelt with them. And John also was baptizing in 'Ain Nun[4] near to Salim, because there was much water there: and the people came, and were baptized. For John was not yet cast into prison.

Then there was a question between one of John's disciples and a Jew about purifying. And they came unto John, and said unto him, Our Master,[5] he that was with thee beyond Jordan, to whom thou barest witness, behold, he also baptizeth, and many come to him. John[6] said unto them, A man can take nothing at all, except it be given him from

---

[1] Cureton.
[2] Cureton.
[3] Cureton.
[4] Or, 'the Fish spring.'
[5] 'Rabban.' Cureton.
[6] Cureton.

28 heaven. But ye bear¹ me witness, that I said, I am not   ¹ Cureton.
29 the Christ, but that I am sent before him. Because
he that hath the bride is the bridegroom: and the
friend of the bridegroom, which standeth and heareth
him, rejoiceth with great joy² because of the bride-   ² Cureton.
groom's voice: this my joy, behold,³ it is fulfilled.   ³ Cureton.
30 Therefore it is fitting to him that he increase, and to
31 me that I decrease. Because he that cometh from
to above is above all: he that is of the earth is on the
34
35 earth, and . . . of the earth; . . . . for . . . giveth
36 . . . . but . . . . . from . . . .
4 . . . many . . . more than . . . because . . . not . . .
2
3 only baptized not, but his disciples. And he left . . .
4 again into Galilee. . . . . . a . . . Samaria, which is
to
7 called Shechem, ... ground which . . . . them-
8 selves meat. And while our Lord sat, it was the
7 sixth hour. And there cometh a certain woman
of Samaria to draw water: and our Lord said unto
9 her, Give me water⁴ to drink. The Samaritan   ⁴ Cureton.
woman said unto him, Lo, thou art a Jew. How
dost thou ask me for water to drink? for the Jews
10 have no dealings with the Samaritans. He said
unto her, If thou knewest the gift of God, and who
it is that saith to thee, Give me to drink; thou
wouldest have asked of him, and he would have given
11 thee living water. She said unto him, Thou hast
not even a pitcher,⁵ and the well is deep: from   ⁵ Cureton.
12 whence hast thou⁶ living water? Art thou perhaps   ⁶ Cureton. Bezae.
greater than Jacob our father, which gave us this
well, and he also drank from it, and his children, and
13 his cattle? Our Lord said unto her, Whosoever
14 drinketh of this water shall thirst again: and whosoever drinketh of the water that I shall give him,

shall never thirst; but the water that I shall give him shall be in him a well of water springing up into everlasting life. The woman saith unto him, Sir, give me to drink of this water, that I thirst not, neither come to draw from here. Our Lord said unto her, Go, call thy husband to me, and come hither. She said unto him, I have no husband. Our Lord said unto her, Thou hast well said, for thou hast had five husbands; and he whom thou now hast is not thy husband: this saidst thou truly. She said unto him, Sir, I perceive that thou art a prophet. Our fathers worshipped in this mountain; and ye say, that Jerusalem is the house[1] of worship. Our Lord said unto her, Woman, believe, the hour cometh, when ye shall neither in this mountain, nor yet at Jerusalem, worship the Father. Ye worship ye know not what: and we worship what we know: for salvation is from Juda. But behold, the hour cometh, and now is, when the true worshippers shall worship the Father in spirit and in truth: for the Father even seeketh these worshippers,[2] those who worship him in spirit and in truth. The woman saith, Behold, the Christ[3] cometh, and when he is come, he will give everything. Our Lord saith unto her, I that speak unto thee am he. And while they were talking,[4] his disciples came and wondered that . . . . with the woman, yet they did not say to him, ... seekest thou? or . . . . talkest . . . The woman . . . water-pot, and . . . to the city, and saith, Come, see a man, which told me all things that I have done: is not this perhaps the Christ? . . . . went out to him. And[5] his disciples prayed him to eat bread with them. He said unto them, I have meat to eat that ye know not of. They[6]

[1] Cureton.
[2] Cureton.
[3] Or, 'Messiah.'
[4] Cureton.
[5] Cureton.
[6] Cureton.

33 said one to another, Hath any man perhaps brought
34 him ought to eat? He saith unto them, My own¹ meat ¹ Cureton.
is to do the will of him that sent me, and to finish
35 his work. Say not ye, There are yet four months,
and the harvest cometh? behold, I say unto you,
Lift up your eyes, and look on the fields; that they
36 are white and have come² to the harvest. And the ² Cureton.
reaper straightway³ receiveth wages, and gathereth ³ Cureton. Bezae.
fruit unto life eternal, and the sower and the reaper
37 shall rejoice together. For herein is a word of
truth,⁴ One soweth, and another reapeth. ⁴ Cureton.

[iv. 38 to v. 5 is lost.]

5 .... had been .... long .... he said unto
7 him, Wilt thou become sound⁵? He⁶ said unto him, ⁵ Cureton. ⁶ Cureton.
Sir, I have no man, who, when the water is troubled,
to will put me into the pool; but while I am coming,
12 . . . .
13 and walk? And that man wist not who it was: for
our Lord had conveyed himself away from one place
14 to another⁷ from the press. After these things our ⁷ Cureton. literally, 'to its fellow.'
Lord findeth him in the temple, and said unto
him, Behold, thou art whole: sin not again, lest a
15 worse [thing] happen unto thee. And the man
went and told the Jews that it was Jesus, which
16 had made him whole. And therefore did the Jews
persecute our Lord,⁸ because he had done these ⁸ R.V. Cureton.
17 things on the sabbath. But our Lord said unto Bezae.
them, My Father worketh hitherto, because of this⁹ ⁹ Cureton.
18 I also work. The Jews then because of this word¹⁰ ¹⁰ Cureton.
. . . . [not] only because he had broken the sabbath,
but because . . . . . called . . . . . had . . . . God.
19
20 . . . our Lord unto them, Verily . . . his Father . . .

Son . . . . . Father . . . . . the dead, and raiseth[1] them up, even so the Son also quickeneth those who believe in him.[2] For the Father judgeth no man, but hath committed . . . . . all judgment unto his Son: . . . . . 21 to 25

- [1] Cureton.
- [2] Cureton.

[vv. 26 to 45 are lost.]

. . . . ye would have believed me also: for he wrote of me. And if ye believe not in his writings, how shall ye believe in my own words? 46 47

After these things our Lord went across the lake of Galilee, of Tiberias. And a great multitude followed him, because they saw the miracles which he did on the sick. And our Lord went up into a mountain, and there he sat with his disciples. And the feast of the unleavened bread of the Jews was nigh. And our Lord lifted up his eyes, and saw a great multitude come unto him; he saith unto Philip, Whence shall we buy bread for these people, that they may eat? But he asked[3] him this, as proving him: for he knew what he was about to do. Philip said unto him, Two hundred pennyworth of bread is not sufficient for them, while they eat little by little.[4] One of his disciples, whose name was Andrew, Simon Cepha's brother, saith unto him, A certain lad here hath five barley loaves, and two[5] fishes: but what are they to all these? 6 2 3 4 5 6 7 8 9

- [3] Cureton.
- [4] Cureton.
- [5] R.V. Cureton. Bezae.

He said unto them, Make the men sit down. Now there was much grass in the place. He said unto them, Go, make the men sit down on the green. And when they had made them sit down, then Jesus took those loaves; . . . . baskets, remains of those five barley loaves, and of those two fishes. 10 11 to 13

13 And the men which did eat of this bread were
14 five thousand. And those people when they saw that
   sign which he did, said, This is of a truth that
15 prophet that cometh into the world. And they were
   considering that they might snatch him away, that
   they might make him a king, . . . left them . . . to
16 the mountain . . . And when it was evening, ...
17 to Capernaum, because . . . . to him . . . . Jesus
18 . . . . to them . . . . And the lake was tumultuous
19 against them, . . . and a wind . . . And when . . .
   five . . . . thirty . . . . upon them, and as he drew
20 near unto their ship: . . . . . . their fear . . . . . .
to
22 And on the day . . . . was . . . . ship came from
to
24 T . . . . place . . . . were . . . . . . found him
25 . . . . Verily I say unto you, that not . . . . . .
26 because ye saw . . . . but because ye did
27 eat . . . . not . . . . the meat . . . . the meat
   . . . which . . . of man . . . shall give unto you:
28 . . . for him hath . . . the Father sealed. They say
   unto him, What shall we do, that we might work
29 . . . . of God? Jesus . . . . of God, ... whom
30 he hath sent . . . . that we may see, ... thee?
31 Our fathers did eat manna in the desert; as it is
32 written, He gave them bread from heaven. Verily,
   verily, I say unto you, Moses gave you not the bread
   from heaven; but my Father giveth you the bread of
33 truth from heaven. For the bread of God is he[1] which
   cometh down from heaven, and giveth life unto the
34 world. They say unto him, Lord at all times . . . give
35 us of this bread. He said unto them, I am the bread
   . . . that cometh . . . hunger; and he that . . . on me
36 . . . But . . . unto you, that ye have seen . . . believe
37 . . . giveth me . . . shall come . . . cometh . . . not

[1] Or, 'that which.'

.... For I came down from heaven, not that I 38
might do my will, ... that I might do his will
.... that sent me. This .... what he hath 39
given me I should not lose even one, but should raise
up ... in the ... day. Because this 40
who believeth in the Son .... hath everlasting life:
and I will raise him up at the last day. .....
murmured .... I am the bread which came down 41
from heaven. And they said, Is .... Jesus, ... 42
and we know .... how saith he .... heaven?
.... unto them, Murmur not one to another. No 43
man can come .... Father .... last .... For 45
it is written in the prophets, And they shall be all
taught of God. Every ..... Father, and hath

[1] Cureton.

learned of him, cometh unto me. It is not because[1] 46
any man hath seen the Father, but he which is with
God, he hath seen God the Father. Verily, verily, 47

[2] Cureton.

I say unto you, He that believeth on God[2] hath life.
I am that bread of life. Your fathers did eat manna 48
49
in the wilderness, and are dead. This is the bread 50
which cometh down from ..... that a man may
eat ... and not .... I .... which came down 51
that .... eat .... for ever: .... I will give is

[3] Cureton.

my body, which is[3] for the life of the world. And 52
the Jews strove with each other, saying, How can
.... give us .... to eat? Jesus .... Verily, 53
verily, I say unto you, That if ye eat not the body of
the Son of man, and drink his blood, ye have no life
in you. But whoso eateth his body, and drinketh his 54
blood, hath eternal life; and I will raise him up at
the last day. My body is meat indeed, and my blood 55
is drink indeed. He that eateth my body, and 56
drinketh my blood, ... and I in him. As the 57

THE GOSPEL OF JOHN

57 living Father hath sent me, and I live because¹ of my Father: he that eateth my body shall be alive   ¹ R.V. Cureton. Bezae.
58 because of me. This is that bread which came down from heaven: not like that which your fathers did eat,² and are dead: he that eateth of this bread shall   ² R.V. Cureton. Bezae.
59 live for ever. These things said he in Capernaum,
60 in the synagogue as he taught. And many of his disciples said, This saying is hard; who can hear it³?   ³ Or, 'him.'
61 But when Jesus knew⁴ that his disciples murmured,   ⁴ Cureton.
62 he said unto them, Doth this offend you? But if ye shall see the Son of man ascend up to the place where
63 he was before? It is the spirit that quickeneth the body; ... but ye ... the body profiteth nothing: the
64 words that I speak with you, ... spirit ... But there are some of you that believe not. For Jesus knew
65 from the beginning who⁵ should betray him. He said   ⁵ Cureton. unto them,⁶ Therefore said I unto you, that no man   ⁶ Cureton. can come unto me, except it were given unto him of
66 the Father. Because of that saying many of his disciples went their way, and walked not⁷ with him.   ⁷ Cureton.
67 He said unto his twelve, And ye also, ye will surely
68
69 ... we go? ... that thou art the Christ, the Son of
70 God. He said unto them, Have not I chosen you
71 all,⁸ and [one] even of you is Satan? .... of Juda   ⁸ Cureton. Iscariot .... was ready⁹ to betray him, [being] one   ⁹ Cureton. of the twelve.

7   After these things Jesus walked in Galilee: for he would not walk openly in Judæa, because the
2 Jews ... to kill him. .... of tabernacles of the Jews
to
4 ... at hand ... and ... came near ... who doeth any-thing ... and he desireth ... openly. If ... shew
5 .... to the world. Until .... then not even his
6 brethren believed in him. Jesus ... unto them,

My time is not yet come: but your time is alway. And the world cannot hate you; ... the world ... because I testify against it, that its works are evil. Go ye up unto this feast: I go not up[1] unto the feast; for my time is not yet full come.[2] .... openly, but .... And the Jews sought him there at the feast, and said, Where is he? .... was .... unto them, My doctrine is not mine, but his that sent me. Whoso will do his will, he shall know this doctrine, whether it be of God, or whether I speak from my own mind. He who speaketh of his own mind, seeketh glory to himself: and he who seeketh the glory of him that sent him, is true, and iniquity ...... Thou hast .... who seeketh to kill thee? Jesus[3] said unto them, I have done one work in your sight,[4] and ye all marvel. Moses therefore gave unto you circumcision; not because it is of Moses, but because it is of your fathers; and ye on the sabbath day circumcise a man. For if a man be circumcised[5] on the sabbath day, that the law of Moses should not be broken; are ye angry because I have made a man every whit whole on the sabbath day? Judge not by faces,[6] but judge righteous judgment. Then said some of them of Jerusalem, Is not this he whom they seek to kill? And lo, he [speaketh] openly, and no man says anything to him. Perhaps the elders know in truth that this is the Christ? But behold,[7] we know this [man] whence he is: and the Christ when he cometh, no man knoweth whence he is.

And Jesus lifted up his voice, and taught in the temple, saying, Ye know me, and ye know whence I am: and I am not come of myself, but he that sent me is true, and ye know him not. For I

---

[1] R.V. marg. Cureton. Bezae.
[2] Or, 'accomplished.'
[3] Cureton.
[4] Cureton.
[5] Cureton.
[6] Cureton.
[7] Cureton.

29 know him: because I was with him, and he hath
30 sent me. And they sought to take him: but no
man laid hands on him, because his hour was not
31 yet come. And many of the town believed on him,
and said, The Christ when he cometh, will he shew
more signs than this man shews?

32 And the chief priests and Pharisees heard that
the people murmured; and they sent officers to take
33 him. Jesus said unto them, Yet a little while I am
34 with you, and I go unto him that sent me, and ye
shall seek me, and shall not find me: and whither I
35 go, ye cannot come. The Jews said among themselves, Whither will this [man] go, that we shall not find him? will he perhaps go teaching the seed of the
36 Gentiles, that we shall not find him? And what is the word that he said, I go away, and ye shall not find me: and that he said, Whither I go, ye cannot
37 come? And in the great day of the feast, Jesus stood and cried, saying, If any man thirst, let him
38 come unto me, and drink. Every one that believeth on me, as the scripture hath said, rivers of living
39 water shall flow out of his belly. But this he spake of the Spirit, which they that believed on him should receive: for till that time . . . . . was not yet given; because Jesus had not . . . . received
40 his glory. Then some people of the crowd . . . . .
41 said, Of a truth this is the Christ. And others said,
42 How shall the Christ come out of Galilee? Is it not written thus, That the Christ shall be of the seed of David, and shall come from Bethlehem, David's own
43 town? And there was a division among the crowd
44 because of him. And there were others who would have taken him, but no man was able to lay hands

on him. And those officers returned, and came to that 45 multitude and to the Pharisees; and the priests and Pharisees said, Have ye not brought him? The officers 46 said to them, Never man spake what this man spake. Then said the Pharisees to those officers, Are ye also 47 deceived? For who of the chief men or of the Pharisees 48 has believed on him? only this mob who knoweth not 49 the law. Nicodemus[1] said unto them, he that came unto him before by night, The law, doth it judge any 50 man, until we hear him, and know what he did? 51 They say unto him, Art thou perhaps also of Galilee? 52 Search, and look, for no prophet ariseth out of Galilee.[2]

Again[3] Jesus said unto them, I am the light of 8 the world: he that followeth me doth not walk in darkness, but findeth the light of life. The Jews 13 said unto him, Thou bearest record of thyself; thy record is not true. Jesus said unto them, Even if I 14 bear record of myself, my record is true: because I know whence I came, and whither I go; and ye neither [know] whence I came, nor whither I go. Ye 15 judge after the body; I judge no man. And if I judge, 16 my judgment is true: because I am not alone, but I and he[4] who sent me. It is also written in your law, 17 that the testimony of two men is true. I am one that 18 beareth witness of myself, and the Father that sent me beareth witness of me. They say unto him, Where 19 is thy Father? He said unto them, Ye neither know me, nor my Father: if ye had known me, ye should have known my Father also. These things spake he 20 in the treasury, and in the temple: and no man took hold of him, because his hour was not yet come.

Again he said unto them, I go my way, and ye 21 shall seek me, and shall die in your sins: and whither

---

[1] Ms. 'Nicodemus.'
[2] Omit v. 53. R.V.
[3] Omit vv. 1 to 11. R.V. marg.
[4] Bezae.

22
23 I go, ye cannot ... kill himself? ... ye ... beneath;
... from above: ... ye ... of ... world; and I am
24 not of it ... ye shall die in your sins: if ... ye ...
25 not that I am he, ye shall die in your sins. They say
26 ... Who art thou? He said unto them ... I have ...
to say concerning you and to judge: ... but he who
sent me is true; and these things which I have heard
27 of him speak I in the world. And they knew not that
he spake unto them of the Father.

28   Again Jesus said unto them, When ye have
lifted up the Son of man, then shall ye know that
I am he; and ... I do nothing of myself; but as
29 the Father hath taught me ... thus I ... And he
who sent me is with me: ... because I do ... him.
30
31 And as ... these ... many ... on him. ... Jesus ...
which believed on him, ... ye ... my disciples indeed;
32 and ye shall know the truth, and the truth shall make
33 you free. They say unto him, ... were in bondage ...
34 how sayest thou, Ye shall become free men? Our
Lord said unto them, Verily, verily, I say unto you,
35 Whoso committeth sin is a slave. And the slave ...
abideth ... for ever ... in the house: the son ...
36 abideth ever. ... shall make you free, ... ye shall
37 be ... I know ... ye ... and ye seek ... to kill me
38 because my word has no free course with you. What I
39 have seen with ... ye ... your father. ... our own
father Abraham. He said unto them, If ye were
40 children ... But now, behold, ye seek to kill me, a
man ... am speaking ... which ... God ... but ...
41
42 Ye ... deeds ... If God were ... love ... for I ...
to myself, ... who sent me. ... And when he speaketh
44 a lie, he speaketh of his own: for he is a liar, and the
45 father of it.[1] I who speak the truth, ye believe me

[1] Or, 'his father,' i.e. 'father of the liar.'

not. Which of you reproveth me concerning sin? 46
And if I say the truth, why do ye not believe?
For he who is of God heareth God's word: ye there- 47
fore hear it not, because ye are not.¹ The Jews 48
said, Say we not well that thou art a Samaritan, and
hast a demon? Jesus said unto them, I have not a 49
demon; but I honour my Father, and ye do dis-
honour me. And I seek not mine own glory: there 50
is one that seeketh and judgeth. Verily, verily, I 51
say unto you, Whoso keepeth my word, he shall
never taste death. The Jews say unto him, Now we 52
know it, that truly thou hast a demon. For Abraham is dead. Thou sayest, Whoso keepeth my word
shall not taste death. Art thou perhaps greater than² 53
Abraham, and than the prophets, who are dead?
whom makest thou thyself? Jesus said to them, If 54
I glorify³ myself, my glory³ is nothing: it is the
Father who glorifies³ me; he of whom ye say that he
is God: ye have not known him; I know him: 55
and if I should say, I know him not, I should
be a liar to myself, like unto you: but I know him,
and I keep his word. Abraham was longing to see 56
my day: and he saw it, and was glad. The Jews 57
say unto him, Thou art not fifty years old, and hath
Abraham seen thee? He said unto them, Verily, 58
verily, I say unto you, Before Abraham was, I have
been. Then took they up stones to cast at him: and 59
Jesus went out secretly from the temple.⁴

And as he passed by, he saw a certain blind man, **9**
who had been blind from his mother's womb. His 2
disciples ask him, Who did sin, this man, or his
people, when he was born blind? He said unto 3
them, He hath not sinned, nor yet his people: but

---

¹ A line must have been dropped here. Cod. Bezae drops the whole clause from 'because.'

² Bezae.

³ R.V. Bezae.

⁴ R.V. Bezae.

3 that the works of God should be seen in him.
4 And I must work the works of him that sent me,
while it is day: for the night cometh, when no man
5 can work. For so long as I am in the world, I am
6 the light of the world. When he had spoken these
things, he spat on the ground, and formed clay of his
spittle, and taking it up, painted it upon the eyes of
7 that blind man, and said unto him, Go, wash thy face
in the pool of Shiloah.[1] And when he had washed
8 his face, his eyes were opened. And when his neighbours saw him, and they who had seen[2] that he had
begged, they say, Is not this he who was begging?
9 Some were saying, This is he: and some were saying,
He is like him. The blind man said unto them, I am
10 he. They say unto him, How were thine eyes opened?
11 He said unto them, That man whose name is Jesus
painted clay upon them, and said unto me, Go, wash
thy face in the pool of Shiloah: and I went and
12
13 washed, and I saw. They say unto him . . . and they
14 brought him . . . Now it was the sabbath . . . But others
to
16 said . . . sinner do these . . . And they were disputing
17 one with another. And they say unto him that was
cured, What sayest thou concerning him? He said
18 unto them, . . . He is a prophet. And . . . did not
19 believe in him . . . he had been blind, . . . If this
is your son, ... Ye say that he was born blind,
20
21 . . . . now see. . . . . that this our son . . . . now
seeth, who hath given . . . . we know not. Behold
22 he too is of age,[3] ye can know it of him. These
things said his parents, because they feared the
Jews: because the scribes and Pharisees had decreed
that whoso said, He is the Christ, they would dismiss
23
24 him. Therefore said his parents, Ask him. And

[1] Hebrew Syriac— 'Sent.'
[2] Literally— 'by whom' he had been seen.'
[3] Syriac— 'master of his years.'

again they called him that was healed, and said unto 24
him, Praise God: for we know that this man is a
sinner. He that was healed said unto them, If he 25
be a sinner, I know not: but one thing I know, that
I was blind, and because of him, lo, I see. They say 26
unto him, ... healed thee? . . . . But I have 27
told you one,[1] . . . and ye heard: why do ye ask me
again? or perhaps ye desire to become his disciples?
Then they reviled him, and said unto him, Thou art 28
his disciple; and we are Moses' disciples. And we 29
know that God spake unto Moses: but we know not
this man, whence he is. The man who was healed 30
said unto them, This is to marvel at, that ye know
not from whence he is, and he hath opened my own
eyes. And we know that God heareth not the voice 31
of sinners: but whoso feareth him, and doeth his
will, him he heareth. Since the day that the world 32
was, was it not heard that [the eyes of] a blind man
were opened who was blind from his mother. If this 33
man were not of God, how did he do this? They say 34
unto him, Thou wast altogether born in sins, thou
comest teaching us? And they cast him out. And 35
Jesus heard that they had cast him out; and when
Jesus had found him, he said unto him, Dost thou
believe on the Son of man?[2] He that was healed 36
said unto him, Who is he, Lord, that I might believe
on him? Jesus said unto him, Thou hast seen him, 37
and it is he that talketh with thee. He said, Lord, 38
I believe. And falling down, he worshipped him.
Jesus said unto him, I am come for the judgment of 39
this world, that they who are blind may see; and
they who see may become blind. And when the 40
Pharisees who were near him heard, they said unto

[1] Or, 'once.'
[2] R.V. marg. Bezae.

41 him, Is it we who are blind? He said unto them, If ye were blind, ye should have no sin: but ye say, We see; therefore your sins[1] remain.

[1] Bezae.

10 Verily, verily, I say unto you, He that entereth not by the door to the fold in which the sheep are, but climbeth up by another way, he is a robber and
2 a thief. And he that entereth in by the door is the
3 shepherd . . . . . . The porter[2] openeth the door to him; and the sheep hear his voice: and he calleth his flock, the sheep, by name, and he leadeth
4 them out. And when he leadeth out his flock, he goeth before them, and his own sheep follow him,
5 because the sheep know his voice. But a stranger will the sheep not follow, but will take themselves away . . . . because they know not the voice of a
6 stranger. These things Jesus spake with them in a parable: and they did not understand.

[2] Syriac— 'keeper of the door.'

7 Again Jesus said unto them, Verily, verily, I say unto you, I am the door of the sheep.
8 And all those who came are thieves and robbers:
9 but the flock did not hear them. I am the door of the sheep: and by me every one who enters shall live,
10 and shall go in and out, and find pasture. But the thief cometh not but that he may steal, and kill and destroy: but I am come that they might have life,
11 and that they might have abundance. I am the good shepherd: and the good shepherd giveth his
12 his life for . . . . But the hireling, ... are not, ... when . . . . wolf coming, leaveth the sheep, ... and the wolf coming, snatcheth and scattereth.
13 Because he is an hireling in it, and careth not about
14 it. I am the good shepherd, and know mine own,[3] and mine own know me; and I am known of mine

[3] R.V. Bezae.

[1] R.V. Bezae.

own,[1] even as my Father knoweth me, and I know 15 my Father. And I lay down my life for the sheep. And other sheep I have, which are not of this fold: and 16 them also I must bring, and they also shall hear my voice; and the flock shall all be one, and one shepherd. Therefore doth my Father love me, because I lay 17 down my life, that I might take it up again. No 18 man taketh it from me, but I lay it down of myself; for I have power to lay it down, and to take it up again; because this commandment have I received of my Father. And as he was saying these things, 19 there was a division among the Jews; because some 20 of them were saying, He hath a demon, and is mad; why are ye standing and hearing him? But others 21 said, These words are not of a demon. Can a demon open the eyes of the blind?

[2] 'honour.'

And it was the feast at Jerusalem which is called 22 the dedication[2] of the sanctuary, and it was winter. And Jesus was walking in Solomon's porch. . . . unto 23 him, How long dost thou take . . . . If thou be the 24 Christ, tell us plainly. He said unto them, ... I 25 speak . . . . ye believe not: and the works that I do in my Father's name, they bear witness of me. But ye believe not, because ye are not of my sheep, 26 . . . . . I said unto you. . . . . . my voice, ... 27 to The Father, which gave me, is greater than all; and 29 there is no man who snatcheth them out of the Father's hand. I and my Father are one. When he 30 31 had said these things, they took up stones to stone him. Jesus said unto them, Many works of the 32 Father I have shewed you; for which of these works are ye stoning me? The Jews say unto him, Not for 33 a good work do we stone thee, but because whilst thou

34 art . . . . a man, thou makest . . . . God. Jesus
35 said unto them, Is it not . . . . . . written . . . . . .
36 gods? . . . . whom the Father hath sanctified, and
sent into the world, ye say, Thou blasphemest;
37 because I said, the Son of God? And if I do not
38 . . . . believe me not. But if I do, even if ye believe
to
41 me not, ... spake . . . .
42 And many . . . . . . in him.

11 And there was . . . . of Beth . . . . the brother
1
to . . . . and of Martha . . . is not . . . Son of . . . .
5 Lazar. And when he heard that Lazar was sick,
6
7 he stayed in his place two days. And he said to his
8 disciples, Come, let us go to Judaea. His disciples
say unto him, Our Master, behold, the Jews have
been seeking to stone thee; and goest thou thither
9 again? Jesus said unto them, Are there not twelve
hours in the day? He who walketh in the day . . . .
stumbleth not, because he seeth the light of this world.
10 But he who walketh in the night stumbleth, because
11 the light is not in him. And when he had said
these things, he said unto them, Lazar, our friend, is
12 sleeping; but I go, that I may wake him.[1] They say [1] Bezae.
unto him, Our Lord, if he is sleeping, he will be
13 healed.[2] But Jesus had said to them concerning [2] Bezae.
Lazar that he was dead; and they were thinking
14 that he had spoken about sleep. Jesus said again
15 to them plainly, Lazar is dead. And I am glad for
your sakes, that ye may believe, that I was not there;
16 but come, let us go to him. Thomas[3] said to his [3] Or, 'the twin.'
fellow-disciples, Come, let us go also, let us die
17 with him. And when Jesus came to Bethany,[4] [4] Bezae.
he found that they had buried Lazar four days
18 before. Now Bethany was distant from Jerusalem

fifteen[1] stadia. . . . . And many . . . . came out to 19
Bethany to console Martha and Mary. And when 20
Martha heard that Jesus was coming, she went
out to meet him: and Mary returned home. And 21
Martha said unto him, If thou hadst been here, my
brother had not died. But even now[2] I know, that 22
what thou shalt ask, God will give it thee. Jesus 23
. . . . . unto her, Thy brother . . . . Martha 24
that in the resurrection . . . . at the last day. Jesus 25
. . . . I am the resurrection, and whosoever believeth
in me, even if were dead, he shall live: and whoso- 26
ever liveth and believeth in me shall never die.
Believest thou these things? Martha saith unto 27
him, Yea, Lord: I believe that thou art the Christ,
the Son of God, which shall come into the world.
And when she had said these things,[3] she went 28
silently, and called Mary, and said unto her, Our
Master is come, and calleth thee. And when Mary 29
heard, she sprang up, and went to him eagerly.
And Jesus had not until now entered into the town, 30
but was in that place where Martha met him. Also 31
those who had consoled Mary, when they saw that
she was thus amazed and had gone out, followed her.
They supposed that she was going to the grave to weep.
And when she, Mary, reached Jesus, she fell at his 32
feet, and said unto him, If thou hadst been here,
Lord, my brother had not died. And when Jesus 33
saw her weeping, and saw the Jews who were with her
weeping, he was troubled in his soul, and was disturbed[4] in his spirit, and said, Where have ye laid 34
him? They say unto him, Our Lord, come, see.
And the tears of Jesus were coming. And when 35
the Jews saw, they were saying, Behold how 36

---

[1] Bezae.

[2] R. V. Bezae.

[3] Bezae.

[4] 'disturbed' or 'angry.'

37 he loved him! And there were some of them who said, This man, who hath opened the eyes of him who was blind from his mother's womb, could he not have caused that this man should not have
38 died? But Jesus, being troubled in himself, came to the grave. And the grave was hollowed out like
39 a cave, and the door was covered by a stone. Jesus said, Take ye away this stone. Martha saith unto him, Lord Why are they lifting away the stone?
40 Behold, he stinketh, for he hath been four days. He said unto her, I said unto thee, that, if thou wouldest
41 believe, thou shouldest see the glory of God. Then those men who were standing, came near, and raised the stone. But he lifted up his eyes to heaven, and said, Father, I thank thee that thou hast heard me.
42 And I know that thou hearest me always: but because of this crowd of people I say these things,
43 that they may believe that thou hast sent me. And when he had said these things,[1] he cried with a loud
44 voice, and said, Lazar, come forth, come out. And in that hour that dead man came forth, bound hand and foot with graveclothes: and his face was bound with a linen napkin. Then said our Lord,
45 Loose him, and let him go. And many Jews which came to Jesus because of Mary, believed in Jesus
46 from that hour. And there were some of them who believed not, but went their ways to the Pharisees, and related to them what Jesus had done.
47 Then the chief priests and the Pharisees assembled, and made a council, and they were saying, What shall we do? for this man doeth many miracles.
48 And if we let him alone thus,[2] all men will believe on him: and the Romans will come, taking away

[1] Bezae.
[2] Bezae.

our city and our nation. Now one of them, whose 49
name was Caipha, their own high priest of that year,
this same Caipha said unto them, Ye know nothing,
nor con . . . . . that it is expedient for us, that one 50
man should die for all the nation, and that the whole
nation perish not. But this word he spake not of 51
his own mind: but because he was high priest, he
prophesied, because Jesus was about to die for the
nation; and not for the nation only, but also that 52
the children of God who are scattered abroad should
be gathered into one. Now from that day forth 53
they took counsel together to kill him. But Jesus 54
walked no more boldly in sight of the Jews but
went his way to a country which was near to . . . .
which is called Ephraim, and there he went about
with his disciples.

And . . . . . was nigh at hand: and many went 55
up out of the country to Jerusalem to sanctify themselves. And they were seeking for Jesus, and saying 56
one to another in the temple, Do ye suppose that
perhaps he will not come to the feast? And the 57
chief priests and the Pharisees commanded, that
whosoever should see him, should come and shew it
to them, that they might take him.

And six days before it was the unleavened bread, 12
Jesus came to the village of Bethany, to Lazarus, he
who had been dead, and was alive. And he[1] made 2
him a supper there; and Lazarus was one of those
seated at meat who were sitting with him; but
Martha was cumbered with service. Now Mary 3
took an alabaster box of a pound of ointment of
pure[2] spikenard, of great price, and poured it on
the head of Jesus while he sat at meat, and she

[1] MS. has 'he made,' but a slight change would give 'they made.'

[2] Syriac keeps πιστικῆς.

3 anointed his feet, and wiped them with her hair: and
all the house was filled with the odour of the oint-
4 ment. And Juda Scariota, one of the disciples, he
5 who should betray him, said, Why was not this ointment sold for three hundred pence, and given to the
6 poor? Now Juda did not care for the poor, but
because he was a thief, and the bag of the poor was
7 with him.[1] When Jesus heard it, he said unto him,
Let her alone: she is keeping it .... of my burial.[2]
9 And much people of the Jews knew that he was
there: and they came there, not in order that they
might see Jesus, but Lazar, whom he had raised from
10 amongst the dead. And the chief priests consulted
11 that they might kill Lazar also; for because of Lazar
12 many believed on Jesus. And on the next day ... he
went out, and came to the Mount of Olives .... and
those great multitudes ..... to the feast, when they
13 heard that Jesus was coming to Jerusalem, they took
branches of palm-trees, and went forth to meet him,
and they were crying and saying .... who cometh
14 in the name of the Lord, the King of Israel. But
Jesus ... on ... that is written by Zakaria the pro-
15 phet. Fear not, daughter of Sion: behold, thy King
cometh unto thee, and he is riding on a foal the son
16 of an ass. These things his disciples knew not from
the first: but when our Lord received his glory, they
remembered that these things were written concerning him, and [that] they did these things unto
17 him. ..... that was with him related how he
had called Lazar from the grave, and raised him up
18
19 ... that they heard ... done ... The Pharisees
.... saying .... See ye that ye prevail nothing?
behold, all the world is gone after him.

[1] Or, 'he had the bag of the poor.'
[2] c. 8 is omitted.

And there were some heathens who had come up 20
to worship at the feast: and they came and said to 21
Philip, which was of Bethsaida of Galilee, Sir, we
would see Jesus. And Philip went and told Andrew: 22
and they both came and told Jesus. Jesus said unto 23
them, The hour is come, ... the Son .... Verily 24
unto you, That a grain of wheat, unless it fall and die
in the earth, it is alone: but if it falls and dies, it
yieldeth much fruit. He that loveth his life shall lose 25
it; and he that hateth his life in this world shall
keep it unto life eternal. Whoso will serve me, let 26
him follow me; and where I am, there shall also my
servant be: and whoso serveth me, him will the
Father honour. Behold, now is my soul troubled; 27
and what shall I say? Father, save me from this
hour: but for this cause came I unto this hour.
Father, glorify thy name. And in that hour a voice 28
was heard from . . . . . . I have glorified . . . . . I to
. . . . . . were . . . . . because of me . . . . . . now 31
. . . . of the world . . . . to
abideth for ever: and how sayest thou, The Son of 34
man must be lifted up? .... this Son of man?
Jesus saith unto them, A little while 35
light . . . . with you . . . . . . ye have the
light, lest . . . . believe . . . . that the 36
children . . . . . .
. . . . done . . . . . on him: . . . . that 37
of Isaia the prophet might be fulfilled; he had said 38
. . . . our report? . . . . to whom . . . . said 39
their eyes, that they should not see 40
. . . . . . and should hear . . . . . prophet 41
said . . . . and his glory, ... and spake . . . . .
But . . . . believed in Jesus; . . . . because of the 42

42 Pharisees .... confess him, ... should dismiss
43 them ..... the glory¹ of man .... more than ¹ R.V.
44 .... But ....   Bezae.
to
47 my words, ... him ..... for I came not to
48 judge the world, but to save the world. Whoso .. r
   .... me, and receiveth not my words, hath ....
49 him : .... with him, ... in the last day. For
   I have not spoken my own words; but the Father
   which sent me, he hath commanded me what I
50 should say, and what I should speak. And I know
   that his commandments are life everlasting: and
   what I speak, as he hath commanded me, so I speak.

13 Now before the unleavened bread, Jesus knew
that his hour was come that he should depart out of
this world unto his Father, loving his own which are
2 in this world, he loved them unto the end. And
there was a supper, and Satan had put into the heart
of Juda, son of Simon Scariota, so that he might
3 betray him. And because Jesus knew that the
Father had given all things into his hands, and he
knew that he was come from God, and went to God;
4 he rose, and laid aside his garments; and took
5 a towel, and cast it about his loins. And he took
water, and poured it into a wash-basin, and began to
wash the feet of his disciples, and to wipe them with
6 the towel which he had cast about his loins. And
when he came to Simon Cepha, Simon said unto
7 him, Lord, dost thou wash my feet? Jesus said unto
him, What I do unto thee thou knowest not; but
8 after a while thou shalt know. Simon said unto him,
Thou shalt never wash my feet. Jesus said unto
him, Except I wash thee, thou hast no part with me.
9 Simon saith unto him, Then, Lord, thou shalt wash

not my feet only, but also my hands and my head. 9
Jesus saith to him, He that is bathed needeth not 10
save to wash his feet only, because he is clean every
whit: and ye also are clean, but not all of you. For 11
he knew who was betraying him; therefore he said
this word. Now when he had washed their feet, he 12
took his garment, and sat down. He said unto them,
Know ye what I have done to you? Behold, ye call 13
me Our Master and Our Lord: and ye say well;
for so I am. And if I, your Master and your Lord, 14
have washed your feet; how much is it fitting that
ye also should wash one another's feet? But I have 15
shewed you this example, that as I have done to you,
ye should do.¹

Verily, verily, I say unto you, There is no servant 16
who is greater than his lord; and no messenger²
greater than he who hath sent him. If ye know 17
and do these things, blessed are ye. I speak not of 18
every man: because I know those whom I have
chosen: but in order that the scripture may be fulfilled which saith, He that eateth bread with me
hath lifted up his heel against me. . . . . I tell you 19
before it come to pass, that when it is come to pass,
ye may know that I am he. Verily I say unto you, 20
He that receiveth whomsoever I send receiveth me;
and he that . . . . me . . . . . he receiveth. And 21
when Jesus had said these things, he was troubled in
his spirit, and testified, and said, Verily I say unto
you, that one of you shall betray me. Then his dis- 22
ciples looked one on another, wondering of whom he
thus spake. Then one of his disciples said 23
who . . . . . who was leaning . . . . . Simon Cepha 24
beckoned to him, that he should ask about whom

¹ Bezae.

² Or, 'apostle.'

25 . . . . the disciple . . . . on . . . . unto him . . . .
26 he who dips . . . . the bread I shall give unto him.
27 And Jesus dipped the bread, and gave it to Juda, the son of Simon Scariota. And after the bread Satan had entered into him. . . . Jesus . . . unto him, That
28 thou doest, do quickly. And . . . . . not . . . . .
29 they supposed . . . . . . Juda had the bag,[1] that he had commanded him what he should buy for the feast, and what he should give to the poor.

[1] Or, 'the bag was with Judas.'

30 Then when Juda had risen and received the bread,
31 he went out, and the time was night. And when he was gone out, Jesus said, Behold, henceforth is the Son of man glorified, and God is glorified in him.
32 And God who glorifies him in himself, shall straight-
33 way glorify him. Children, yet a little while I am with you. And ye shall seek me: as I said unto the Jews, that whither I go, they cannot come; and behold,
34 I say unto you also. But now a new commandment I give unto you, That ye love one another; as I have
35 loved you. For by this shall all men know that ye are my disciples, if there be love in you one to
36 another. Simon Cepha said unto him, Lord, whither goest thou? He said unto him, Whither I go thou canst not come now; but afterwards thou shalt follow
37 me. Simon said unto him, Why cannot I follow thee?
38 I will lay down my life now for thy sake. Jesus said unto him, Wilt thou lay down my life for my sake? Verily I say unto thee, Before the cock has yet crowed twice, thou shall deny me thrice.

14 Jesus said, Let not your heart be troubled: believe
2 in God, and in me ye are believing. There are many mansions in the house of my Father, and if it were not so, I would have told you that I go to prepare a place

for you. And if I go and prepare for you, I will 3
come again, and lead you unto myself; that where I
am, there ye may be also. And whither I go ye 4
know, and the way ye know. Thoma said unto him, 5
Lord, we know not whither thou goest; how can
we know the way, what it is? Jesus said unto 6
him, I, I am the way, and the truth, and the life:
no man cometh unto my Father, but by me. If 7
.... me, ye would have known my Father also: and
from henceforth ye know him, and have seen him.
Philip said unto him, Our Lord, shew us the Father, 8
and it sufficeth us. Jesus said unto him, All the 9
long .... with you, and not .... he who hath
seen me .... my Father; .... and how ....
thou, shew us the F ... Believe ye ... that I am 10
in the Father, ... and my Father in me¹? Verily 12
I say ..... he that believeth ..... these works
.... that I do, he .... and greater than .....
that the Father may be glorified in his Son 13
²If ye love me, keep my commandments. And I 15 16
will pray my Father, and he shall give you .....
Comforter,³ ... with you for ever; ... truth; whom 17
the world .... receive him, ... has seen him
.... neither known him; but ye know him, who
dwelleth with you ... and shall be [in] you. And 18
I will not leave you orphans: but I will come unto
you. Yet a little while, and the world seeth me 19
not; and ye shall see me: and I am living, and ye
shall live also. And in those days ye shall know that 20
I am in my Father, and ye in me, and I in you. He 21
that hath my commandments, and keepeth them, he it
is that loveth me: and he that loveth me, he also shall
be loved of my Father, and I also will love him, and

¹ v. 11 is wanting, with part of v. 10.

² v. 14 is omitted.

³ Syriac— 'Paraclete.'

22 will manifest myself to him. Thoma saith unto him, Our Lord, how is it that thou wilt manifest thyself unto us, and dost not manifest thyself unto
23 the world? Jesus said unto him, He who loveth me will keep my word: and my Father will love him, and we come unto him, and will make abode
24 with him. He who loveth me not, keepeth not my words: and the word . . . . . and that word is[1] not
25 mine, but his that sent me. These things have I
26 spoken unto you, whilst I am present with you. But that Spirit, the Comforter,[2] whom my Father will send unto you in my name, he shall teach you all things, and he shall remind you of all that I have
27 said. Peace I leave with you, my own peace I give unto you: not as . . . . . I give . . . . be troubled,
28 . . . . and I come . . . . my Father who is greater
29 than I. And now . . . . . . you, when it is not yet come to pass, that when it is come to pass, ye might
30 believe. Henceforth I will not talk with you: for the prince of the world cometh, and hath nothing in me.
31 But that the world may know that I love my Father; as my Father commanded me, even so I do. Arise, let us go hence.

15 I am the vine of truth, and my Father is the
2 husbandman. Every vine . . . . . not fruit . . . . .
to
4 that beareth . . . . much . . . . . so also . . . . ye
5 can do nothing, without me. I am the vine, and ye are the branches: He that is in me, and
6 I in him, . . . ye can do no . . . . . out as a
to branch which is withered, and is cast out; and they
10 gather it, and throw it . . . . . in my love; even as I have kept my Father's commandments, and abide
11 in his love. These things have I spoken unto you,

[1] Or, 'was.'
[2] Syriac—'Paraclete.'

. . . . 12
. . . . . I call you . . . . . . because the servant to 15
knoweth not what his lord doeth: but I have called
you friends; because all that I have heard from¹ my
Father . . . . you. And ye have not chosen me, 16
but I have chosen you, and ordained you, that ye
should go and bring forth . . . . and your fruit . . . .
that when ye shall ask anything of my Father in my
name, he may give it you. But this I command you, 17
that ye be loving one another. And if the world 18
. . . . . know . . . . . me before you. . . . . . the 19
world, the world . . . . its own : . . . . not . . . . .
the world . . . . . and I have chosen you out of the
world, therefore the world hateth you. And re- 20
member that I said unto you, The servant is not
greater than his lord. If they have persecuted me,
they will also persecute you; and if they have heard
and kept my word, they will keep yours also. All 21
these things will they do unto you for my own name's
sake, because they know not him that sent me. And 22
if I had not come and spoken unto them, they had not
had sins: but now they have no excuse for their sins.
Because that whoso hateth me hateth my Father also. 23
And if I had not done in their presence² the works 24
which none other man did, they had not had . . . now
. . . both seen and hated . . . also. But . . . word . . . 25
in their law . . . when . . . Comforter³ . . . unto you 26
from my Father, . . . from before . . . with me . . . 27

But . . . . . . have I spoken unto you, that ye **16**
should not be offended. For they shall put you out 2
of their synagogues: and the hour cometh, that whoso
killeth you will think that he serveth God.⁴ These 4
things have I spoken with you, that when the hour

¹ R.V. Bezae.

² Syriac— 'eyes.'

³ Syriac— 'Paraclete.'

⁴ v. 3 is omitted.

4 shall come, ye may remember that I told you these
things, which I told you not from the beginning,
5 because I was with you. But now that I go to him
that sent me, none of you asketh me, Whither goest
6 thou? For because I have said these things unto
you, sorrow hath come and hath filled your hearts.
7 But I tell you the truth; It is expedient for you that
I go away: because if I go not away, the Comforter[1]   [1] Syriac—'Paraclete.'
will not come unto you; but when I have gone, I will
8 send the Comforter unto you. But when he is come, he
will reprove the world for its sins, and about its[2] right- [2] Or, 'his.'
9 eousness, and about judgment: and about sins, that
10 they have not believed on me; but about righteousness,
11 because I go to my Father, ... ye see me ... about
to
13 judgment, ... will guide you ... truth: because
to
16 ... of ... mind; but all ... he heareth ... my
17 Father. And his disciples say to each other, What is
this that he saith, ... A little while ... and ye shall
not see me: and again a little while, and ye shall
see me: and that he said, I go my way to my
18 Father? What then is this little while that he said?
19 .... Jesus knew what ..... were .... to ask
him; he said unto them, ... Do ye seek for this
that I said unto you, ... and ye shall not see me: ...
20 a little while and ye shall see me? Verily, verily,
I say unto you, That ye shall weep, and wail, and
sigh, and the world shall rejoice: ye shall be anxious,
21 but your sorrow shall become[3] joy. A woman   [3] Bezae.
to who is in travail is sorrowful, because ......
23 say ..... anything of my Father in my name
24 .... Hitherto ye have asked .... that ... may
25 be fulfilled ... cometh .... in proverbs ....
I shall shew you concerning my Father ......

ye shall ask in my name 26
. . . . God . . . . into the world : to 28
unto . . . . . His disciples said unto him, . . . now 29
speakest thou, . . . and . . . proverb. Now we know¹ 30
that thou . . . all . . . and . . . not . . . we believe
that thou art sent . . . from God. Jesus said unto 31
them, Behold, now ye believe in me. Behold, 32
the hour cometh, and² is come, that ye shall be
scattered, every man to his place, and shall leave me
alone: and I am not alone, because the Father is
with me. These things I have spoken unto you, that 33
in me ye might have peace: and in the world ye
shall have tribulation: but fear not, for I have over-
come the world.

And when Jesus had said these things, he lifted **17**
up his eyes to heaven, and said, My Father, the hour
is come; glorify thy Son, that thy Son may glorify
thee: as thou hast given him power over all flesh, that 2
to every one whom thou hast given him, he should give
eternal life. This is life eternal, that they should know 3
thee, that thou art the only . . . God, and him whom
thou hast sent, Jesus, the Christ. I have glorified thee 4
on the earth: and the work which thou gavest me to
do I have finished. And now also give me the glory, 5
my Father, from beside thyself, from that which thou
gavest me when the world was not yet. And I have 6
manifested thy name unto the men which thou gavest
me out of the world; for thine they were, and thou
gavest them me; and they have kept thy word.
And now they³ have known that all which thou hast 7
given me is from thee. . . . . . For the words which 8
. . . . I have given . . . . received . . . . and have
known surely . . . . . but for them which thou hast 9

¹ R.V. Bezae.

² Bezae.

³ Or, 'I.'

10 given me; for they are thine. And all that is mine is thine, and thine is mine; and I am glorified in them.
11 And henceforth I am not in the world, and these are in the world, and I come to thee. O my holy
12 Father, take, keep them in thy name.¹ While I was with them in the world, I kept them . . . . . . of them . . . . except the son of perdition; that . . . .
13 is written might be fulfilled. Now . . . . . . and
14 these . . . . . in the world, ... not . . . . .
15 of the world. I pray thee . . . . . them . . . . . .
16 . . . . of the world, ... not . . . .
17 Sanctify . . . . thy . . . . is truth.
18 . . . . hast sent . . . .
19 . . . their sakes . . . . myself, ... through the
20 truth. . . . . for . . . I pray . . . but also for . . . .
21 them which shall b . . . . through their word; that they all may be one, as thou . . . . . that the world
22 may believe that thou hast sent me. And the glory which thou gavest me I have given them; that they
23 may be one, even as we are one: I shall be with them, and thou with me, that they may become perfect in one; that the world may know that thou hast sent me, and hast loved them, even as, Father,
24 thou hast loved me. And what thou hast given me, I will that where I am, these may also be with me; that they may behold the glory which thou hast given me; and that thou hast loved me before the world
25 was, O my righteous Father. And the world hath not known thee: but I have known thee, and those have
26 known that thou hast sent me. And I have made known unto them thy name, and will make it known²: so that the love wherewith thou hast loved me may be in them, and I also may be in them.

¹ The last clause of r. 11 is omitted.

² R.V. Pezae

These things spake Jesus, and went forth with his **18** disciples over the brook Kedron, [to] the mountain, the place where there was a garden, and he entered there, he and his disciples. But Juda, the betrayer, 2 knew that place: for many times Jesus came there together with his disciples. But Juda, the betrayer, 3 brought with him a band, and some of the chief priests and Pharisees, and officers, and a crowd of people carrying lanterns and lamps, and he came thither. And when Jesus saw all that came against[1] 4 him, he went forth, saying unto them, What seek ye? They say unto him, Jesus of Nazareth. He 5 saith unto them, I am he. But Juda also stood with them. And as Jesus said these things, I am he, 6 they went backward, and fell to the ground. And 7 Jesus said to them again, Whom seek ye? They say unto him, Jesus of Nazareth. He said unto them, I 8 have told you that I am he: if ye seek me, let [these] go their way: that the word might be fulfilled which 9 he spake, Of them which thou gavest me have I lost none. Then Simon Cepha drew a sword, and smote 10 the high priest's servant, and took off his right ear; and the name of the man was Malchus. And Jesus 11 said unto Cepha, Put back the sword . . . . into its place: the cup which my Father hath given me, shall I not drink it? And the band and the chiliarch 12 and the officers of the Jews bound him, and brought 13 him first to Hannan, the father-in-law of Caiapha, which was the high priest of that year. Now 24 Hannan sent him bound unto Caiapha . . . . . . counsel to the Jews, ... that one man 14 should die for the people. [2]But Simon Cepha and 15 one of the disciples, who was known to the high

---

[1] Bezae.

[2] The scribe has evidently omitted a line here— 'followed Jesus, and so did another disciple.'

priest, because of this he went with Jesus into the palace.

19 Then the high priest asked Jesus about his disciples, who they were, and about his doctrine, what
20 it was. Jesus said unto him, I spake openly with the world; and at all times I taught in the synagogue, and in the temple, and where all the Jews are assembled; and in secret have I said nothing.
21 But now why dost thou ask me? Ask them which heard me, what I have spoken with them: behold,
22 they know what I have spoken. When he had thus spoken, one of the officers which stood by struck Jesus on the cheek, and said unto him, Dost thou thus give
23 an answer to the high priest? Jesus said unto him, I have spoken well: why smitest thou me?

16 But Simon Cepha was standing without at the [door]. And the disciple, which was known unto the high priest, went out, and spoke to the
17 keeper of the door, and brought in Simon. When . . . . the handmaid of the door-keeper saw him, ... she said to him, Art thou not also one of this man's disciples? He saith unto her, ... not.
18 Now there was there . . . . . . and the officers, and they had laid for themselves a fire in the court to warm themselves, for it was freezing. Now Simon also was standing with them, and warming himself.
25 . . . these people . . . Art not thou also . . . of his disciples? But he denied it, and said, I am not.
26 And one of the servants of the high priest answered (being his kinsman whose . . . . Simon had cut off), ... to Simon . . . . I . . . . in the garden with
27 him? And again he denied . . . . that not . . . . . the cock . . . . .

¹ Or, 'prae- torium.'

.... led they Jesus from Caiaphas ..... to 28 the hall of judgment,¹ to deliver him to the governor: but they went not into the judgment-hall, that they should not be defiled whilst they were eating the unleavened bread. And Pilate went out unto them, 29 and said unto them, What accusation have you against this man? They answered, and said, If he 30 were not a malefactor, we would not even have delivered him up unto thee. Pilate said unto them, 31 Then take him, and judge him according to law. The Jews said unto him, We have no power to put .... to death:

[xviii. 32 *to* xix. 39 *are lost.*]

..... the body of Jesus, wrapped it in linen 19 clothes with the aromatic ointment, as was the law of 40 the Jews that they should be buried. And there 41 was a garden in that place, and in the garden was a sepulchre, in which no man had been buried. And 42 with haste they laid him there .... sabbath .... for it was near to the place ....

...... the first day of the week, while it was 20 yet dark in the early morning, ... Mary Magdalene to the sepulchre, and saw that the stone was rolled away, and lifted from the mouth of the sepulchre. And she ran, she came to Simon Cepha, 2 and to that disciple whom Jesus loved, and saith unto them, They have taken away our Lord out of the sepulchre, and I know not where they have borne him. And the two went forth to go to the sepulchre, 3 and they were running: .... disciple .... Simon, 4 and came .... and stooped down, ... they when 5 .... to the sepulchre .... reached ..... and 6

7 saw the linen clothes, and the napkin that was rolled
8 up together and placed apart. And then went in also that disciple to the grave, and they saw and believed.
9 Because that until now they did not know from the
10 scriptures that he was to rise from among the dead. But when the disciples saw these things, they went their
11 way. But Mary was standing by the grave and weeping:
12 and while she was weeping, she looked at the sepulchre, and saw there two angels in white garments, sitting one at the pillows of the place in which Jesus had been
13 lying, and one at the [place of the] feet. Those angels say unto her, Woman, why weepest thou? and whom seekest thou? She saith unto them, Because they have lifted away my Lord, and I know not where they
14 have laid him. And when she had said these things, she turned herself back, and saw Jesus standing, and
15 knew not that he was Jesus. But he said unto her, Woman, why weepest thou? and whom seekest thou? And she supposed that he was the gardener. She said unto him, Sir, if thou hast taken him away, tell me where thou hast laid him. I will go and take
16 him away. Then Jesus saith unto her, Mary. And she understood him, and answered, saying unto him, Rabbuli.[1] And she ran towards him that she might
17 touch him. But he said unto her, Touch me not; for I am not yet ascended to my Father: but go unto my brethren, and say unto them, Behold, I ascend unto my Father, and your Father, and to
18 my God, and your God. And Mary came and told the disciples that she had seen our Lord, and the things he had revealed to her she told unto them.[2]
19 And on the same day, which was the first of

[1] Or, 'my master.'
[2] Berae.

the week, in the place where the disciples were, and 19
the doors were shut for fear of the Jews, came Jesus,
and stood amongst them, and saith unto them, Peace
be with you. And when he had so said, he shewed 20
them his hands and his side. And when the disciples 21
saw him, they were glad. Again he said unto them,
Peace be with you: even as my Father hath sent
me, send I you. And when he had said these things, 22
he breathed in their faces, and said unto them, Receive ye the Holy Ghost: whose soever sins ye remit, 23
they are remitted unto him; and whose ye retain
against him, they[1] are retained.

[1] Cod., 'he is retained.'

But Thoma, one of the twelve, was not there 24
with the others when Jesus came unto them. They 25
say unto him, Our Lord is come, and we have seen
him. He saith to them, Except I shall see his hands,
and the place of those nails, and shall stretch forth
my finger into the places, and shall stretch forth my
hand into his side, I will not believe.

And after eight days, on the next first [day] of the 26
week, the disciples were assembled together in the
house, and Thoma with them: and the doors were
shut. Jesus came and stood amongst them, and said
unto them, Peace be with you. Then he said to 27
Thoma, Reach hither thy finger, and see my hands;
and put thy hand on my side: and be not faithless.
Thoma said unto him, My Lord and my God. Jesus 28 29
saith unto him, Now that thou hast seen me, thou
hast believed in me: blessed are they that have not
seen, and have believed in me.

And many [other] signs did Jesus shew to his 30
disciples, which are not written in this book: but 31
these that are written, are that ye may believe that

31 Jesus is the Christ, the Son of God; that ye may believe in him, and may live by his name.

21 After these things Jesus appeared to his disciples at the lake of Tiberias; and appeared to 2 them on this wise. When they were assembled all together, Simon Cepha, and Thoma, and Nathanael, he who was of Catana of Galilee, and the sons of Zebedee, and two others of the disciples, 3 Simon saith unto them, I go a-fishing. They say unto him, We also go with thee. And they went up, and sat in the boat; and on that night they caught 4 nothing. And when the day was breaking,[1] Jesus [1 R. V.] came and stood on the shore of the lake: and his 5 disciples understood not that it was he. He said unto them, Children, have ye aught to eat[2]? They [2 R.V. Bezae.] 6 say unto him, No. He said unto them, Cast your net on the right side of the ship, and ye shall find. And when they had cast as he had said unto them, they sought to pull the net into the ship, and they could not for the weight of many fishes which it 7 held. Then said the disciple whom Jesus loved unto Simon, This is our Lord. So when Simon heard that it was our Lord, he took his coat, and girt it about his loins, and cast himself into the lake, and was swimming, and came, for they were not far from the 8 land. But the rest of the disciples were coming in 9 the boat, dragging the net; and as they went up on the dry land, they found before Jesus live coals of fire, 10 and fish lying thereon, and bread also laid. Jesus saith unto them, Bring ye of those fish which ye 11 have now caught. And Simon went up, and drew the net to the dry land quite full: and they found in it great fishes, a hundred and fifty and three: and with all this weight the net was not rent.¹ Jesus ¹² saith unto them, Come and break your fast.² And none of the disciples durst ask him, Who he was. for they were believing that it was he. And Jesus ¹³ took the bread and the fish, and blessed them, and gave to them. This was the third time that Jesus ¹⁴ appeared to the disciples after he rose from the dead. And when they had eaten, Jesus saith to ¹⁵ Simon, Thou [art] Simon, son of Jonah, lovest thou me? He saith unto him, Yea, Lord. He saith unto him, Feed my lambs. Again Jesus saith to him, ¹⁶ Thou [art] Simon, son of Jonah, lovest thou me much? He saith unto him, Yea, Lord. He saith unto him, Feed my sheep. Again Jesus saith unto ¹⁷ him, Simon, son of Jonah, lovest thou me? Simon was grieved because three times Jesus spake thus unto him. Simon said unto him, Thou knowest all things; thou knowest that I love thee. And he said, Feed my flock. Verily, I say, When ¹⁸ thou wast a young man, thou didst gird thy loins, and didst walk whither thou wouldest: and when thou shalt be old, thou shalt lift up thy hands, and another shall gird thy loins, and shall drive thee whither thou wouldest not. But this he said, by ¹⁹ what death Simon should g . . . God. And when he had said these things, he saith unto Simon, Follow me. Simon turned about, and saw that disciple whom ²⁰ Jesus loved following him; he who had lain on Jesus' breast at supper, and had said to him, Lord, which is he that betrayeth thee? When Simon saw him follow- ²¹ ing him, he said unto him, And what of this man, Lord? Jesus saith unto him, If I will that this one tarry till ²² I come, what is that to thee? Follow thou me now.

---

¹ R.V. Bezae.
² R.V.

23 And this saying went abroad among the brethren, that that disciple should not die: but Jesus had not said concerning him, that he should not die; but, If
24 I will that he tarry till I come. This is the disciple which testified about these things, and wrote them:
25 and we know that his testimony is true. And Jesus did many other things, which, if they were written one by one, the world would not suffice for them.

Here endeth the Gospel of the *Mĕpharrĕshē* four books. Glory to God and to his Christ, and to his Holy Spirit. Let every one who reads and hears and keeps and does [it] pray for the sinner who wrote [it]. May God in his tender mercy forgive him his sins in both worlds. Amen and Amen.

APPENDIX I.

List of words and phrases in the "Textus Receptus" which are omitted in this Version without a full equivalent.

MATTHEW.

I.

6. ὁ βασιλεὺς before ἐγέννησε. 17. οὖν.
18. Ἰησοῦ. 20. ἰδού.
25. καὶ οὐκ ἐγίνωσκεν αὐτὴν, ἕως οὗ—αὐτῆς τὸν πρωτότοκον.

II.

8. ἀκριβῶς. 9. καὶ ἰδού. 10. σφόδρα. 13. ἰδού.
19. ἰδού. 22. ἐπὶ τῆς Ἰουδαίας. 23. ὅπως.

III.

3. γὰρ—φωνὴ βοῶντος ἐν τῇ ἐρήμῳ—εὐθείας ποιεῖτε τὰς τρίβους αὐτοῦ.
9. δόξητε—ἐν ἑαυτοῖς. 10. οὖν—καλόν.
16. Ἰησοῦς—εὐθὺς—αὐτῷ. 17. ἰδού.

IV.

2. ὕστερον. 7. Πάλιν. 9. πάντα. 11. ἰδού.
12. ὁ Ἰησοῦς. 13. κατῴκησεν—ἐν ὁρίοις. 16. μέγα.
17. Μετανοεῖτε—γάρ.
18. τῆς Γαλιλαίας—τὸν λεγόμενον Πέτρον.
21. τὸν τοῦ Ζεβεδαίου—τὸν ἀδελφόν αὐτοῦ. 22. εὐθέως.
24. καὶ ἀπῆλθεν ἡ ἀκοὴ αὐτοῦ εἰς ὅλην τὴν Συρίαν—κακῶς ἔχοντας—καὶ δαιμονιζομένους, καὶ σεληνιαζομένους, καὶ παραλυτικούς—ἠκολούθησαν αὐτῷ.

V.

2. ἀνοίξας τὸ στόμα αὐτοῦ ἐδίδασκεν.
11. ῥῆμα—ψευδόμενοι.   12. τοὺς πρὸ ὑμῶν.
13. δέ—ἔτι.   19. οὖν.   27. τοῖς ἀρχαίοις.   28. ἤδη.
30. καὶ εἰ ἡ δεξιά σου χεὶρ σκανδαλίζει σε, ἔκκοψον αὐτὴν καὶ βάλε ἀπὸ σοῦ· συμφέρει γάρ σοι ἵνα ἀπόληται ἓν τῶν μελῶν σου, καὶ μὴ ὅλον τὸ σῶμά σου βληθῇ εἰς γέενναν.
31. δέ.   33. Πάλιν—τοῖς ἀρχαίοις—σου.   39. δεξιάν.
44. εὐλογεῖτε τοὺς καταρωμένους ὑμᾶς, ποιεῖτε τοὺς μισοῦντας ὑμᾶς—ἐπηρεαζόντων ὑμᾶς καὶ.
47. καὶ ἐὰν ἀσπάσησθε τοὺς ἀδελφοὺς ὑμῶν μόνον, τί περισσὸν ποιεῖτε; οὐχὶ καὶ οἱ τελῶναι οὕτω ποιοῦσιν;

VI.

1. Προσέχετε—εἰ δὲ μήγε.   2. οὖν.   4. σου.
5. καὶ ὅταν προσεύχῃ, οὐκ ἔσῃ ὥσπερ οἱ ὑποκριταί, ὅτι φιλοῦσιν ἐν ταῖς συναγωγαῖς καὶ ἐν ταῖς γωνίαις τῶν πλατειῶν ἑστῶτες προσεύχεσθαι, ὅπως ἂν φανῶσι τοῖς ἀνθρώποις· ἀμὴν λέγω ὑμῖν, ὅτι ἀπέχουσι τὸν μισθὸν αὐτῶν.
6. σου after ταμιεῖον—σου after θύραν—ἐν τῷ φανερῷ.

VIII.

5. Εἰσελθόντι δὲ τῷ Ἰησοῦ εἰς Καπερναούμ.   6. Κύριε.
7. ὁ Ἰησοῦς.   8. μόνον.   16. τὰ πνεύματα.
17. τοῦ προφήτου.   20. αὐτῷ.   21. Κύριε.
22. ὁ δὲ Ἰησοῦς.   24. ἰδού.   28. εἰς τὸ πέραν.
32. ἰδού—καὶ ἀπέθανον ἐν τοῖς ὕδασιν.

IX.

9. ὁ Ἰησοῦς.   12. Ἰησοῦς—αὐτοῖς.   14. αὐτῷ.
20. ὄπισθεν.   21. μόνον.   22. Ἰησοῦς—ἰδὼν αὐτήν.
25. τὸ κοράσιον.   27. καὶ λέγοντες.
28. Ἰησοῦς.   32. ἰδού.
34. οἱ δὲ Φαρισαῖοι ἔλεγον, Ἐν τῷ ἄρχοντι τῶν δαιμονίων ἐκβάλλει τὰ δαιμόνια.
35. ἐν τῷ λαῷ.   37. μέν.

X.

1. μαθητὰς—πᾶσαν before μαλακίαν.
2. ὁ λεγόμενος—ὁ ἀδελφὸς αὐτοῦ after Ἰωάννης.
3. καὶ Λεββαῖος ὁ ἐπικληθεὶς Θαδδαῖος.*
6. μᾶλλον.   11. ἡ κώμην—ἐν αὐτῇ.   13. ἦ ἀξία.
19. πῶς ἤ.   24. οὐδὲ δοῦλος ὑπὲρ τὸν κύριον αὐτοῦ.
32. οὖν—ἔμπροσθεν τῶν ἀνθρώπων.

XI.

10. σου after ὁδόν.   17. καὶ λέγουσιν.

XII.

36. περὶ αὐτοῦ.   38. ἀπεκρίθησαν.
45. μεθ' ἑαυτοῦ—ἐκείνου.
47. εἶπε δέ τις αὐτῷ, Ἰδού, ἡ μήτηρ σου καὶ οἱ ἀδελφοί σου ἔξω ἑστήκασι, ζητοῦντές σοι λαλῆσαι.
49. Ἰδού.

XIII.

1. ἀπὸ τῆς οἰκίας.   2. ὥστε.
5. διὰ τὸ μὴ ἔχειν βάθος γῆς.   9. ἀκούειν.
11. τῶν οὐρανῶν.   12. καὶ περισσευθήσεται.
15. καὶ ἐπιστρέψωσι, καὶ ἰάσωμαι αὐτούς.   20. εὐθύς.
25. αὐτοῦ.   26. τότε.   27. δέ—οὖν.   28. δέ—οὖν.
29. δέ.   30. μου.   31. παρέθηκεν.
32. ὥστε—τοῦ οὐρανοῦ.   33. ἐλάλησεν αὐτοῖς.
35. ἀπὸ καταβολῆς κόσμου.   36. ὁ Ἰησοῦς—αὐτῷ.
39. ὁ δὲ ἐχθρός.   40. τούτου.   43. ὡς ὁ ἥλιος.
44. Πάλιν.   45. καλούς.   48. εἰς ἀγγεῖα.
51. λέγει αὐτοῖς ὁ Ἰησοῦς—Κύριε.   53. καὶ ἐγένετο.
55. τοῦ τέκτονος.

XIV.

2. ἐνεργοῦσιν ἐν αὐτῷ.   6. ἐν τῷ μέσῳ.   7. ὅθεν.
12. προσελθόντες.   13. ὁ Ἰησοῦς.   35. ὅλην—ἐκείνην.

* We have instead καὶ Ἰουδαῖος ὁ τοῦ Ἰακώβου.

XV.

1. τῷ Ἰησοῦ.   8. ἐγγίζει μοι—τῷ στόματι αὐτῶν.
13. μου.   14. τυφλοί.   16. ὁ δὲ Ἰησοῦς.   22. αὐτῷ.
27. γὰρ—ἀπὸ τῶν ψιχίων τῶν πιπτόντων.
28. ὁ Ἰησοῦς—αὐτῇ.   30. τοῦ Ἰησοῦ.
31. κυλλοὺς ὑγιεῖς.   33. αὐτῷ—τοσοῦτοι.

XVI.

2. Ὀψίας γενομένης λέγετε, Εὐδία· πυρράζει γὰρ ὁ οὐρανός.
3. καὶ πρωΐ, Σήμερον χειμών· πυρράζει γὰρ στυγνάζων ὁ οὐρανός. ὑποκριταί, τὸ μὲν πρόσωπον τοῦ οὐρανοῦ γινώσκετε διακρίνειν, τὰ δὲ σημεῖα τῶν καιρῶν οὐ δύνασθε;
6. Ὁρᾶτε καί.   7. λέγοντες.   8. αὐτοῖς.
12. τοῦ ἄρτου.

XVII.

12. οὕτω.   13. τοῦ Βαπτιστοῦ.   14. αὐτῷ after προσῆλθεν.
15. Κύριε.   19. τῷ Ἰησοῦ.
20. ὁ δὲ Ἰησοῦς—ἐντεῦθεν ἐκεῖ.
21. τοῦτο δὲ τὸ γένος οὐκ ἐκπορεύεται, εἰ μὴ ἐν προσευχῇ καὶ νηστείᾳ.
26. ὁ Πέτρος.   27. ἐκεῖνον λαβών.

XVIII.

1. τῷ Ἰησοῦ.   7. ἐκείνῳ—τὸ σκάνδαλον.
9. ὀφθαλμοὺς after δύο.   10. ἐν οὐρανοῖς.
11. ἦλθε γὰρ ὁ υἱὸς τοῦ ἀνθρώπου σῶσαι τὸ ἀπολωλός.
14. ἔμπροσθεν.   15. ὕπαγε καί—μόνου.   20. ἐκεῖ.
22. ὁ Ἰησοῦς—λέγω σοι ἕως.   25. καὶ ἀποδοθῆναι.
26. σοι.   27. ὁ κύριος τοῦ δούλου ἐκείνου.
29. εἰς τοὺς πόδας αὐτοῦ—πάντα—σοι.   30. ἀπελθών.
31. σφόδρα.   34. πᾶν—αὐτῷ.   35. τὰ παραπτώματα αὐτῶν.

XIX.

2. ἐκεῖ.   3. αὐτῷ.   4. ἀπ' ἀρχῆς—αὐτούς.
5. καὶ εἶπεν.   7. οὖν—καὶ ἀπολύσαι αὐτήν.
9. καὶ ὁ ἀπολελυμένην γαμήσας μοιχᾶται.   15. ἐκεῖθεν.
16. ἰδού.   17. δὲ—οὐδεὶς—εἰ μὴ—ὁ Θεός.
27. Ἰδού.   29. ἢ πατέρα—ἢ γυναῖκα.

XX.

1. γάρ.   2. τῶν ἐργατῶν.   4. οἱ δὲ ἀπῆλθον.
6. ἀργούς.   7. καὶ ὃ ἐὰν ᾖ δίκαιον λήψεσθε.
8. τοῦ ἀμπελῶνος.   17. μαθητάς.
21. Εἰπέ.
22. καὶ τὸ βάπτισμα, ὃ ἐγὼ βαπτίζομαι, βαπτισθῆναι—αὐτῷ.
23. καὶ τὸ βάπτισμα, ὃ ἐγὼ βαπτίζομαι, βαπτισθήσεσθε.

XXI.

23. διδάσκοντι.   25. οὖν.
28. καὶ προσελθὼν—σήμερον—μου.   29. ὁ δὲ ἀποκριθείς.
30. προσελθών.   32. οὐ before μετεμελήθητε.
34. αὐτοῦ after καρπούς.   38. ἐν ἑαυτοῖς.
41. αὐτῷ after ἀποδώσουσιν.   43. αὐτῆς.
44. καὶ ὁ πεσὼν ἐπὶ τὸν λίθον τοῦτον συνθλασθήσεται, ἐφ᾽ ὃν δ᾽ ἂν πέσῃ, λικμήσει αὐτόν.

XXII.

4. τὸ ἄριστόν μου ἡτοίμασα, οἱ ταῦροί μου καὶ τὰ σιτιστὰ τεθυμένα.
7. Ἀκούσας.   9. διεξόδους.
17. εἰπὲ οὖν ἡμῖν.
24. καὶ ἀναστήσει σπέρμα τῷ ἀδελφῷ αὐτοῦ.
25. παρ᾽ ἡμῖν—γαμήσας.   34. ἐπὶ τὸ αὐτό.   35. νομικόν.

XXIII.

2. λέγων.   3. οὖν—τηρεῖν, τηρεῖτε καί.
4. γάρ—καὶ δυσβάστακτα—τῷ δὲ δακτύλῳ αὐτῶν—θέλουσι.
8. δὲ—γάρ—ὁ Χριστός.   10. εἷς γάρ—ἐστιν.
13. Οὐαὶ δὲ ὑμῖν, γραμματεῖς καὶ Φαρισαῖοι, ὑποκριταί, ὅτι κατεσθίετε τὰς οἰκίας τῶν χηρῶν, καὶ προφάσει μακρὰ προσευχόμενοι· διὰ τοῦτο λήψεσθε περισσότερον κρίμα.
14. κλείετε.   17. γάρ.   19. μωροὶ καί—γάρ.
26. καὶ τῆς παροψίδος.
27. οἵτινες ἔξωθεν μὲν φαίνονται ὡραῖοι.   31. ἑαυτοῖς.

XXIV.

2. ὁ δὲ Ἰησοῦς—οὐ.   3. αὐτῷ.   7. καὶ λοιμοί.   17. τι.
26. οὖν.   31. αὐτῶν.   38. ἐν ταῖς ἡμέραις ταῖς—ἧς ἡμέρας.

XXV.

4. αὐτῶν after ἀγγείοις.   8. ἡμῶν.
9. Ἀπεκρίθησαν δὲ—μᾶλλον.   11. καὶ αἱ λοιπαί—κύριε.

XXVI.

22. αὐτῷ.   23. ὁ δὲ ἀποκριθείς.
24. ὁ υἱὸς τοῦ ἀνθρώπου before παραδίδοται—ὁ ἄνθρωπος ἐκεῖνος.
25. αὐτόν.   28. γάρ.   29. τούτου—ἐκείνης.
33. δὲ—αὐτῷ—καί.   36. ἐκεῖ.   42. ἀπ' ἐμοῦ.
46. ἰδού.   51. αὐτοῦ after μάχαιραν.   52. σου.
53. ἄρτι—μου.   61. τοῦ Θεοῦ.   64. ὁ Ἰησοῦς—πλήν.
71. ἐκεῖ.   73. δῆλόν σε ποιεῖ.

XXVII.

2. Ποντίῳ.   3. αὐτόν.   9. Ἰερεμίου.
11. ὁ ἡγεμὼν before λέγων.   21. ἀπὸ τῶν δύο.
22. οὖν—αὐτῷ.   23. ὁ δὲ ἡγεμών.   24. τοῦ δικαίου.
27. ὅλην.   28. καὶ ἐκδύσαντες αὐτόν.
33. ὅς ἐστι λεγόμενος κρανίου τόπος.
35. ἵνα πληρωθῇ τὸ ῥηθὲν ὑπὸ τοῦ προφήτου Διεμερίσαντο τὰ ἱμάτιά μου ἑαυτοῖς, καὶ ἐπὶ τὸν ἱματισμόν μου ἔβαλον κλῆρον.
37. Οὗτός ἐστιν.
46. τοῦτ' ἐστι, Θεέ μου, Θεέ μου, ἱνατί με ἐγκατέλιπες;
51. ἰδού—εἰς δύο—ἕως κάτω.
58. τότε—τὸ σῶμα after ἀποδοθῆναι.

XXVIII.

2. προσελθών—ἀπὸ τῆς θύρας.   3. λευκόν.
4. καὶ ἐγένοντο.   5. δέ.   6. γάρ—ὁ Κύριος.
7. ἀπὸ τῶν νεκρῶν.

MARK.

I.

13. ἐν τῇ ἐρήμῳ. 14. τῆς βασιλείας. 15. καὶ λέγων. 17. γενέσθαι. 19. ἐκεῖθεν. 21. καὶ εἰσπορεύονται εἰς Καπερναούμ—εὐθέως—εἰσελθών. 22. αὐτούς. 24. Ἔα. 27. ὥστε συζητεῖν—Τί ἐστι τοῦτο; 28. εὐθύς. 29. εὐθέως. 30. κατέκειτο. 31. τῆς χειρός. 32. ὀψίας δὲ γενομένης—πρὸς αὐτόν—καὶ τοὺς δαιμονιζομένους. 34. κακῶς ἔχοντας ποικίλαις νόσοις—τὰ δαιμόνια. 35. ἔννυχον—ἀναστάς. 37. Ὅτι. 39. αὐτῶν. 42. καὶ εἰπόντος αὐτοῦ—ἀπῆλθεν ἀπ' αὐτοῦ ἡ λέπρα. 43. εὐθέως ἐξέβαλεν αὐτόν.

II.

22. ὁ νέος. 27. οὐχ ὁ ἄνθρωπος διὰ τὸ σάββατον. 28. καί.

III.

5. ἡ χεὶρ αὐτοῦ. 6. κατ' αὐτοῦ. 7. ἠκολούθησαν αὐτῷ. 8. καὶ ἀπὸ τῆς Ἰδουμαίας—πλῆθος πολύ. 11. ὅταν αὐτὸν ἐθεώρει. 17. τοῦ Ἰακώβου—ὅ ἐστιν Υἱοὶ βροντῆς. 19. καὶ—αὐτόν.

IV.

4. καὶ ἐγένετο—τοῦ οὐρανοῦ. 5. ὅπου οὐκ εἶχε γῆν πολλήν—εὐθέως. 11. γνῶναι. 15. ὅπου σπείρεται ὁ λόγος.

V.

2. εὐθέως—ἐκ τῶν μνημείων. 4. διὰ τὸ αὐτὸν πολλάκις πέδαις καὶ ἁλύσεσι δεδέσθαι. 10. πολλά. 12. πάντες—λέγοντες. 13. εὐθέως ὁ Ἰησοῦς—κατὰ τοῦ κρημνοῦ. 14. τοὺς χοίρους. 19. ὁ δὲ Ἰησοῦς. 21. ἐν τῷ πλοίῳ πάλιν—καὶ ἦν—Καὶ ἰδού. 23. πολλά—ὅπως σωθῇ.

VI.

10. καὶ ἔλεγεν αὐτοῖς.
11. ἀμὴν λέγω ὑμῖν, ἀνεκτότερον ἔσται Σοδόμοις ἢ Γομόρροις ἐν ἡμέρᾳ κρίσεως, ἢ τῇ πόλει ἐκείνῃ.
14. ἐνεργοῦσιν αἱ δυνάμεις ἐν αὐτῷ.   16. ἐκ νεκρῶν.
21. καὶ γενομένης ἡμέρας εὐκαίρου.   22. ὃ ἐὰν θέλῃς.
23. Ὅτι ὃ ἐάν με αἰτήσῃς, δώσω σοί.
25. μετὰ σπουδῆς—ᾐτήσατο.   26. αὐτὴν ἀθετῆσαι.
27. εὐθέως—ὁ βασιλεὺς—ἐπέταξεν.   28. τὴν κεφαλὴν αὐτοῦ.
31. ὑμεῖς αὐτοί—τόπον.
33. ὑπάγοντας οἱ ὄχλοι—ἐκεῖ, καὶ προῆλθον αὐτούς.
34. ὁ Ἰησοῦς—πολλά.   35. αὐτῷ.
36. καὶ κώμας—τί γὰρ φάγωσιν οὐκ ἔχουσιν.
37. ὁ δὲ ἀποκριθείς.   38. καὶ γνόντες.
39. συμπόσια συμπόσια—χλωρῷ.   44. ὡσεί.
48. καὶ περὶ τετάρτην φυλακὴν τῆς νυκτός.
49. καὶ ἐταράχθησαν.   51. λίαν ἐκ περισσοῦ—καὶ ἐθαύμαζον.
53. καὶ προσωρμίσθησαν.
55. ἐκείνην, ἤρξαντο—ὅπου ἤκουον ὅτι ἐκεῖ ἐστι.
56. αὐτοῦ after ἥπτοντο.

VII.

1. τίνες τῶν.
2. τινὰς τῶν—κοιναῖς—τοῦτ' ἔστιν—ἐμέμψαντο.
3. πυγμῇ.   4. ἄλλα—καὶ χαλκίων καὶ κλινῶν.
6. δὲ ἀποκριθεὶς—τῶν ὑποκριτῶν.
8. Ἀφέντες γὰρ τὴν ἐντολὴν τοῦ Θεοῦ, κρατεῖτε τὴν παράδοσιν τῶν ἀνθρώπων, βαπτισμοὺς ξεστῶν καὶ ποτηρίων, καὶ ἄλλα παρόμοια τοιαῦτα πολλὰ ποιεῖτε.
9. καὶ ἔλεγεν αὐτοῖς.   11. ὅ ἐστι, δῶρον.   12. ἔτι.
13. ᾗ παρεδώκατε.   14. μου.   18. δύναται.
19. εἰς τὸν ἀφεδρῶνα.   20. ἔλεγε δέ.   21. ἔσωθεν.
24. ἐκεῖθεν—καὶ Σιδῶνος.
25. γὰρ—περὶ αὐτοῦ—τοὺς πόδας.   26. Ἑλληνίς—τῷ γένει.
27. γάρ.   28. ἀπεκρίθη καὶ—Ναί—ὑποκάτω τῆς τραπέζης.
34. ὅ ἐστι, "Διανοίχθητι."

VIII.

1. ὁ Ἰησοῦς.   10. εὐθέως.   12. αὐτοῦ.   19. ἔκλασα.
26. μηδὲ εἴπῃς τινὶ ἐν τῇ κώμῃ.   29. Ἀποκριθεὶς δέ.
34. μοι.   35. ἕνεκεν ἐμοῦ.   38. γάρ.

IX.

3. λίαν—οἷα γναφεὺς ἐπὶ τῆς γῆς οὐ δύναται λευκᾶναι.
4. τῷ Ἰησοῦ. 6. γάρ. 7. λέγουσα. 8. μεθ' ἑαυτῶν.
11. δεῖ. 12. μέν. 16. τοὺς γραμματεῖς.
19. ἕως πότε before ἀνέξομαι—πρός με.
23. δύνασαι—τῷ πιστεύοντι. 24. μετὰ δακρύων.
25. τῷ ἀκαθάρτῳ. 27. καὶ ἀνέστη. 34. ἐν τῇ ὁδῷ.
36. καὶ ἐναγκαλισάμενος αὐτό. 37. καὶ ὃς ἐὰν ἐμὲ δέξηται.
38. ὃς οὐκ ἀκολουθεῖ ἡμῖν. 39. Ἰησοῦς—δύναμιν—ταχύ.
44, 46. ὅπου ὁ σκώληξ αὐτῶν οὐ τελευτᾷ, καὶ τὸ πῦρ οὐ σβέν-
46. εἰς τὸ πῦρ τὸ ἄσβεστον. 47. τοῦ πυρός. [νυται.
49. καὶ πᾶσα θυσία ἁλὶ ἁλισθήσεται.

X.

1. πάλιν before εἰώθασκεν.
2. καὶ προσελθόντες οἱ Φαρισαῖοι.
7. καὶ προσκολληθήσεται πρὸς τὴν γυναῖκα αὐτοῦ.
8. ὥστε. 11. ἐπ' αὐτήν.
16. καὶ ἐναγκαλισάμενος αὐτά. 19. μὴ ἀποστερήσῃς.
21. δεῦρο. 25. εἰσελθεῖν. 26. λέγοντες· 27. δέ.
28. καὶ ἤρξατο. 29. ἢ γυναῖκα.
32. ἀκολουθοῦντες—πάλιν. 37. εἷς . . . εἷς.
38. ὃ ἐγὼ βαπτίζομαι. 39. μέν.
42. ὁ δὲ Ἰησοῦς—δοκοῦντες—καὶ οἱ μεγάλοι αὐτῶν κατεξουσιά-
ζουσιν αὐτῶν.
47. Ἰησοῦ. 52. ὁ δὲ Ἰησοῦς—τῷ Ἰησοῦ.

XI.

1. αὐτοῖς. 3. Τί ποιεῖτε τοῦτο;—αὐτοῦ. 4. ἀμφόδου.
5. αὐτοῖς. 6. καὶ ἀφῆκαν αὐτούς. 7. τὸν πῶλον—αὐτῷ.
8. ἄλλοι δὲ στοιβάδας ἔκοπτον ἐκ τῶν δένδρων, καὶ ἐστρώννυον εἰς τὴν ὁδόν.
10. ἐν ὀνόματι Κυρίου—Ὡσαννά. 11. ὁ Ἰησοῦς.
13. ἐπ' αὐτήν—γάρ. 14. ὁ Ἰησοῦς.
15. ὁ Ἰησοῦς—κατέστρεψε. 17. αὐτοῖς. 21. ἴδε.
23. γάρ—αὐτῷ ὃ ἐὰν εἴπῃ. 24. αἰτεῖσθε.
26. εἰ δὲ ὑμεῖς οὐκ ἀφίετε, οὐδὲ ὁ πατὴρ ὑμῶν ὁ ἐν τοῖς οὐρανοῖς ἀφήσει τὰ παραπτώματα ὑμῶν.
28. ἵνα ταῦτα ποιῇς; 31. πρὸς ἑαυτούς. 32. ὄντως.
33. καὶ ἀποκριθέντες—τῷ Ἰησοῦ.

XII.

1. αὐτοῖς.   2. παρὰ τῶν γεωργῶν.
4. καὶ πάλιν ἀπέστειλε πρὸς αὐτοὺς ἄλλον δοῦλον· κἀκεῖνον λιθοβολήσαντες ἐκεφαλαίωσαν, καὶ ἀπέστειλαν ἠτιμωμένον.
6. ἔτι οὖν—καὶ αὐτὸν—ἔσχατον.   9. οὖν.   10. ταύτην.
14. ἢ οὔ; δῶμεν.   16. Καὶ.   33. *καὶ ἐξ ὅλης τῆς συνέσεως*.
36. γὰρ.   37. οὖν.   38. αὐτοῖς.
44. ὅλον τὸν βίον αὐτῆς.

XIII.

2. ἀποκριθεὶς—μεγάλας.   4. πάντα.
5. ἀποκριθεὶς—ἤρξατο.
9. Βλέπετε δὲ ὑμεῖς ἑαυτούς—*καὶ εἰς συναγωγὰς δαρήσεσθε*.
11. μηδὲ μελετᾶτε.   14. *τὸ ῥηθὲν ὑπὸ Δανιὴλ τοῦ προφήτου*.
18. ἡ φυγὴ ὑμῶν.   20. κύριος.   23. ἰδού.
33. Βλέπετε—πότε—ἐστιν.

XIV.

3. τὸ ἀλάβαστρον.   5. ἐπάνω.   7. εὖ.
8. ὃ εἶχεν αὕτη.   9. τοῦτο—λαληθήσεται.   10. αὐτοῖς.
19. Καὶ ἄλλος, Μή τι ἐγώ;   20. Ὁ δὲ ἀποκριθεὶς.
22. φάγετε.   23. πάντες.   27. ἐν τῇ νυκτὶ ταύτῃ.
31. ἐκ περισσοῦ.   33. μεθ' ἑαυτοῦ.
34. μείνατε ὧδε καὶ γρηγορεῖτε.   36. ὁ πατήρ.
41. τὸ λοιπὸν—ἀπέχει.   43. εὐθέως.   45. ἐλθὼν—ῥαββί.
46. αὐτῶν.   63. χρείαν ἔχομεν μαρτύρων.
65. καὶ περικαλύπτειν τὸ πρόσωπον αὐτοῦ—αὐτῷ after λέγειν.
66. κάτω, ἔρχεται.   68. καὶ ἀλέκτωρ ἐφώνησε.
70. καὶ ἡ λαλιά σου ὁμοιάζει.   71. ὁ δὲ ἤρξατο.
72. καὶ ἐπιβαλών.

XV.

1. εὐθέως—τὸ συνέδριον.   4. ἐπηρώτησεν.   8. καθὼς ἀεί.
11. μᾶλλον.   21. παράγοντα.   22. τόπος.   23. πιεῖν.
24. τίς τί ἄρῃ.   26. ἐπιγεγραμμένη.
28. *καὶ ἐπληρώθη ἡ γραφὴ ἡ λέγουσα, Καὶ μετὰ ἀνόμων ἐλογίσθη*.

29. καὶ οἱ παραπορευόμενοι. 33. ἐφ' ὅλην τὴν γῆν.
34. ὁ Ἰησοῦς—ὅ ἐστι μεθερμηνευόμενον, ὁ Θεός μου, ὁ Θεός μου, εἰς τί με ἐγκατέλιπες.
35. Ἰδού. 40. ἐν αἷς ἦν καί.
42. καὶ ἤδη ὀψίας γενομένης, ἐπεὶ ἦι παρασκευή, ὅ ἐστι προ. . . .
44. πάλαι. 46. καὶ καθελὼν αὐτόν.

XVI.

3. ἐκ τῆς θύρας. 4. ἦν γὰρ μέγας σφόδρα.
8. ἀπὸ τοῦ μνημείου. εἶχε δὲ αὐτὰς τρόμος καὶ ἔκστασις.
Also vv. 9—20.

LUKE.

I.

7. αὐτῶν. 9. τοῦ Κυρίου. 10. ἔξω. 12. Ζαχαρίας.
48. ἰδού. 49. ὁ δυνατός. 60. ἀποκριθεῖσα.
63. λέγων—καὶ ἐθαύμασαν πάντες.
64. Ἀνεῴχθη δὲ τὸ στόμα αὐτοῦ—ἐλάλει. 65. τὰ ῥήματα.
66. πάντες οἱ ἀκούσαντες—ἄρα. 68. Κύριος.
70. ἐλάλησε. 76. γάρ.

II.

4. καὶ πατριᾶς. 5. μεμνηστευμένῃ. 17. τούτου.
19. τὰ ῥήματα ταῦτα. 20. καὶ αἰνοῦντες—πᾶσιν. 22. ὅτε.
25. ἰδού. 27. περὶ αὐτοῦ. 40. πνεύματι.
46. ἐγένετο. 51. ἐν τῇ καρδίᾳ αὐτῆς.

III.

3. ἦλθεν. 4. λέγοντος. 5. καὶ πᾶν. 7. ὑπ' αὐτοῦ.
8. ἐν ἑαυτοῖς. 10. λέγοντες—οὖν. 11. Ἀποκριθεὶς δὲ.
12. Διδάσκαλε. 15. πάντων. 16. ὁ Ἰωάννης.
19. Φιλίππου. 21. ἐγένετο. 22. λέγουσαν.
23. ἀρχόμενος. 36. τοῦ Καϊνάν.*

* We have instead of this "Of Helam."

IV.

2. καὶ οὐκ ἔφαγεν οὐδὲν ἐν ταῖς ἡμέραις ἐκείναις.
4. καὶ ἀπεκρίθη—ἀλλ' ἐπὶ παντὶ ῥήματι Θεοῦ.
5. εἰς ὄρος ὑψηλὸν.   6. ὁ διάβολος.   7. οὖν.
8. Ὕπαγε ὀπίσω μου, Σατανᾶ—γάρ.   9. κάτω.
11. τὸν πόδα σου.   12. Ὅτι εἴρηται.   13. πάντα.
16. καὶ ἀνέστη ἀναγνῶναι.
18. ἰάσασθαι τοὺς συντετριμμένους τὴν καρδίαν.
20. ἐν τῇ συναγωγῇ οἱ ὀφθαλμοί.   29. ἀναστάντες.
30. ἐπορεύετο.   38. καὶ ἠρώτησαν αὐτὸν περὶ αὐτῆς.
39. καὶ ἐπιστὰς ἐπάνω αὐτῆς.   41. ὁ Χριστός.
43. ὅτι εἰς τοῦτο ἀπέσταλμαι.

V.

3. ἓν τῶν πλοίων, ὃ ἦν τοῦ Σίμωνος—αὐτὸν.   8. Πέτρος.
12. καὶ ἐγένετο—καὶ ἰδού.   15. ὑπ' αὐτοῦ.

VI.

19. ὁ ὄχλος.   22. ὅταν before ἀφορίσωσιν.   36. οὖν.
38. πεπιεσμένον καὶ σεσαλευμένον.
40. κατηρτισμένος δὲ πᾶς ἔσται ὡς ὁ διδάσκαλος αὐτοῦ.
42. ἢ—οὐ βλέπων.
48. ὅμοιός ἐστιν—τεθεμελίωτο γὰρ ἐπὶ τὴν πέτραν.

VII.

1. αὐτοῦ.   7. διὸ οὐδὲ ἐμαυτὸν ἠξίωσα πρός σε ἐλθεῖν.
10. ἀσθενοῦντα.   11. ἐγένετο—ἱκανοί.   20. οἱ ἄνδρες.
31. εἶπε δὲ ὁ Κύριος.   32. καὶ λέγουσιν.
33. ἄρτον—οἶνον.   37. Καὶ ἰδού.   38. ἤρξατο.
40. καὶ ἀποκριθεὶς.   42. εἰπέ.   43. Ἀποκριθεὶς δὲ.
44. τοὺς πόδας after μου.   46. ἐλαίῳ τὴν κεφαλήν μου.
47. σοι.

VIII.

1. καὶ ἐγένετο—καὶ εὐαγγελιζόμενος.
5. τὸν σπόρον αὐτοῦ—τοῦ οὐρανοῦ.   6. φυὲν.
7. καὶ συμφυεῖσαι αἱ ἄκανθαι.   18. οὖν.

Luke VIII. 20—XI. 33.

20. καὶ ἀπηγγέλη. 21. αὐτόν. 22. καὶ ἀνήχθησαν.
24. καὶ ἐπαύσαντο. 30. εἰσῆλθεν. 34. ἀπελθόντες.
36. καὶ οἱ ἰδόντες—ὁ δαιμονισθείς.
37. τῆς περιχώρου—μεγάλῳ. 40. Ἐγένετο δὲ. 41. ἰδού.
43. ἥτις εἰς ἰατροὺς προσαναλώσασα ὅλον τὸν βίον.
44. παραχρῆμα. 45. καὶ οἱ μετ' αὐτοῦ.
47. αὐτοῦ after ἥψατο—αὐτῷ after ἀπήγγειλεν. 48. Θάρσει.
52. ἀλλὰ. 54. ἐκβαλὼν ἔξω πάντας.

IX.

2. τοὺς ἀσθενοῦντας. 7. ὑπ' αὐτοῦ—ὑπό τινων.
22. ἄρχι... 23. πρὸς πάντας—καθ' ἡμέραν. 29. ἐγένετο.
30. οἵτινες ἦσαν. 35. λέγουσα. 37. Ἐγένετο δὲ.
38. ἰδού. 39. ἰδού—κράζει. 43. ὁ Ἰησοῦς.
45. ἐρωτῆσαι. 48. αὐτοῖς. 51. Ἐγένετο δὲ.
54. ὡς καὶ Ἠλίας ἐποίησε.
55. Στραφεὶς—καὶ εἶπεν, Οὐκ οἴδατε οἵου πνεύματός ἐστε ὑμεῖς.
56. ὁ γὰρ υἱὸς τοῦ ἀνθρώπου οὐκ ἦλθε ψυχὰς ἀνθρώπων ἀπολέσαι, ἀλλὰ σῶσαι.
57. ἐγένετο δὲ—Κύριε. 59. Κύριε. 60. ὁ Ἰησοῦς.
61. καί.

X.

1. ὁ Κύριος. 13. καθήμεναι. 20. μᾶλλον.
23. κατ' ἰδίαν. 25. ἰδού.
30. Ὑπολαβὼν δὲ ὁ Ἰησοῦς—τυγχάνοντα.
31. ἀντι... 32. ἐλθών—ἀντι... 34. ἴδιον.
35. ἐξελθών—αὐτῷ. 36. οὖν. 37. οὖν. 38. Ἐγένετο.
40. πολλὴν—οὖν. 41. μεριμνᾷς καὶ τυρβάζῃ περὶ πολλά.
42. ἑνὸς δέ ἐστι χρεία.

XI.

1. Καὶ ἐγένετο—καὶ.
2. ἡμῶν ὁ ἐν τοῖς οὐρανοῖς—γενηθήτω τὸ θέλημά σου ὡς ἐν οὐρανῷ, καὶ ἐπὶ τῆς γῆς.
4. ἀλλὰ ῥῦσαι ἡμᾶς ἀπὸ τοῦ πονηροῦ. 7. ἤδη.
8. ἀναστάς.
11. τὸν πατέρα—ἄρτον, μὴ λίθον ἐπιδώσει αὐτῷ;—αὐτῷ.
13. Πνεῦμα Ἅγιον. 33. οὐδὲ ὑπὸ τὸν μόδιον.

36. ὅλον—μὴ ἔχον τὶ μέρος—ἔσται φωτεινὸν ὅλον.
37. Ἐν δὲ τῷ λαλῆσαι—εἰσελθὼν. 38. ὁ δὲ Φαρισαῖος ἰδὼν.
44. γραμματεῖς καὶ Φαρισαῖοι, ὑποκριταί—ὡς.
46. τοῖς φορτίοις. 49. αὐτῶν τὰ μνημεῖα.
53. καὶ ἀποστοματίζειν αὐτὸν περὶ πλειόνων.
54. ἐνεδρεύοντες αὐτόν—τι ἐκ τοῦ στόματος αὐτοῦ ἵνα κατηγορήσωσιν αὐτοῦ.

XII.

1. πρῶτον. 3. ἀνθ' ὧν. 6. πέντε.
9. ὁ δὲ ἀρνησάμενός με ἐνώπιον τῶν ἀνθρώπων ἀπαρνηθήσεται ἐνώπιον τῶν ἀγγέλων τοῦ Θεοῦ.
11. πῶς. 16. λέγων.
18. καὶ εἶπε, Τοῦτο ποιήσω—καὶ τὰ ἀγαθά μου.
19. ψυχή. 22. ὑμῶν. 27. αὐξάνει—ἓν. 28. οὕτως.
38. οἱ δοῦλοι. 39. ἐγρηγόρησεν ἄν.
42. ἄρα—καὶ φρόνιμος—αὐτοῦ. 43. ὁ δοῦλος.
47. Ἐκεῖνος δὲ—μηδὲ ποιήσας. 56. πῶς. 58. γάρ.

XIII.

11. ἰδού—ἀσθενείας. 25. ἄρξησθε—Κύριε.
28. ὑμᾶς δὲ ἐκβαλλομένους ἔξω.
30. οἳ ἔσονται after πρῶτοι. 35. ἔρημος—ὑμῖν—ἀμήν.

XIV.

1. ἐγένετο. 2. ἰδού. 3. λέγων. 5. ἀποκριθεὶς.
7. ἐπέχων πῶς. 8. ὑπό τινος—ὑπ' αὐτοῦ.
12. ἢ δεῖπνον. 18. πάντες. 20. καὶ διὰ τοῦτο.
23. ὁ κύριος. 24. μου.
27. καὶ ὅστις οὐ βαστάζει τὸν σταυρὸν αὐτοῦ, καὶ ἔρχεται ὀπίσω μου, οὐ δύναταί μου εἶναι μαθητής.
29. ἄρξωνται. 31. εἰς πόλεμον—καθίσας. 33. οὖν.

XV.

1. πάντες. 3. λέγων. 4. ἄνθρωπος. 12. Πάτερ.
14. ἰσχυρὸς—καὶ αὐτὸς ἤρξατο ὑστερεῖσθαι.
22. εἰς τοὺς πόδας. 28. οὖν. 30. ἦλθεν.

XVI.

5. ἕκαστον.
7. Καὶ λέγει αὐτῷ, Δέξαι σου τὸ γράμμα, καὶ γράψον.
18. ἀπὸ ἀνδρὸς. 19. λαμπρῶς. 20. ἡλκωμένος.
29. αὐτῷ.

XVII.

3. εἰς σέ. 4. εἰς σέ—τῆς ἡμέρας before ἐπιστρέψῃ.
6. ὁ Κύριος. 9. οὐ δοκῶ. 10. πάντα—ἀχρεῖοί.
11. ἐγένετο—αὐτὸς. 12. ἀπήντησαν. 13. αὐτοί.
28. ἐφύτευον, ᾠκοδόμουν. 36. καὶ ἀποκριθέντες.

XVIII.

2. λέγων—τινι. 4. ἐπὶ χρόνον. 5. διά γε.
14. αὐτοῦ. 15. ἰδόντες δὲ. 16. προσκαλεσάμενος αὐτὰ.
21. πάντα. 22. ταῦτα—δεῦρο. 25. εἰσελθεῖν.
35. Ἐγένετο. 40. πρὸς αὐτόν.

XIX.

12. οὖν. 25. καὶ εἶπον αὐτῷ Κύριε, ἔχει δέκα μνᾶς.
29. ἐγένετο ὡς. 30. πώποτε.
33. εἶπον οἱ κύριοι αὐτοῦ πρὸς αὐτούς, Τί λύετε τὸν πῶλον;
35. τὸν πῶλον. 37. δυνάμεων. 42. τὰ πρὸς—νῦν.
43. περιβαλοῦσιν—ἐπὶ σε—χάρακά σοι.

XX.

2. λέγοντες—εἰπὲ ἡμῖν. 3. ἕνα. 9. τὸν λαόν.
16. εἶπον Μὴ γένοιτο. 24. Ἀποκριθέντες. 25. τοίνυν.
26. αὐτοῦ after ἀποκρίσει. 29. οὖν.
32. ὕστερον δὲ πάντων. 33. οὖν—γυναῖκα.
35. τυχεῖν—οὔτε γαμοῦσιν. 36. καὶ υἱοί εἰσι τοῦ Θεοῦ.
39. ὑποκριθέντες.

XXI.

2. ἐκεῖ. 3. ἅπαντες—τοῦ Θεοῦ. 4. τὸν βίον.
6. ἐν αἷς. 7. οὖν. 8. οὖν. 10. Τότε ἔλεγεν αὐτοῖς.
11. ἔσονται. 12. αὐτῶν. 14. οὖν. 15. ἀντειπεῖν οὐδὲ.
20. τότε. 23. ἐπὶ τῆς γῆς. 26. καὶ προσδοκίας. 30. ἤδη.

XXII.

11. σοι.   12. Κἀκεῖνος.   14. οἱ δώδεκα.
18. τῆς ἀμπέλου.   20. Ὡσαύτως—τὸ ὑπὲρ ὑμῶν ἐκχυνόμενον.
22. τῷ ἀνθρώπῳ.   23. αὐτοὶ—ἐξ αὐτῶν.   24. δοκεῖ.
31. Εἶπε δὲ ὁ Κύριος.   36. οὖν—ὁμοίως.   38. Κύριε.
39. ἠκολούθησαν δὲ.
43. Ὤφθη δὲ αὐτῷ ἄγγελος ἀπ' οὐρανοῦ ἐνισχύων αὐτόν. καὶ γενόμενος ἐν ἀγωνίᾳ, ἐκτενέστερον προσηύχετο. ἐγένετο δὲ ὁ ἱδρὼς αὐτοῦ ὡσεὶ θρόμβοι αἵματος καταβαίνοντες ἐπὶ τὴν γῆν.
47. ἰδού.   52. ὁ Ἰησοῦς—τοῦ ἱεροῦ.   58. Πέτρος.
60. ἔτι λαλοῦντος αὐτοῦ.   62. ὁ Πέτρος.   63. τὸν Ἰησοῦν.
64. αὐτὸν ἔτυπτον.   69. τῆς δυνάμεως.

XXIII.

1. αὐτῶν.   3. ἐπηρώτησεν.   8. πολλά.
10. εἱστήκεισαν δὲ οἱ ἀρχιερεῖς καὶ οἱ γραμματεῖς, εὐτόνως κατηγοροῦντες αὐτοῦ.
11. ἐξουθενήσας δὲ αὐτὸν ὁ Ἡρώδης σὺν τοῖς στρατεύμασιν αὐτοῦ, καὶ ἐμπαίξας, περιβαλὼν αὐτὸν ἐσθῆτα λαμπρὰν, ἀνέπεμψεν αὐτὸν τῷ Πιλάτῳ.
12. ἐγένοντο δὲ φίλοι ὅ τε Πιλᾶτος καὶ ὁ Ἡρώδης ἐν αὐτῇ τῇ ἡμέρᾳ μετ' ἀλλήλων· προϋπῆρχον γὰρ ἐν ἔχθρᾳ ὄντες πρὸς ἑαυτούς.
14. ἰδού—ἐν τῷ ἀνθρώπῳ τούτῳ.   15. καὶ ἰδού.
18. ἡμῖν.   19. τινὰ γενομένην ἐν τῇ πόλει.
26. τινος—ἐπέθηκαν.   27. πολύ.
29. ἰδού.   32. ἕτεροι.
34. ὁ δὲ Ἰησοῦς ἔλεγε, Πάτερ, ἄφες αὐτοῖς· οὐ γὰρ οἴδασι τί ποιοῦσι.
36. καὶ ὄξος προσφέροντες αὐτῷ.
38. ἐπ' αὐτῷ γράμμασιν Ἑλληνικοῖς καὶ Ῥωμαϊκοῖς καὶ Ἑβραϊκοῖς.
40. Ἀποκριθεὶς.   46. Καὶ ταῦτα εἰπών.
48. ὄχλοι ἐπὶ τὴν θεωρίαν ταύτην—ὑπέστρεφον.
50. ἰδού.
51. οὗτος οὐκ ἦν συγκατατεθειμένος τῇ βουλῇ καὶ τῇ πράξει αὐτῶν.

XXIV.

1 ἀρώματα. 3. τοῦ κυρίου. 4. ἐγένετο—καὶ ἰδού.
9. πάντα—πᾶσι. 12. κείμενα.
13. ἰδού.
18. Ἀποκριθεὶς—μόνος—ἐν ταῖς ἡμέραις ταύταις;
20. ὅπως—ἡμῶν. 21. σὺν πᾶσι τούτοις—σήμερον.
22. ἀλλὰ—ἐξέστησαν ἡμᾶς—ὄρθριαι.
23. ὀπτασίαν.
29. λέγοντες—καὶ κέκλικεν ἡ ἡμέρα.
30. ἐγένετο—μετ' αὐτῶν. 32. ἐν ἡμῖν —ὡς ἐλάλει ἡμῖν.
35. αὐτοῖς. 36. αὐτὸς ὁ Ἰησοῦς.
42. καὶ ἀπὸ μελισσίου κηρίου. 49. ἰδού—Ἱερουσαλήμ.
51. ἐγένετο—διέστη.
52. εἰς τὸν οὐρανόν—προσκυνήσαντες αὐτόν.
53. αἰνοῦντες καὶ—Ἀμήν.

JOHN.

I.

26. Ἀπεκρίθη. 27. ὃς ἔμπροσθέν μου γέγονεν.
31. διὰ τοῦτο. 35. πάλιν. 37. δύο—τῷ Ἰησοῦ.
38. θεασάμενος αὐτοὺς ἀκολουθοῦντας.
39. ὃ λέγεται ἑρμηνευόμενον Διδάσκαλε.
41. δύο τῶν ἀκουσάντων—Πέτρου—καὶ ἀκολουθησάντων αὐτῷ.
42. πρῶτος—ὅ ἐστι μεθερμηνευόμενον, ὁ Χριστός.
44. ὁ Ἰησοῦς. 46. ἐν τῷ νόμῳ.

II.

18. Ἀπεκρίθησαν οὖν. 19. τοῦτον. 22. αὐτοῖς.

III.

2. οὗτος—ἃ σὺ ποιεῖς. 3. Ἀπεκρίθη. 5. Ἀπεκρίθη.
7. Δεῖ—ἄνωθεν. 8. πᾶς. 9. Ἀπεκρίθη.
10. Ἀπεκρίθη. 11. ἀμήν. 18. ἤδη—τοῦ Θεοῦ.
22. τὴν . . . γῆν. 27. Ἀπεκρίθη. 28. αὐτοί.

IV.

9. οὔσης γυναικὸς Σαμαρείτιδος.   10. Ἀπεκρίθη Ἰησοῦς.
11. ἡ γυνή, Κύριε—οὖν.   17. Ἀπεκρίθη ἡ γυνή.
19. ἡ γυνή.   20. ὅπου δεῖ.   23. αὐτόν.
24. Πνεῦμα ὁ Θεός—δεῖ.
25. αὐτῷ—Οἶδα ὅτι—ὁ λεγόμενος Χριστός—ἐκεῖνος—ἡμῖν.
28. τοῖς ἀνθρώποις.   30. ἤρχοντο.
31. Ἐν δὲ τῷ μεταξὺ—λέγοντες.   33. οὖν οἱ μαθηταί.
34. ὁ Ἰησοῦς.   36. ἵνα.

V.

7. ἀπεκρίθη—ὁ ἀσθενῶν.   13. ἰαθεὶς—ἐν τῷ τόπῳ.
16. καὶ ἐζήτουν αὐτὸν ἀποκτεῖναι.   21. οὓς θέλει.

VI.

7. ἀπεκρίθη—ἕκαστος αὐτῶν.
10. ὁ Ἰησοῦς—οὖν οἱ ἄνδρες τὸν ἀριθμὸν ὡσεὶ πεντακισχίλιοι.
13. τοῖς βεβρωκόσιν.   14. ὁ Ἰησοῦς.
15. Ἰησοῦς οὖν γνοὺς ὅτι—ἔρχεσθαι.   31. φαγεῖν.
32. Εἶπεν οὖν αὐτοῖς ὁ Ἰησοῦς.   39. ἐξ αὐτοῦ.
47. αἰώνιον.   51. ἐγὼ δώσω after ἥν.   55. γάρ.
57. κἀκεῖνος.   58. τὸ μάννα.   60. οὖν ἀκούσαντες.
61. ἐν ἑαυτῷ—περὶ τούτου.
64. τίνες εἰσὶν οἱ μὴ πιστεύοντες, καὶ.
66. εἰς τὰ ὀπίσω—ἔτι.
67. οὖν ὁ Ἰησοῦς.   69. τοῦ ζῶντος.
70. Ἀπεκρίθη—ὁ Ἰησοῦς—τοὺς δώδεκα.

VII.

6. ἕτοιμον.   8. ταύτην— -πω.   11. οὖν.
21. Ἀπεκρίθη.   23. ἐμοί.   28. οὖν.
32. περὶ αὐτοῦ ταῦτα—οἱ Φαρισαῖοι.   33. οὖν.
35. οὖν—μέλλει—τοὺς Ἕλληνας.   37. ἐσχάτῃ.
40. Οὗτός ἐστιν—ὁ προφήτης.   41. Ἄλλοι ἔλεγον—γάρ.
42. ὁ Χριστὸς after Δαβίδ.   45. οὖν—Διατί.
46. Ἀπεκρίθησαν.   47. οὖν.   49. ἐπικατάρατοί εἰσι.
50. εἷς ὢν ἐξ αὐτῶν.   52. Ἀπεκρίθησαν.

VIII.

12. οὖν—ἐλάλησε. 13. οὖν. 14. Ἀπεκρίθη—οἴδατε.
16. πατήρ. 19. οὖν—Ἀπεκρίθη ὁ Ἰησοῦς.
20. τὰ ῥήματα—ὁ Ἰησοῦς—ἐδίδασκων. 21. ὁ Ἰησοῦς.
34. Ἀπεκρίθη—τῆς ἁμαρτίας. 46. μοι.
47. ἐκ τοῦ Θεοῦ before ἐστέ.
48. Ἀπεκρίθησαν οὖν.
49. Ἀπεκρίθη. 52. οὖν—καὶ οἱ προφῆται—εἰς τὸν αἰῶνα.
53. τοῦ πατρὸς ἡμῶν—ὅστις ἀπέθανε;
55. ὑμῶν after Θεός.
56. ὁ πατὴρ ὑμῶν. 57. οὖν. 58. ὁ Ἰησοῦς.
59. οὖν—διελθὼν διὰ μέσου αὐτῶν· καὶ παρῆγεν οὕτω.

IX.

1. ἄνθρωπον. 2. λέγοντες—Ῥαββί.
3. ὁ Ἰησοῦς—ἥμαρτεν.
7. ὁ ἑρμηνεύεται, ἀπεσταλμένος. ἀπῆλθεν οὖν.
8. ὁ καθήμενος. 10. οὖν.
11. Ἀπεκρίθη—ἐποίησε, καὶ—τοὺς ὀφθαλμούς.
17. ὅτι ἤνοιξέ σου τοὺς ὀφθαλμούς;
21. αὐτὸς περὶ αὐτοῦ λαλήσει. 22. ἤδη.
23. Ὅτι ἡλικίαν ἔχει. 24. οὖν—ὃς ἦν τυφλός.
25. Ἀπεκρίθη. 27. οὐκ before ἠκούσατε.
30. Ἀπεκρίθη.
32. ὀφθαλμούς. 33. οὐκ ἠδύνατο. 34. Ἀπεκρίθησαν.
35. τοῦ Θεοῦ. 36. Ἀπεκρίθη. 40. ἐκ—ταῦτα—καί.
41. ὁ Ἰησοῦς—νῦν.

X.

6. τίνα ἦν ἃ ἐλάλει αὐτοῖς. 8. πρὸ ἐμοῦ.
12. αὐτά after ἁρπάζει—τὰ πρόβατα.
13. ὁ δὲ μισθωτὸς φεύγει—περὶ τῶν προβάτων.
18. ἐξουσίαν ἔχω before πάλιν. 20. πολλοί.
21. ὀφθαλμούς.
29. μου after πατήρ—ἁρπάζειν—μου after πατρός.
31. πάλιν—οἱ Ἰουδαῖοι. 32. καλά. 33. Ἀπεκρίθησαν.
34. Ἀπεκρίθη. 36. εἰμί.

XI.

6. τότε.   7. ἔπειτα μετὰ τοῦτο—πάλιν.   9. Ἀπεκρίθη.
11. μετὰ τοῦτο.   12. οἱ μαθηταὶ αὐτοῦ.
13. τῆς κοιμήσεως.   14. οὖν.   16. οὖν—ὁ λεγόμενος Δίδυμος.
18. ὡς.   19. περὶ τοῦ ἀδελφοῦ αὐτῶν.
21. οὖν—πρὸς τὸν Ἰησοῦν, Κύριε.   25. καὶ ἡ ζωή.
26. πᾶς.   28. τὴν ἀδελφὴν αὐτῆς.
31. οἱ οὖν Ἰουδαῖοι οἱ ὄντες μετ' αὐτῆς ἐν τῇ οἰκίᾳ—τὴν Μαρίαν—ἐκεῖ.
32. οὖν—ἰδοῦσα αὐτόν.   33. συνελθόντας.
39. ἡ ἀδελφὴ τοῦ τεθνηκότος.   40. ὁ Ἰησοῦς, Οὐκ.
41. οὗ ἦν ὁ τεθνηκὼς κείμενος—Ἰησοῦς.
42. τὸν περιεστῶτα.   44. αὐτοῖς.
45. οὖν—καὶ θεασάμενοι ἃ ἐποίησεν ὁ Ἰησοῦς.
51. τοῦ ἐνιαυτοῦ ἐκείνου.
55. τῶν Ἰουδαίων—πρὸ τοῦ πάσχα.   56. οὖν—ἑστηκότες.

XII.

1. οὖν—ὃν ἤγειρεν ἐκ νεκρῶν.   2. οὖν.
4. οὖν—αὐτοῦ—Σίμωνος.
6. Εἶπε δὲ τοῦτο—καὶ τὰ βαλλόμενα ἐβάσταζεν.   7. οὖν.
8. τοὺς πτωχοὺς γὰρ πάντοτε ἔχετε μεθ' ἑαυτῶν, ἐμὲ δὲ οὐ πάντοτε ἔχετε.
9. μόνον.   11. ὑπῆγον.   21. οὖν—ἠρώτων.
22. πάλιν Ἀνδρέας καὶ Φίλιππος.   23. ἀπεκρίνατο.
50. οὖν—ὁ πατήρ.

XIII.

1. τῆς ἑορτῆς.   2. ἤδη.   4. ἐκ τοῦ δείπνου.   7. ἄρτι.
9. Πέτρος.   11. Οὐχὶ πάντες καθαροί ἐστε.
12. πάλιν.   14. οὖν.   15. γάρ.   18. ὑμῶν.
21. ἀμὴν.   29. ὁ Ἰησοῦς—χρείαν ἔχομεν.
32. εἰ ὁ Θεὸς ἐδοξάσθη ἐν αὐτῷ.   33. ὑμεῖς.
34. ἵνα καὶ ὑμεῖς ἀγαπᾶτε ἀλλήλους.   36. ὁ Ἰησοῦς.
37. Κύριε.   38. Ἀπεκρίθη—ἀμὴν.

XIV.

3. τόπον.
10. τὰ ῥήματα ἃ ἐγὼ λαλῶ ὑμῖν, ἀπ' ἐμαυτοῦ οὐ λαλῶ· ὁ δὲ πατὴρ ὁ ἐν ἐμοὶ μένων, αὐτὸς ποιεῖ τὰ ἔργα.

11. πιστεύετέ μοι ὅτι ἐγὼ ἐν τῷ πατρί, καὶ ὁ πατὴρ ἐν ἐμοί· εἰ δὲ μή, διὰ τὰ ἔργα αὐτὰ πιστεύετέ μοι.
14. ἐάν τι αἰτήσητε ἐν τῷ ὀνόματί μου, ἐγὼ ποιήσω.
19. ἔτι—ἔτι after οὐκ—ὅτι. 23. Ἀπεκρίθη. 24. πατρὸς.
26. τὸ Ἅγιον—ὑμῖν. 30. πολλὰ—τούτου.

XV.

16. μένῃ. 20. τοῦ λόγου. 21. ἀλλά.

XVI.

2. ἀλλ'.
3. καὶ ταῦτα ποιήσουσιν ὑμῖν, ὅτι οὐκ ἔγνωσαν τὸν πατέρα οὐδὲ ἐμέ.
7. γὰρ. 19. μετ' ἀλλήλων. 32. νῦν. 33. ὑμῖν.

XVII.

5. ᾗ εἶχον—παρὰ σοί.
11. οὓς δέδωκάς μοι, ἵνα ὦσιν ἓν, καθὼς ἡμεῖς. 24. τὴν ἐμήν.

XVIII.

2. αὐτόν. 3. καὶ ὅπλων. 4. οὖν.
5. ὁ Ἰησοῦς—ὁ παραδιδοὺς αὐτὸν. 6. οὖν—αὐτοῖς.
8. ὁ Ἰησοῦς—οὖν—τούτους. 9. οὐδένα.
10. ἔχων—αὐτήν. 12. συνέλαβον τὸν Ἰησοῦν. 13. γὰρ.
15. Ἠκολούθει δὲ τῷ Ἰησοῦ—ἄλλος—ὁ δὲ μαθητὴς ἐκεῖνος ἦν—τοῦ ἀρχιερέως.
16. τῇ θύρᾳ—ὁ ἄλλος ὃς ἦν. 17. Πέτρῳ.
23. Ἀπεκρίθη—εἰ κακῶς—μαρτύρησον περὶ τοῦ κακοῦ· εἰ δὲ.
28. ἀλλ' ἵνα. 29. οὖν. 30. αὐτῷ.
31. οὖν—ὑμῶν—οὖν.

XIX.

41. ὅπου ἐσταυρώθη—καινόν.

XX.

2. ἄλλον. 3. ὁ Πέτρος καὶ ὁ ἄλλος μαθητής.
7. κείμενα—ὃ ἦν ἐπὶ τῆς κεφαλῆς αὐτοῦ, οὐ μετὰ τῶν ὀθονίων κείμενον, ἀλλὰ—εἰς ἕνα τόπον.

8. ἄλλος—ὁ ἐλθὼν πρῶτος.   10. πάλιν.   11. ἔξω—οὖν.
12. τὸ σῶμα.   15. ὁ Ἰησοῦς.
16. Στραφεῖσα ἐκείνη—ὃ λέγεται, Διδάσκαλε.
17. ὁ Ἰησοῦς—γάρ.   18. ἡ Μαγδαληνὴ,
19. Οὔσης οὖν ὀψίας—συνηγμένοι.
20. τοῦτο—ἰδόντες τὸν κύριον.   21. οὖν—ὁ Ἰησοῦς.
24. ὁ λεγόμενος Δίδυμος.
25. οὖν—οἱ ἄλλοι μαθηταί—ἐν -τῶν ἥλων before καὶ βάλω τὴν χεῖρά μου.
26. πάλιν.   27. ὧδε—καὶ φέρε—ἀλλὰ πιστός.
28. καὶ ἀπεκρίθη.   29. Θωμᾶ.   30. ἐνώπιον.

XXI.

1. πάλιν.   2. ὁ λεγόμενος Δίδυμος—αὐτοῦ.
3. Πέτρος—ἐξῆλθον καὶ—εὐθύς.   4. ἤδη—μέντοι—Ἰησοῦς.
5. οὖν—ὁ Ἰησοῦς—Ἀπεκρίθησαν.   6. οὖν—ἔτι.
7. Πέτρος—ἦν γὰρ γυμνός.
8. ἀλλ' ὡς ἀπὸ πηχῶν διακοσίων—τῶν ἰχθύων.
9. οὖν—κειμένην.   11. Πέτρος.   12. ὁ Κύριος.
13. ἔρχεται οὖν—ὁμοίως.   14. ἤδη.
15. οὖν—Πέτρῳ—πλεῖον τούτων—σὺ οἶδας ὅτι φιλῶ σε.
16. δεύτερον— σὺ οἶδας ὅτι φιλῶ σε.
17. τὸ τρίτον—φιλεῖς με; καὶ—Κύριε—ὁ Ἰησοῦς.
18. ἀμὴν—σοι.   19. σημαίνων.   20. Κύριε.
23. οὖν—αὐτῷ —τί πρός σε;
25. ὅσα—οὐδὲ αὐτὸν οἶμαι—τὰ γραφόμενα βιβλία—Ἀμήν.

APPENDIX II.
INTERPOLATIONS.
MATTHEW.
I.

16. Joseph—to whom was betrothed—the Virgin.
21. to thee.   22. Isaia.   25. to him.

II.

15. the mouth of Isaia.

III.

4. of the mountain.   5. they of.   6. each man.
14. unto him.   15. to be baptized.   17. to him.

IV.

5. and brought him.   6. to keep thee.
9. These kingdoms and their glory thou hast seen—before—until a time.
18. preparing their.
24. and on each of them he laid his hands—everyone.

V.

1. began to.   11. own.   12. in that day.
17. them.   35. beneath.   41. again.

VIII.

8. unto him.   14. Simon.   21. and I will come.

IX.

18. of the synagogue—falling down.
30. immediately—behold.   31. to every man.

X.

5. disciples.
23. and if they persecute you in the other city, flee ye to another—of the house.
41. For.

XIII.

2. of the sea.   3. seed.
6. and with the shining of the sun which was upon it, it sank down.
7. with it.   13. that they may never be converted.
48. of the sea—very.

XIV.

34. dry.

XV.

1. unto him.   15. Simon.   27. and live.   28. very.

XVI.

9. who ate them—from before them.
10. who ate of them—from before them.   13. What—this.
14. to him—say he is—say he is—say he is—say he is.

XVII.

15. a spirit of epilepsy seizes on him.

XVIII.

1. unto him.   7. that are coming.   10. verily.
21. Simon.   22. seven.   30. receive the entreaty.

XIX.

4. also.   22. rich.

XX.

2. for one workman.   7. my.

XXI.

23. tell us.   29. his soul—to the vineyard.   37. haply.

XXII.

25. by her.

XXIII.

5. the straps of.

XXIV.

2. stones.

XXV.

8. and bride.

XXVI.

20. unto them.   33. Simon—in thee (before 'Jesus').
35. Simon.   38. Behold.   43. with sleep.
70. neither do I understand—of the court.

XXVII.

5. and was strangled.
16. Jesus (before 'Bar-Abba')—He had been thrown into prison because of the evil he had done, and because he was a murderer.
17. the Jews—Jesus (before 'Bar-Abba').   26. with whips.
28. of purple and.   35. upon them.
36. while they were sitting.   41. and insulting him.

MARK.

I.

19. sitting.   26. threw him down.
28. and many followed him.   29. Cepha.   38. Up.

II.

21. than before.

V.

10. these demons.

VI.

24. the damsel.   43. of those five loaves—two.
48. with the fear of the waves.

VII.

5. these things.   6. that he said.   26. a widow.
28. woman—which are over.

VIII.

27. some say—say.
32. Simon—as though he pitied him, said to him, Be it far from thee.

IX.

8. again—his disciples.   10. this word that he said.
25. coming.   26. of him.
27. and delivered him to his father.

X.

4. and give it to her.   23. who trust in.   48. again.

XI.

3. unto him.   11. and he entered (before 'into the temple').
15. of God.   17. thus.

XII.

1. in it—in it.   2. to him.   5. servant.   6. perhaps.
33. a man.

XIV.

8. behold, she hath done [it].   14. My time is come.
18. verily.   20. his hand.   30. verily.   31. Simon.
36. My.   40. sleep.   41. the end is at hand.
62. answered and—unto him.   63. Then.

XV.

3. but he gave no answer.   26. This is.   31. again.
44. sent and.   46. and brought [it].   47. daughter.

XVI.

1. daughter.   7. behold.
8. when they had heard—and went.

LUKE.

I.

1. to write.   7. in all their manner of life.
10. standing and.   11. to Zacharia.
12. and shook—the angel.   42. to Mary.   44. great.
49. glorious.   50. and on the tribe.   62. also.   68. for them.

II.

18. what they had seen and heard, wondered.
19. in her mind.   22. as it is written in—up.   28. Simeon.
30. behold.   34. of contention.
37. and the rest of her life—and prayer.
39. and Joseph and Mary—on the first-born—that is written.
41. of unleavened bread.   44. Jesus.   48. his parents.

III.

4. in the plain—for our God.*   6. shall be revealed--together.
9. behold.   14. we also.   15. who heard him—and saying.
16. unto them—Behold.   17. holds.   19. of Herod.
22. of the body.

IV.

1. took him out.   2. that—might be—and he was there.
5. took him.   6. these kingdoms.
23. ye will say unto me.   24. unto them.   25. the prophet.

V.

4. dry.   7. They brought up fish—from the weight of them.
8. on his face.   10. to salvation.   14. Jesus.

VI.

35. to them—of men—in heaven.   39. this.
40. in teaching.   42. and behold.   48. was full.

VII.

12. of the people.   17. the region.

VIII.

13. hastily.   22. and sat.   37. from them.
48. answered and.

IX.

6. apostles—and the cities.   39. and it throweth him down.
53. set.   54. unto him.

X.

1. two.   12. much.   13. perhaps.   27. unto him.
40. about me.

XI.

36. when there is in it no lamp that hath shone is dark.
53. in the sight of all the people.

XII.

7. hair of.   47. stripes.   48. stripes (after 'few')—his hand.
56. to prove.

* See Isaiah xl. 3 in the Revised Version.

XIII.

23. came, asking him—Jesus.   27. Verily.

XIV.

5. pull him.   13. and the despised, and many others.
22. at the feast.

XV.

13. that came to him—with harlots.   22. quickly.   30. that.

XVI.

23. being cast into.

XVII.

6. from hence.

XVIII.

21. lo.   36. the voice of.   39. Jesus—saying.

XIX.

7. Zachai.   36. and came.   39. that they shout not.

XX.

9. and surrounded it.   10. one of the.   11. his.
17. When they heard these things, they knew certainly that he spoke this parable about them.
29. amongst us.   33. behold.   34. are begotten and beget.
37. when God spake with him.   38. behold.   39. unto him.
41. the scribes concerning.   43. beneath.

XXI.

5. to them.   6. stones.   8. unto them.
11. in divers places (after 'pestilences').   18. of the hair.
23. unto her.   24. all.   25. weakness of the hands.
30. and yield their fruit.

XXII.

8. unto them.   11. Our.   12. Behold—for us.   14. he.
30. own.   34. unto him.   38. for you.
39. which is called Beth.   47. there appeared a great.
58. unto him—unto him, Let me alone.
59. And it came to pass that.   71. lo.

XXIII.

3. that I am.   7. Herod (after 'because').   9. Jesus.
13. all.   20. and said unto them.
21. unto them (after 'said').
37. Hail to thee—And they placed also on his head a crown of thorns.
40. behold.   41. behold.
48. saying, Woe unto us, what hath befallen us! woe unto us, for our sins!
55. in their footsteps.

XXIV.

4. there appeared.
5. and looked on—for their fear—These men.   7. to you.
10. the daughter.   13. he appeared.   19. in power.
21. behold.   22. where he had been laid.
23. to us—and they were amazed.   25. Jesus.   29. began to.
31. immediately.   36. was found.   38. Jesus.
39. Behold.   46. Lo.

JOHN.

I.

34. chosen one.   35. with him.   41. My brother.
42. and he came (42. into Greek).   45. by his family.

II.

23. of unleavened bread.   25. The heart.

III.

1. and this man was.   6. because God is a living Spirit.

IV.

9. Lo.   16. to me.   34. own.   36. straightway.

V.

17. because of this.   18. word.   21. believe in him.   47. own.

VI.

4. of the unleavened bread.   7. by little.
10. He said unto them, Go, make the men sit down on the green.
13. and of these two fishes—of this bread.   63. the body.

VII.

35. that we shall not find him?   49. before.

VIII.

39. own.

IX.

6. and taking it up.   7. thy face.
8. and they who had seen that he had begged.
9. were saying (before ' He is like him ')—The blind man.
11. thy face.   30. own.   38. falling down.

X.

3. flock.   4. his own—the sheep.
14. and mine own know me.   20. are ye standing.
22. the feast—which is called.

XI.

15. come.   16. Come.   19. to Bethany.   20. went out to.
29. eagerly.   31. was thus amazed.   35. and when—saw.
37. from his mother's womb.
38. the grave was hollowed out—and the door was.
41. those men who were standing, came near.
42. of people—these things.   43. come out.
44. in that hour.   45. from that hour.
46. And there were some of them who believed not.
47. and made.   49. whose name was—their own—this same.
57. to them.

XII.

2. seated at meat—cumbered with.
3. and poured it on the head of Jesus while he sat at meat.
6. of the poor.   7. When—heard it—to him.
12. he went out, and came to the Mount of Olives.
13. and saying.   14. by Zacharia the prophet.

XIV.

1. Jesus said.   5. what it is.   6. I.   27. own.

XV.

20. heard and.   21. own.   23. because that.

XVI.

20. and sigh.

XVII.

11. take.   26. may be (after 'also').

XVIII.

1. [to] the mountain.   3. and a crowd of people.
15. because of this.   19. who they were—what it was.
21. But now.   17. unto her.   25. these people.
28. to deliver him to the governor.   30. even.

XIX.

42. with haste—to the place.

XX.

12. the pillows of the place.   13. angels.
16. and she ran towards him that she might touch him.
18. she told unto them.   23. against him.   25. is come.
29. in me.

XXI.

4. of the lake.
6. as he had said unto them, they sought to—the weight—which it held.
7. and was swimming.   9. before Jesus.
11. and they found.   21. following him.   22. now.

J PALMER, PRINTER, ALEXANDRA STREET, CAMBRIDGE.

www.ingramcontent.com/pod-product-compliance
Lightning Source LLC
Chambersburg PA
CBHW031930230426
43672CB00010B/1873